MR. DARWIN MISREAD
MISS PEACOCK'S MIND

*A New Look at Mate Selection
in Light of Lessons From Nature*

Merle E. Jacobs, Ph.D.

NatureBooks

Additional copies of this book are available through your local bookstore. Or contact the distributor:
BookMasters, Inc.
P.O. Box 388
Ashland, OH 44805-0388
1-800-247-6553
E-mail: order@bookmaster.com
Internet: http://www.bookmasters.com

A two-hour VHS videotape (of the same title) illustrating the book is also available from the distributor.

PRINTED IN THE UNITED STATES OF AMERICA

Book production: Phelps & Associates
Illustrations: Janice Phelps
Cover design: Sierra Gamma

Cataloging-in-Publication
(prepared by Quality Books, Inc.)

Jacobs, Merle E.
        Mr. Darwin misread Miss Peacock's mind : a new look at
mate selection in light of lessons from nature / Merle E.
Jacobs. -- 1st ed.
        p. cm.
Includes bibliographical references and indexes.
Preassigned LCCN: 98-72865
ISBN: 0-9665916-1-5

    1. Courtship of animals. 2. Animal psychology.
I. Title.

QL761.J33 1998   591.56'2
                                     QBI98-941

To Mother,
who encouraged us
to study and appreciate
nature

TABLE OF CONTENTS

A C K N O W L E D G M E N T S

I wish to thank my wife, Elizabeth, for her faithful aid in this project in all its phases. I also want to thank Richard Hostetler who worked with me on the studies of the house finch and Cooper's hawk, Dwight Jacobs who helped with studies of the white-breasted nuthatch, and Eric Kirk who assisted with studies of the cicada-killer wasp.

I also am greatly indebted to Janice Phelps for her dedication, artistry, and personal interest in helping to produce this book. And I greatly admire the concentrated copy-editing efforts of Dan Shenk of CopyProof as he worked tirelessly to incorporate improvements into this story, showing intense interest in the project.

To personnel at the Lalor Foundation and the National Institutes of Health: I am grateful for your encouragement and financial assistance in this research.

— Merle Jacobs

OVERVIEW

*T*HIS IS A STORY. IT'S A STORY OF SIMPLE THINGS — such as birds, fish, and insects. It's about years of careful observations of nature, as well as times of reflection on what those observations mean. How do animals "think"? How do they select their mates? What implications does all this have for us — the human creatures of the world?

This is also a very personal story, beginning with growing up in the Appalachian Mountains in the 1920s among scarlet tanagers and canaries. Questions about the brilliant coloration of the males in contrast to the concealing coloration of the females led to research into the significance of these differences in pigmentation among dragonflies, fruit flies, guppy fish, birds, and a variety of other creatures. Out of this study have grown some novel ideas about the roles of body pigmentation in mate choice relative to niche specialization. A revision of the theory of sexual selection resulted.

Charles Darwin (1809–92) had developed this special theory as a supplement to the general theory of natural selection. He said that fancy-male species arise in nature the way fancy-male varieties of birds are produced by human breeders — in response to an aesthetic sense (beauty for the sake of beauty), implying an element of consciousness. Darwin claimed that female birds, insects, and the like are endowed with such a sense and choose their mates on this basis.

At the beginning of the sexual reproductive cycle, according to Darwin, the females watch as the males strut around and compete with each other, as males are wont to do. The females, lacking notebooks, make mental conceptualizations of the contest. It is a reverse beauty contest, sort of a free-time exercise.

Physical prowess is part of the dossier of the males. After a victorious male has intimidated his rivals, openly proving his physical condition by means of brute force, he entertains the females with various types of prancing-displays of his grandeur. This is where subjective judgment of the female, along with a high degree of intellectual visualization, enters the picture. Beauty, to be sure, is a subtle thing, dependent on the eyes of the beholder. After prolonged and intensive observation, like a human artist squinting at a subject from various angles, the female finally makes her choice. This is Darwin's reading of the mind of the female.

According to this view, the males, by such a process of sexual selection, become more physically and ornamentally endowed generation after generation. In time, the males may become so loaded with ornaments that they can hardly walk, or fly. In spite of these encumbrances, the males perform their competitive exhibitions in plain view of predators. But the females are satisfied; they have given vent to their artistic bent. After all, the males are expendable, and there are plenty of runner-up males waiting in line. The females set the rules here, and they are exceedingly cunning and perceptive in their judgments.

To the author, Darwin's explanation of the origin of male adornment appears artificial and out of tune with nature. In fact, it appears to violate the natural law of energy conservation. But after all, the adorned males are still out there, blatantly violating the law of natural selection. According to Darwin, it's the females who are to blame for this violation of natural law. Could Adam have phrased it better? In Darwin's own words:

> When we behold two males fighting for possession of the female, or several male birds displaying their gorgeous

plumage and performing strange antics before an assembled body of females, we cannot doubt that, though led by instinct, they know what they are about, and consciously exert their mental and bodily powers. ... Just as man can give beauty, according to his standards of taste, to his male poultry, or more strictly can modify the beauty originally acquired by the parent species, can give to the Seybright bantam a new and elegant plumage, an erect or peculiar carriage — so it appears that female birds in a state of nature have by a long selection of the more attractive males added to their beauty or other attractive qualities. No doubt this implies powers of discrimination and taste on the part of the female, which will at first appear extremely improbable; but by the facts to be adduced hereafter, I hope to be able to show that the females actually have these powers. ... The exertion of some choice on the part of the female seems to be almost as general as the eagerness of the male. ... On the whole, birds appear to be the most aesthetic of all animals.

Darwin's practice of attributing to non-humans a human-like mentality (anthropomorphism) soon fell into disrepute. It was realized that such subjective methods could lead investigators astray. Little unequivocal support for female choice of male beauty was found in the non-human world of animals. The whole idea was finally considered dead "nonsensical" and anthropomorphism became taboo in scientific writings.

Studies of newborn animals were showing that much animal behavior formerly considered as under conscious direction was innate. In fact, the idea that life was directed by a sort of vital spiritual force was rapidly giving way to the firmer foundation of physical-chemical interpretations. A revolution was underway. The new movement came to be known as "behaviorism" (interpretation of animal behavior in mechanistic terms).

But we are now experiencing a counter revolution "the cognitive revolution" which has spawned an enormous number of anthropomorphic interpretations of animal behavior. We now have books such as that of Theodore Barber, *The Human Nature of Birds* (1993). Even the eminent explorer of bird life, Alexander Skutch (1992), supports Darwin's anthropomorphic idea of an aesthetic sense among birds:

> The widespread reluctance to admit that birds have an aesthetic sense, and that this influences their selection of mates, is but a special case of a much more widespread phenomenon, human materialization of the non-human world, our blindness to its psychic aspects. ... The more we study the courtship of birds, the more convinced we become that Darwin was right when he attributed the adornments of birds and other animals to their choice of mates, which implies that they are not devoid of aesthetic sensibility.

How significant are anthropomorphic analogies? The answer depends on how human-like the minds of the animals in question are. Beyond this, we must be careful lest our studies of the animal mind amount merely to thinly disguised studies of our own minds, with little or no relevance to the mind of the animal in question. The present book deals extensively with the animal mind, particularly that of the female. Even the supposedly wise Solomon had trouble fathoming the female mind, though the enormous number of "specimens" he had available should have enabled him to draw statistically significant conclusions.

Darwin had included dragonflies in support of his female-choice idea. In studying populations of amber-winged dragonflies in the 1950s, I discovered that these insects are territorial. Males select territories and defend them against rival males by means of displays of their amber-colored wings. Females are later attracted to these beautiful, amber-winged males and select them for mates.

But it soon became clear that the females, in making their selections, had more on their minds than beauty. It was plain, old-fashioned home economics. Up-close research revealed that it was the nature of the reproductive site and the food located there that were determining female choice of mates. This related sexual selection to niche specialization rather than abstract art. Attraction of both sexes to a specific type of reproductive site, along with a courtship period that allows time for the female to make a selection of the reproductive site, would lead to genetic segregation and, eventually, species formation.

As a simple hypothetical scenario, let us consider a habitat containing an abundance of both red berries and blue berries — and a species that uses both red and blue berries for food. Let us say that an economic advantage were to be gained by splitting that species into two so that one of the resulting species was physiologically and psychologically predisposed to feed on red berries, while the other favored blue berries. The split could be achieved by a segregating mating system involving the use of red berries in one case — and blue berries in the other — in the courting and mating ceremony.

The male, being of the pioneering sex, would arrive first at the breeding ground as attracted to the fruit of his choice. The females, arriving later, would be attracted to the fruit of choice by the male. The male would display the fruit, or even better, bear permanent representations of the fruit on his plumage. The same could be said of flowers.

Over time the two populations might be naturally selected not only for a love of red — or blue — berries, but also for related features of the habitat, including ripening time of the berries as coordinated with breeding time of the species. Eventually, we would have a species of blue-berry lovers and another of red-berry lovers. This may help explain why fruit-eating species bear "florid" or "fruity" plumage. Use of plumage markings in the courtship ceremony would finally result in species identification. The markings would not evolve in an arbitrary way, but as directed by niche requirements, the mind of the female being directed primarily by adaptive economics.

In this view, the female sees the male as a representative of a good territory rich in the foods of her choice, matching her tastes and physiology. Of course, his tastes also match his territory, which he therefore vigorously defends. In doing this, the male appears to be fighting for females. Though access to females appears to be the motivation for fighting by the male, the underlying motivation is defense of food supplies available in the general defended territory. Observers who are not environmentally sensitive may easily get the impression that the female is choosing her mate solely on the basis of his "sexy physique." But his physical appearance and vigorous display tactics may be simply the result of an adequate supply of nutritious foods found in his territory.

It is realized that pictorial representations of the food of the species may have developed in ages past when the representative food played a more important role in the diet of the species than is the case today. After the years of human encroachment into the environment, various species may have needed to change their dietary menus to survive.

The food-courtship theory developed in this book is intended to account for only a *portion* of the adornment displayed by animals. It is acknowledged that many such signals may be employed in various forms of communication. The subject of "gestures" is not elaborated in this book.

To explore the roles of food supplies in mating systems, I began a long series of studies with a variety of creatures. In the 1990s my research led to far-flung places, including Australia, for the observation of bowerbirds. Is a female attracted to the bower because she sees it as a kind of modern artwork, or does she see it as a display representing the food supply of the territory in which she might raise a family? Given the fact that it has been demonstrated by bird psychologists that birds are attracted to, and peck at, pictures of food, it appears reasonable that females are attracted to such representations — even as displayed on the plumage of the male.

But it is not necessary to go so far as Australia to explore these questions; there are plenty of opportunities at home. The studies on which this book is based were started, and are continuing, with observations of *local* creatures. Numerous examples were found of the use of specific foods, or representations of such foods, in courtship and selective mating.

The value of any theory is finally judged by its spin-off fruits, regardless of whether the results do or do not support the theory. Darwin's theory of sexual selection is no exception to this. My early studies of amber-winged dragonflies raised questions not only about the sexually selective role of body-color pigments, ranging from light tan to dark brown, but also about possible physiological roles of these pigments. This led to many years of laboratory work involving biochemical and behavioral genetics. Out of this came discoveries of a new role for an unusual amino acid (beta-alanine) in insect pigmentation, physiology, and adaptation.

This book was prepared in an attempt to summarize results accumulated over the years, including extensive studies in the 1990s in North America, Central America, South America, and Australia.

In addition, an evaluation of the validity of anthropomorphic interpretations is presented. Humans are obviously prone to emphasize beauty for the sake of beauty, even though the effort involves sacrifice of time, energy, and natural resources. But are all of nature's creatures — from Protozoa on — capable of such higher mentality as a human-like aesthetic sense? Are they conscious of beauty, ugliness, pleasure, pain? In fact, are they conscious at all? And if so, to what extent?

Donald Griffin — whose reputation stems from his studies of echo-location among bats — contends in his book, *Animal Minds* (1992), that anthropomorphism, along with the attendant question of animal consciousness, is due for re-examination.

Griffin's advice opened the gates to a *new* anthropomorphism, differing from the original in that many of today's observers (newly influenced both by population genetics and the sexual revolution of the 1960s) now ascribe to the mind of the animal these "developments" in animal psychology. Female creatures are now said to be evaluating their potential mates not only in romantic terms, including an aesthetic sense, but in terms of their "fitness genes." They are inclined to contrive schemes for leaving their partners for more promising prospects, as their genetic sense directs. The female black grouse is said to possess a genetic sense of near mystical proportions. By walking through an arena of gathered males, she is able to pick the one with the greatest potential for longevity. (See Chapter 3.)

The pendulum, which has historically swung from anthropomorphic to mechanistic interpretations, is now swinging back. Where will it come to rest? If anthropomorphism leads to scientifically correct interpretations of animal behavior, it may well become enshrined in the halls of science. On the other hand, if anthropomorphism leads to error, it will be relegated to the murky mists of mysticism. The merits of these methodologies will be evaluated on the basis of their fruits.

If carried too far, anthropomorphism might change the rules of science. Instead of universal science, we may end up with male science and female science, both being at once politically, but not at once scientifically, correct. Ethologist James Gould (1982) well describes this predicament: "One lesson of field ethology is that male ethologists generally find the females of the species being studied to be relatively passive elements in the social system, while female ethologists find case after case of female-dominated societies."

Interpretation of the animal mind on the basis of our own mind is a very tricky process. On watching a frog scrape from its skin a piece of irritating filter paper soaked with acetic acid, we may conclude that the frog is conscious of what it is doing. It is indeed acting as if it knows what it's doing. However, the frog will behave similarly when its brain is removed. Either the brain is not necessary for consciousness, or the frog is behaving unconsciously, by simple reflex reaction to the stimulus. Similar reflex actions occur continuously throughout the body of any organism. They control vital functions even when the brain is unconscious, as it is for about a third of our lifetime, when we are sound asleep. Single-celled organisms, with no centralized brain, perform all vital functions, even including trial-and-error learning. It should be pointed out here that this type of learning amounts simply to use of results discovered by accident.

Associative learning, on the other hand, requires recognition of the cause-and-effect relationships between separate events, a type of reasoning in which the animal anticipates the results. An element of consciousness may be involved in *associative* learning. Consciousness involves decisions made on the basis of internal reflections. These decisions lead to *voluntary* responses to stimuli rather than *automatic* responses. Determination of whether a certain behavior is consciously or automatically directed is often ambiguous. Since consciousness is due to private, internal processes, an investigator is tempted to employ subjective, anthropomorphic methods to fathom the mind of the animal. On the other hand, another investigator may explain the same behavior in terms of simple response mechanisms.

This dichotomy of interpretations is seen in studies of sexual selection. For example, in applying anthropomorphic interpretations to help explain the origin of display features of male animals, Amotz and Avishag Zahavi in their book, *The Handicap Principle* (1997), claim that these features have evolved by female choice of males on the basis of "handicaps." The females choose the males most encumbered with ornaments, associating physical fitness with these "handicaps." Any male able to survive under duress of such adornment must be a strong candidate for a mate:

> The adult males of many species of birds are far more colorful than females and young males: examples include peacocks, ducks, birds of paradise, and sunbirds. Colorful plumage attracts rivals and predators and thus serves as a reliable signal of quality: only males of high quality can risk advertising their location. Conspicuous coloration also emphasizes the exact shape, posture, and movements of its bearer. A high-quality individual "wears"

The male peacock wears fruity plumage atop his head.

bright coloring well; on a low-quality one the same coloring accentuates imperfections. ... Each aspect of the display seems to convey specific, reliable information about a particular feature of the male. The long tail feathers are grown over a period of several months, during a time of the year when food is scarce. Unhealthy birds arrest the process, so a male who displays a set of perfect tail feathers advertises that he has been in good health and has managed to find food even during molt season. ... Each of these criteria seems to be minutely scrutinized by females. ... Any improvement in a signal must be accompanied by a cost to the signaler — that is, it *must* make the signal's bearer *less* well-adapted to its environment.

This explanation attributes remarkable powers of association to the female. It presupposes that the female is capable of associating colorful plumage with predation and male physical fitness relative to adaptation.

But such powers of association on the part of the female would not be necessary for deriving an adaptive advantage from the predation of the conspicuous males. Along with removal of such males from predation-prone territories would go elimination of male attraction of females to those potentially dangerous reproductive sites. This principle is dramatically illustrated among dragonflies. (See Chapter 2.)

The Zahavis emphasize the importance of detailed ornamental designs in influencing female choice. For example, the intricate circular lines of the "eyespots" on the tail of the peacock bring out the perfect symmetry of the markings and therefore indicate to the female the physical fitness of the male bearer. Also, the huge tail on which these spots are arrayed must be difficult to erect, and successful elevation of this train toward the female indicates that the male is physically fit. The Zahavis suggest that the peacock turns his back toward the female during courtship with the aim of administering to the female an interest test. If the female bothers to go around the male to examine his display from the front, this is proof that she is interested enough in him to warrant further courtship effort.

However, it may well be that the male is intuitively programmed to direct his display away from the female with the function of warding off potential male rivals that might otherwise interfere with courtship and mating.

According to the Zahavis, even the redness of appendages such as combs of birds are capable of a "handicap" interpretation:

> There are cases in which coloring itself signals health, as do the red of cocks' combs, the color of human lips, and similar structures that show off blood circulation, and the color of flamingoes and other birds that get their hue

from foods rich in carotenoids. Carotenoids are active molecules and can cause damage within the body; we speculate that high levels of carotenoids in the blood at the time the bird is growing its feathers may well be a handicap that can be sustained only by a high-quality bird.

Mr. Darwin Misread Miss Peacock's Mind develops the thesis that red-yellow colors of males of some fancy-male varieties of animals are capable of mechanistic stimulus-response interpretations. Since carotenoids increase redness of the plumage, along with physiological fitness of a male, a female being programmed for attraction to such colored males may reap nutritional benefits for herself and her offspring. If a certain territory is rich in carotenoids essential for nutrition, a male feeding in that territory would develop reddish color attractive to a female. Nutritionally conditioned physical fitness of the male would add to the effectiveness of his advertising display.

Are animals capable of making conscious choices? Do they "know" what they are doing, or are they essentially "robots" so extensively programmed that they merely give the appearance of consciousness?

In recent years increasing attention has been paid to the question of animal consciousness. Charles Darwin deduced that all animals, which have heredity in common with humans, must show at least rudiments of human-like consciousness. Darwin therefore felt secure in interpreting the consciousness of animals anthropomorphically.

Even today it appears that the majority of people feel intuitively that animals, from worms to dolphins and chimpanzees, experience human-like mental states. In the book, *Anthropomorphism, Anecdotes, and Animals* (1997), edited by Mitchell, Thompson, and Miles, there is a chapter by Harold Herzog and Shelly Galvin titled "Common Sense and the Mental Lives of Animals: An Empirical Approach." The authors questioned 169 Social Psychology students regarding their opinions about the mentality of animals. Among the students, 96 percent thought dolphins are conscious. Only 47 percent thought mice are conscious. A mere 15 percent believed ants to be conscious. With regard to suffering, roughly the same pattern was displayed. Interestingly, 92 percent thought dogs are conscious, but only 59 percent considered pigs conscious. Commenting on this, the authors state, "We know of no systematic research findings that would support the belief that dogs and cats are more conscious than pigs, but our subjects intuitively felt that their mental capacities were quite different." These results reveal the weakness of subjective interpretations of animal behavior, particularly regarding pets.

In the present book the question of consciousness, its origin, and its adaptive significance is considered. A comparison is made of the nervous systems and behavior of animals, beginning with the Protozoa. An attempt is made to describe the behavior of *wild* animals with a view toward deciphering their mentality, including possible consciousness. Darwinian sexual selection is set as a frontispiece, for it appears that consciousness reaches its apex in the sexual phase of the life cycle. A close relationship between consciousness and sexual selection was already recognized by an early student of animal mentality, Conway Morgan (1852–1936), who noted in his *Habit and Instinct* (1896):

> Natural selection begins by eliminating the weakest, and so works up the scale from its lower end until none but the fittest survive; there is no conscious choice in the matter. Sexual selection by preferential mating begins by selecting the most successful in stimulating the pairing instinct, and so works down the scale until none but the hopelessly unattractive remain unmated. The process is determined by conscious choice.

Resolving the problem of animal consciousness could well influence the way we treat nature — and thereby affect the direction of environmental movements. The debate is waged today as the biosphere-centered environmentalists take on the human-centered environmentalists. The human-centered environmentalist, Gregg Easterbrook (1995), for one welcomes the encroachment of the human with optimism and open arms. He contends that brutally cruel nature needs to be tamed. Nature, being unconscious and incapable of such taming, is therefore in dire need of humanity to "civilize" it. The procedure would be to supplant the cruel, brutish forces of nature with conscious planning by humankind. Easterbrook proposes, for instance, that genetic engineering be used to make non-killers out of the predators. He further suggests that nature could remain as at present, "except for the gruesome part." Easterbrook expresses no concern about the problem of switching the feeding habits of a species while leaving that species remain as at present. He repudiates conservationists who wish to maintain cruel nature as it is.

Biosphere-centered naturalists, on the other hand, view the human not as a *savior* of nature, but as a *curse,* a pest introduced into the ecosystem, a cancer in the superorganism, a species that has played God with itself to create a genetically engineered monster. Maintaining that Mother Nature has done a creditable job of creation, biosphere environmentalists would like to preserve this system intact. In the huge family of species on earth, if the human does not perceive its proper place and put itself into it, "Mother" will do the job — with her traditional "inhumane" methods. Nature's cardinal rule seems to be, "Many must die that some might live."

It is not the human physique that is the problem, it is the *conscious psyche*. Has the origin of consciousness into nature produced artificial misfits? Is the human a unique example of such a misfit, or are all animals conscious, as maintained by Darwin? *Mr. Darwin Misread Miss Peacock's Mind* gives attention to the problem of whether the general animal mind is sufficiently conscious to be capable of such human-type intangibles as would allow for choice of mates on the basis of an abstract aesthetic sense. If so, we could expect consciousness to expand, genetically, to its outer limits.

Indeed, early students of sexual selection claimed that this process could lead to "dysgeny" (defined as a genetically maladapted condition).

This book includes a review of the history of sexual selection and animal psychology. My intent as author is to place the problem of sexual selection and the accompanying problem of animal mentality — and rights — into context and so help formulate balanced interpretations. This is admittedly a broad-brush approach to sexual selection and animal ingenuity. The daunting challenge here is no less than the integration of three major disciplines: aesthetics, dietetics, and genetics.

In my view, since the mind of the animal is centered on environmental issues, particularly the food chain, proper interpretation of that mind must be in line with natural economics. The interpretations in this book are based on the premise that, at its core, life is driven by solar energy. In line with the physical law of energy conservation, species form as a result of specialization to maximize efficient use of such energy bound up in food molecules in the various ecological niches found on earth. Any species violating this principle will be ousted from its niche, to be replaced by a more efficient species. Keeping this emphasis in mind results in the resolution of an astounding number of paradoxes now prevailing in interpretations of animal behavior.

In line with this theory, the answer to questions about what is the most important drive in nature is simply the *food* drive. Wild animals appear to know this but humans invariably think the answer is the *sex* drive. Yet sex is merely subservient to the aim of the food drive, providing the exploratory variability from which nature can select the most efficient genotypes.

Since the liberal, consuming sexual phase of the life cycles is characterized by an extravagant exploitation of energy — as contrasted with the conservative, producing vegetative phase — natural selection counteracts over-extension of the sexual phase. But the human species, through its ability to override nature, elaborates the sexual phase inordinately. According to the author, this has contributed to the fall of a succession of human empires.

The general thesis of sexual selection has been hidden as a molehill in a mountain of natural selection for far too many years. It has remained as a spark with the potential of creating a great conflagration. Sexual selection allows creatures to design their own genotypes — just as geneticists can design the genotypes by a process of artificial selection. It is, like the human mind itself, a terrible thing.

Sexual selection can take a species outside the boundaries of the laws of Mother Nature. In this respect, sexual selection can be *antithetical* to natural selection. Once the intellect has been directed to the point of consciousness, the artificial selective process could enable this special enlightened species to erase its nearest competitors, leaving a wide gap in the fossil record. An observer such as Alfred Wallace (1823–1913) might then naturally conclude that humans cannot trace their ancestry to ape-like species.

But sexual selection, like artificial selection, may also be a *wonderful* thing. If it works to make rapid improvements in adaptation to nature, it is laudable indeed. Part of the purpose of the present work is to assist in such a value judgment.

It is hoped that the present contribution, including laboratory and field studies involving genetics and biochemistry in one package, will be helpful. It would be especially gratifying if potential students of the topic of sexual selection and the animal mind would gain some inspiration from the ideas presented and the questions raised.

Some portions of the book, being admittedly but necessarily somewhat technical, may be summarily skimmed by the general reader. Presumably, the inclusion of these technicalities, though of interest to the specialist, will not detract from the overall simple message of the book.

The illustrations in *Mr. Darwin Misread Miss Peacock's Mind* are from the many hours of videos on animal behavior recorded in the course of these studies. A two-hour illustrative VHS tape under the title of this book is available. (See copyright page.)

CHAPTER 1

LESSONS FROM THE AUTHOR'S EARLY YEARS

*E*ACH OF US HAS A STORY TO TELL, life experiences woven into a fabric we call the web of life. My story starts in the wilds of the Appalachian Mountains of southwestern Pennsylvania where my ancestors landed after escaping the tyrannies of Europe. Nature was all around us. We knew where the staff of life (food) originated: from the earth! There was no question of origins here. Food was not created; it arose spontaneously from the ground. The only outside force needed was solar energy, pure and simple.

Just outside the door on every hand we found food, ripe for the plucking. This food contained not only carbohydrates for energy, but proteins for amino acids, essential vitamins and minerals, and who knows what else. We didn't know all this; we simply matched our biochemistries, physiologies, and psychologies (our tastes) with what was available. Soon therefore we associated food with localities and seasons. We shared the chokecherries with the cedar waxwings and the huckleberries with the ruffed grouse.

As a boy I raised canaries, in which both male and female birds are a brilliant yellow. Starting with one pair, donated by an aunt, I ended up with 67 birds, in a sun porch adjacent to my bedroom. The birds were given free rein there, and they developed strong powers of flight. In my family of origin, we were not merely bird watchers, we *lived* with the birds. They were free to fly into the bedroom and back into the sun porch voluntarily. All of us — parents and children — became intimately involved with the canaries and came to understand their nuances of behavior and mentality.

We needed no alarm clock, only the birds. I traded one good singer for an antique Victrola on which especially good canary songs were played for the canaries to imitate. Other records were played for our own entertainment. Some of the birds picked up bars of "It's Raining Sunbeams," sung by a young girl, Deanna Durbin. We also raised, in the canary room, a family of deer mice we had found in an old apple tree. They ate the same bird seed as the canaries. They also trilled the song of the canaries.

One day all 67 birds escaped through an open window. They perched atop trees throughout the community, singing. Our uncle, who had lost one eye in an accident, was asked if he had seen any of the birds. He pointed to a crow. This was my first lesson in the cooperation of both eyes in size/distance perception. Toward evening all the birds homed back into the sun porch, entering the window through which they had left.

We were assigned chores. I raised the chickens. Except in winter they were free-ranging. Some of them were "banties" (Seybright bantams), not far removed from their red jungle-fowl ancestors. I became intensely interested in their behavior. Noting that they appeared to be more energetic and stronger when they had to hunt for what they got, I would hide their food in various scattered areas and watch them search for it and scratch it up. We started the newly hatched chicks ("peepies") up in the attic — our former bedroom. We not only woke up with the chickens, we grew up with them.

As the chicks matured, we placed them in the chicken house from which they could exit or enter at will through a little door. As the cocks matured, some of them fought, kicking each other, sometimes knocking out feathers. Certain cocks appeared to defend the places where I customarily hid food for them.

One vigorous cock, with especially ornate plumage and bright red comb, seemed very defensive of a spot where I often hid food under the decomposing leaves. Occasionally, this cock, upon discovering food, would pick at it while uttering soft clucking noises. Hens would come running and begin feeding there. The cock might then lower his wing toward a certain female as she crouched, and mating would ensue.

Early in the morning the cock would perch on his roosting tree, and announce his "cock-a-doodle-doo." Our aunt's rooster, about a quarter-mile away, would answer. The chickens, especially the roosters, appeared to be highly space-conscious. They would repeatedly return to the location where the food was normally hidden. The roosters in particular seemed likely to engage in cock fights in the vicinity of such sites.

We discovered that a chicken could be "hypnotized" by holding it gently, then getting its attention fixed on a stick. If the stick were slowly withdrawn, the chicken would remain motionless when carefully placed on its side on the ground. Later, I found that blue jays, captured in a trap for banding, would stay still when gently held and turned on their backs. They would also remain motionless when released upside down on the ground or on top of a post. Captured dragonflies behave similarly when they are slowly lowered to the ground.

Having constructed a telescope, I early became fascinated with the beauty of wild birds, especially the brilliant-scarlet male tanager with contrasting black wings, which we called the "tit bird" because of his alarm note. He was strikingly visible in spring, as he sang in the open. His demure green mate, on the other hand, could hardly be seen, as she blended in with the foliage. The nest was discovered as she was building it, on a horizontal limb of an oak tree. The bottom was so thin that the eggs were visible from below. No rainstorm would flood that nest.

What accounts for the striking difference in plumage between the sexes of the scarlet tanager? The obscure green color of the female, matching the foliage, made sense, but the scarlet male looked like a Christmas-tree ornament, surely not designed for concealment. Actually, this is an apt description. The ornaments hung on Christmas trees often represent highly ornamental foods. The male golden bowerbird erects a "tree" over which he strews green-gray beard lichens (fungi with green algae in them). Later, he decorates the structure with colorful, eye-catching flowers and seeds.

Not only was the male scarlet tanager himself imprinted on my memory, but also the perplexing problem of the significance of the color differences between the sexes. Our devout mother, an ardent nature observer, explained that the highly ornamented male birds merely show that God loves beauty. It did not appear to bother her that God liked beauty particularly in males.

As with the plumage contrasts in the scarlet tanager, those of the goldfinch were equally intriguing. In this species both sexes are a cryptic, greenish color in the winter, but in spring the male dons a bright-yellow plumage, with contrasting black wings, while the female maintains her obscure, greenish color. Possibly the plumage change has something to do with the breeding activities. Much later, I discovered that the male rose-breasted grosbeak sometimes breeds before attaining the mature plumage.

In high school the class got into the study of the binomial theorem. At the time, little did we realize that it was this simple theorem — dealing with chance combinations of occurrences involving two alternatives — that led to discovery of the normal curve and the laws of heredity. In physics I admired the precision with which the principles of triangulation could be used to calculate the end result of forces operating in different directions at the same time.

But it was the chemists who seemed to get the biggest bang out of their efforts. The chemistry professor held up a yellow pencil and said, "There is enough energy in this pencil to blow up all of Ferndale." This was in 1934, more than a decade before Hiroshima. The use of a pencil as an illustrative symbol was most appropriate. Margarita Ryutova-Kemoklidze (1995), who reviewed the history of the development of quantum theory, stated, "Theoreticians have no trouble obtaining such energies; all they need is a pencil and paper." Modern quantum physicists realize that unification of gravitational and nuclear-attractive forces into a single mathematical description would require such enormous amounts of energy as would be experienced only in the early stages of the original Big Bang.

At Goshen College, Goshen, Indiana, where my kin went to college, I met S.W. Witmer (1890–1990) who, though having a Ph.D. in botany from Indiana University, was fascinated also with birds. He was amusingly methodical. Witmer's dictum was: "Describe what you see and add no effects." This, of course, was not to denigrate the important role of imagination and deduction in the sciences. It was simply to admonish students, usually in a hurry, not to report deductive conclusions as observations.

Witmer had learned this lesson (somewhat negatively) at Indiana University from his mentor there. In his cytological studies of plant tissues, he was sure he had observed the pairing of chromosomes during formation of gametes. His excitement abated when he was told not to be carried away by the new-fangled chromosome theory. (This was before the principles of cytogenetics had been developed.) I spent many hours with Witmer, banding birds and individually marking cardinals and blue jays for study of their territorial behavior. In due course I entered Indiana University as a graduate student in zoology.

The minute I stepped onto the IU campus I knew this was a good place for nature study, not only because of the relatively natural campus, but because of the intellectual traditions relative to nature studies. I thought it would be interesting to investigate the birds that frequent the campus and environs. While exploring that natural environment, I met an upper-level student, James Watson (1928–), who had studied birds in the Chicago area. But by the time I met him his main thoughts were not about birds, though he showed admiration for the work Margaret Nice had done on territorialism among song sparrows. Watson's thoughts were more on genes, especially the "naked" variety, as in virus particles.

At that time Indiana University was taking leave of its emphasis on field studies and was pushing ahead in laboratory studies, particularly in the area of genetics. In the zoology department at IU, Hermann Muller

(1890–1967) was studying gene mutations in the fruit fly, *Drosophila melanogaster*. Muller had much to do with the development of modern genetics from its beginnings in the "fly room" at Columbia University. In 1927, at the University of Texas, he discovered that irradiation destabilizes genes and therefore leads to their mutation. This caught the immediate attention of atomic physicists, including Erwin Schrödinger (1887–1961). Since radiant energy destabilizes atoms and molecules, Muller's discovery led to the view that the gene might be a molecule.

The physicist Max Delbrük (1906–81), having found a home at Vanderbilt University after fleeing the Nazi regime in Germany, presented a theoretical model of the gene. Schrödinger popularized this model at Trinity College in England in a 1943 lecture series. The lectures were published in 1944 as the classic, *What Is Life?*

Delbrük was fascinated by the work of the "fly people," including T.H. Morgan and his colleagues from Columbia University, who had settled at the California Institute of Technology in 1928. Delbrük, who collaborated there, was naturally interested in fly chromosomes but, along with Morgan himself, realized that to determine the fundamental nature of the ultimate particle of life, the gene, something smaller than fly chromosomes must be found. (Incidentally, the pairing of chromosomes, gene by gene, a type of sexual selection at the microscopic level, has gone largely unnoticed by biophysicists. In the salivary chromosomes, this pairing is seen as a permanent, large-screen representation of what occurs in the reproductive cycle of the flies.)

To see tiny examples of the gene at its most fundamental level, the bacteriologists and virologists entered the picture. Salvador Luria (1912–91), who had escaped the fascist regime in Italy by fleeing to America, turned his early interest in physics to biology after meeting Delbrük in 1940 at a science conference. Luria had long been interested in collaborating with Delbrük in his studies of the structure of the gene. What materials could be simpler to work with than viruses? Luria established a virus group at IU. The students were excited by the way viruses that were killed with irradiation could be brought back to life by other forms of radiation. Watson, who avidly read *What Is Life?* worked with Luria in performing experiments on the effects of radiation on viruses.

The DNA molecule was under attack on three fronts: physics, biology, and chemistry. By Watson's time the chemistry of the nucleic acids had been thoroughly worked out. Furthermore, among different samples of DNA it was known that there were pairing relationship among the ring bases of these nucleic acids. It was also known that chromosomes have both a protein and DNA component. What was *not* known, however, was whether it was the protein or the DNA that is the genetic material. Fortunately, this problem could be solved by studies of virus particles, which are still genetically active after the DNA has lost its protein coat. The coat is left outside the cell as the viral DNA takes over the metabolism of the cell and uses the cellular ingredients to make more of the viral DNA. The viral DNA is left free of protein and ready for analysis. All the pieces of the DNA jigsaw puzzle are waiting to be assembled to reveal the picture of life as we know it.

Watson dreamed about these "naked" genes — and about ways to put the pieces of DNA into physically, chemically, and biologically sound relationships. Being a biologist, he was sure that the parts had a double-pairing nature, for the gene is a biological thing, and "Everything biological comes in pairs." All that remained was to unscrew the double helix. A helix of triple-paired ring bases was being proposed by Linus Pauling (1901–94).

Muller, in his class on mutation and the gene, would go through the most remarkable contortions trying to figure out how a three-dimensional object, such as a gene, could replicate. Muller's diagrams were bigger than he was as he stood beside them. Sometimes when he was so engaged the wind would blow his yellow lecture notes across the floor. The students would watch in bemusement as he bounced around gathering them up. Muller had little trouble keeping the attention of his students. He had a special step-up platform behind the lecture table so he could see out better. The students were occasionally startled and, of course, stimulated when he suddenly popped up to lecture.

In Muller's presentation itself it was obvious there was a huge gap in knowledge about the structure and function of the gene. Watson, during a walk on campus, complained that everyone was talking about the gene, but nobody knew anything about it. Reflecting that folks back home in Chicago expected great things of him, Watson decided to determine the structure of the gene. He seemed elated when I told him his work was of universal importance. On getting back to the lab he announced this to a certain gifted graduate student who happened to be the object of his attention at the time. She obviously was not impressed. In fact, she was infuriated. Watson had repeatedly reported to her how quickly he could do his experiments with viruses, one experiment per night. She, on the other hand, needed months to do an experiment involving the effects of testosterone on the development of combs in chickens.

As it turned out, this was not the only lady Watson was to infuriate. His abrasive dealings with crystallographer Rosalind Franklin, who had confidentially shown him her X-ray pictures of the DNA molecule, are related by Anne Sayre in the book, *Rosalind Franklin & DNA* (1975). It was in these pictures that Watson first saw direct evidence that DNA was a double helix. Evidently, though, he and Franklin didn't see eye to eye on the significance of this evidence.

Watson's advisory committee was waiting for him. It was time for the oral part of the Preliminary Examinations. This inquisition aims, among other things, to show that a particular graduate student knows significantly less than the faculty. The whole process is not only to determine whether a potential graduate student is worth keeping around but also to knock off a few rough edges. Although I don't know how the committee members treated Watson, or even what he was asked, he related later at lunch that he couldn't eat, for his stomach was full of butterflies.

In his attempts to decipher the gene, Watson had a choice between a physical or a chemical approach. Ironically, in spite of the fact that he hated chemistry, which he thought was a lot of kitchen work, he bit the bullet and tried the chemical approach. For these studies he went to Europe where DNA was under investigation by seasoned chemists and physicists. After one year there, he decided on the physical approach.

Biologist Watson and biophysicist Francis Crick (1916–) were the first to describe the double-helical structure of DNA, a discovery for which they would share a Nobel Prize for medicine in 1962, along with biophysicist Maurice Wilkins (1916–).

The double-helix breakthrough led to the rapid development of molecular biology. There is a lesson to be learned from this DNA story. Though the whole may be greater than the sum of its parts, the whole cannot be comprehended without a proper understanding of the parts. The DNA story also shows the immense potential of "reductionism," which amounts to reducing the whole into its parts for study, making the problem as simple as possible. Putting the parts together to create the whole is known as "complementation." Since the parts are sometimes too tiny to be visible, a lot of deduction goes along with the process. Ideally, deductions should be supported by observation.

In the case of DNA, electron microscopy provided the observation. Not only was the double helix seen, but also the mechanism by which DNA makes proteins out of the constituent amino acids. Who would have thought that each cell contains little tape-recorder heads (ribosomes) through which recorded tapes pass? DNA strands serve as templates for stamping the three-lettered codes that instruct the ribosomes how to assemble the amino acids into proteins.

But DNA is not the *whole* story. There is much more to life than four letters of the alphabet, representing four ring bases: C (cytosine), A (adenine), T (thymine), and G (guanine). In fact, the entire gene complement of a cell is the mere clay of life awaiting the sculptors (natural and sexual selection) to shape it into living organisms. Genes do not operate in a vacuum. Their activity depends on the immediate "furniture" within the cell, as well as the environment outside. This is where field biology comes to the rescue.

In recent years Crick has been applying the reductionism used in deciphering the gene toward understanding the human soul. Why not? One good discovery deserves another. But this remarkably insightful investigator may ultimately discover that the soul encompasses all the experiences of life — from head to toe, including even the entire outside world. Reductionist methods may need to be supplemented by field studies showing that the soul is more than the sum of its parts.

Watson, meanwhile, appears to be concentrating not on the whole human soul, but the whole human genome. The aim of the numerous investigators now probing the human genome is to read its entire genetic code. It remains to be seen whether either Watson or Crick, who raced as a team to describe the double helix, will reach their new goals. In any case, reaching goals is often a collaborative effort, requiring input from numerous investigators.

Analyzing nature and studying the parts is a relatively safe procedure. Many scientists therefore are satisfied with stopping here. Isaac Newton (1642–1727) was one of these. Having analyzed the components of light and the motion of bodies, he rested securely in his clockwork view of the universe. He was known for his refusal to make abstract speculations. Albert Einstein (1879–1955) was his exact counterpart. He was addicted to far-flung theories. In fact, he died while attempting to find a unified theory to encompass all the forces of nature. In a sense, he was a physical ecologist.

Whereas analyzing the component parts of nature is a fairly simple procedure, synthesizing the parts to create the whole is inordinately complicated. It's all too easy to come up with false constructs. This is particularly true in the fields of evolution and animal psychology where it is difficult to check theories with direct observation. Extrapolations of laboratory results into the world of nature may be drastically off the mark. Herein lies the basis for the philosophical controversy between the mechanists (behaviorists) and the ethologists in interpretations of animal behavior. Can animal behavior all be interpreted in light of simple immediate responses to stimuli or does an overall view help direct their behavior by a type of consciousness? (This matter is explored in Chapters 6 and 7.)

At IU, Muller taught the evolution class — from the point of view of genetics. He took his personal investigations not much farther than a study of gene mutations, under laboratory conditions. Although it has been reported that he was once lost in the wilds with an insect net, possibly trying to catch fruit flies, we never noticed that he had any interest in fieldwork at Indiana University. He thought nature studies were "old fashioned." Like Darwin in his later years, Muller was a denizen of his den where he could usually be found with his magnifying glass observing fruit flies in little bottles. In his evolution class, when asked why no new species are observed arising in nature, Muller claimed that all these generations of natural selection have led to "the best of all possible worlds." Muller likened the present state of species to precisely engineered watches. A watch would not get any better if dropped, causing a change, a mutation.

During a symposium, Muller once inadvertently demonstrated his perfect-watch mutation theory in a large lecture hall. He accidentally dropped his flashlight pointer. Upon resuming the lecture, he sheepishly remarked that the behavior of the pointer appeared somewhat erratic. This brought forth ripples of empathetic laughter from the audience.

According to Muller, when mutations arise among the perfect species, they may be expected to be harmful, as is indeed found to be the case with radiation-induced mutations. Since Muller by that time was a Nobel laureate, his students avidly entered his sayings into their notebooks, in preparation for the next examination. Even in science, where nature is supposed to be the authority, underlings have a tendency to give undue credit to "overlings." But any student of animal behavior in the class would obviously see a need for field studies to determine whether the professor was right. Are existing species perfectly adapted to their niches?

At IU, students of general animal behavior were conspicuously absent. At that time, studies in any form of psychology were isolated into a separate department, which concentrated on *human* behavior. Even Alfred Kinsey (1894–1956), who had been in the zoology department at IU as a professor doing research on the evolution of isolated populations of gall wasps, turned his back on the wasps when he noticed that studies of human sexuality were more interesting than wasp taxonomy. He developed his own institute and was sort of a misfit insofar as some of the IU constituents were concerned. Many of them wanted him to cease and desist in his investigations. But the administration insisted that it is the policy of the university to allow faculty members to study anything they choose.

Muller invited Kinsey, as well as Julian Huxley (1887–1975), to lecture to his evolution class. Julian was a grandson of Thomas Huxley (1825–95), one of Darwin's chief allies. Julian was author of the textbook, *Evolution, the Modern Synthesis* (1942). Having done studies in sexual selection, he had concluded that Darwin's theory of sexual selection was wrong. Darwin had said male creatures received their special adornment by a process of females choosing beautifully adorned males. Julian, however, supported the view that much, if not all, beautiful male adornment gave males an advantage in the natural battle for survival, independent of any female choice.

Early in his career Julian Huxley had worked on the genetics of freshwater shrimp (amphipods). In class Muller had stated that some amphipods living in caves were eyeless. He explained this on the basis that eyes were not needed in caves and, furthermore, were actually an impediment, since they got scratched when the animals bumped them against the walls of the cave. Eyeless mutants were therefore favored by natural selection. He gave no further particulars.

Muller explained the origin of blind cave fish in these same terms. But a former professor at IU, Carl Eigenmann (1863–1927), a famous student of fish, had maintained that cave fish lost their eyes simply by inheriting an acquired characteristic: Their eyes ceased to exist because they were of no use in the dark caves. Lack of use of the eyes led to their gradual atrophy, and the condition became hereditary.

After Fernandus Payne (1881–?) came to IU as a cytology teacher and researcher, he decided to put the theory of use and disuse of eyes to the test. For this he used the fast-breeding fruit fly, *Drosophila melanogaster*. He cultured the fruit flies for 39 generations in the dark, in an artificial "cave" (a dark room under the steps in the biology building). Upon making meticulous observations of the eyes of the flies, Payne could see no difference between those of fruit flies grown in light and those grown in the dark. Having proved a negative, he went back to his main study, general cytology. Later, Muller said that if this study had been continued, the eyeless mutant in *Drosophila melanogaster* would eventually have arisen spontaneously. What conclusions would Payne have drawn then? Perhaps we'll never know.

Noting the need for field studies, I searched the local caves. I found no eyeless amphipods, but near the entrance of May's cave (a few miles from Bloomington) I found a community of sighted amphipods, which were furiously mating. There were light-bodied as well as dark-bodied forms in the community, and they were mating selectively. The dark ones were in pairs, and the light ones were in pairs. This appeared to be sexual selection in action!

I was excited when all the specimens — light ones and dark ones — sent to an amphipod expert were identified as one species, *Gammarus minus*. My enthusiasm waned, however, when I discovered that the dark forms differed from the light forms in the structure of the antennae. According to all taxonomic rules at the time, these must then be classified as different species. Sexual-selection studies are supposed to be done within a single species.

In the same vicinity 17-year cicadas were emerging. Though all these were supposed to be one species, *Magicicada septendecim*, I again became intrigued after noticing that large and small forms were segregated on the basis of habitat selection. Furthermore, large forms were sexually segregated from the small forms, and the two forms had different mating calls. After at first entertaining thoughts of studying sexual selection in this species, I later suspected that these two separated groups of cicadas are actually two different species. I reported this in the *Proceedings of the Indiana Academy of Science*. Later, cicada taxonomists agreed that these are two different species.

Above the caves are "solution ponds." These are formed after the underlying limestone has been dissolved out by carbonated rainwater, and surface depressions are left on the ground above. Numerous dragonflies were breeding in these ponds. It was soon noted that males of a small, amber-winged dragonfly, *Perithemis tenera*, were perched along the margins of a pond at regular intervals. These males seemed to be attracting females to certain stations around the pond and mating with them. Since their behavior was highly localized and overt — and specimens could be experimentally marked with small dots of paint for studies in sexual selection — it was decided to focus on them.

But first, the game of Preliminary Examinations had to be played in front of the IU zoology legends. The results of this contest left my stomach full, not of butterflies, but dragonflies. The first pitch came from Fernandus Payne, who liked his answers lean, with no hemming and hawing. He threw a hard ball: "Is evolution a fact?" Like many similar queries, I thought that was a dumb question, but I didn't say so. (I consider such questions unanswerable, for they are utterly lacking in precision.) I said I accepted microevolution as a fact, but not macroevolution. I questioned whether the theory of natural selection of mutations was adequate to account for the origin of major categories of organisms. Base hit!

"Mr. Mutation and the Gene," H.J. Muller, was waiting for me in the third-base coaching area, smiling and twiddling his thumbs in his characteristic manner. He also had smiled like that when I was taking the written part of the qualifying exam in his office. I wasn't having that much fun trying to answer the question, "Why are newly arisen mutations usually recessive?" Since all the desks in his office were thoroughly cluttered, he had me sit with my feet stuck in the side of a big wooden box (in which he had received a huge model of a fruit fly he used for lecturing). The box was my desk, and it shook with each stroke of my pen. Not only did

Muller have an office that could have qualified as a disaster area, he wasn't known for his mechanical dexterity. He had a lot of trouble running a stopwatch. During the examination a phone call came in, and he began looking for a number in the directory. When he paged down to the lady's lingerie section, he looked up grinning and said, "This seems to be a Sears catalog." Dr. Muller was a most astute observer!

Pitch #2 was a curve. Queried Payne: "Can you suggest a simpler explanation than the natural-selection-of-mutations theory for the origin of organisms?" Since Payne liked simple, direct answers, I gave one: "The inheritance of acquired characteristics." Another base hit! Muller, who had come close to losing his career, even his life, in Communist Russia for his association with, and promotion of, "Western" genetics — with its ideas about heredity and failure to accept the doctrine of the inheritance of acquired characteristics — smiled and twiddled his thumbs even more now.

The next toss from pitcher Payne was a drop. I saw it coming. "Can you give us an example of evolution," he asked, "which can be better explained in terms of the inheritance of acquired characteristics than on the basis of natural selection of mutations?" Yes! At the swing of the bat, I replied, "The external genital apparatus of the damselfly."

Each species of damselfly, I went on to explain, seems to have its own lock-and-key mechanism counteracting the possibility of hybridization. The female carries a lock on the anterior end of the top of the thorax. The male also has a lock — at the bottom of the abdomen on the second and third anterior segments. The male has a key that matches these two locks. The key resides on the tip of his abdomen. Somehow he knows what to do with his key.

First, bending his long abdomen forward, he inserts it into his lock in a type of self-mating maneuver. This results in the passing of a spermatophore into his lock. Next, he flies to the pond and finds a good place for reproduction. He waits for a female, though not any female. He awaits his specific female. He catches her and inserts his species-identification key into the species-identification lock on the top of the female's

The male damselfly clasps the thorax of the female while she receives sperm from the bottom of his abdomen.

thorax. Coupling results, as the male holds the female dangling from the tip of his abdomen.

The female also carries a key on the tip of her abdomen. This key matches the lock at the base of the male abdomen where the spermatophore is stored. She bends her abdomen forward and, after some effort, inserts her key on the tip of her abdomen into the lock at the bottom of the sternite of the male — and, so engaged, obtains the loot, the spermatophore. Having performed this complicated coital conniption, the female is ready to lay her eggs.

The odd mating method is not without its advantages. The firm hold of the female by the male promotes monogamy by preventing her from being clasped by other males. In fact, extraneous males frequently attempt this clasping, unsuccessfully. The long abdomens of both male and female facilitate the underwater egg-laying. The female sometimes goes several inches beneath the surface to lay her eggs in submerged vegetation, while the male maintains his hold on her thorax. If she goes too far under, the male releases her before his wings get wet. The male then flits about intently above the area where she went down and drives away intruding males.

After the female has finished egg-laying and tries to emerge from the water, she often gets stuck in the surface film. Were she to be blown about over the pond, she might become a ready meal for fish. Fortunately for the poor damselfly in distress, her heroic mate quickly rescues her and lifts her from the water. They can then fly away together, looking for another egg-laying site.

Given the structural and mental complexity of this mating system, it is little wonder that few, if any, hybrid dragonflies are reported. The Odonata have a patent on this mating system. To understand its origin in terms of natural selection of rare mutations may explain why so many entomologists, geneticists, and the like are bald on the top of the head. Scratching of the head over such problems may have produced, after many generations of doctoral candidates, a hairless condition.

Are we to believe that, in past history, locks and keys arose promiscuously over the bodies of damselflies for eons of generations until the proper fits had been matched? This is to say nothing of the origin of the proper mental qualifications for use of the locks and keys. It also overlooks how the species reproduced before the system was operational.

If we start with end-to-end transfer of genetic material between the sexes, characteristic of the rest of the insects, what advantage would be gained by a male bending his abdomen forward and depositing a spermatophore on the front of his abdomen? If this were a wasted effort, would it not have been weeded out by natural selection — instead of persisting for millennia while other parts of the system, similarly energy-wasting, had been perfected? This does not seem natural.

Payne's third question had been a good one. Can you think of a method for explaining evolution that is simpler than the natural-selection-of-mutations theory? The theory of the inheritance of acquired characteristics bypasses the need to wait for trial and error on the road to perfection. It is thereby closer to obeying the natural law of energy conservation than is the mutation theory. Simply stated, the animal gets what it needs. It presupposes a desire, a drive. According to this theory, the wish is the father of the acquisition — and, yes, necessity is the mother of invention. There is no wasted effort. The giraffe, obeying its innate desire to obtain food, a desire shared by all organisms, stretches its neck to reach the leaves high up in the trees. Since offspring resemble their parents, the young giraffes will inherit longer and longer necks until the topmost leaves are reached. After the highest leaves are reached, there is nothing left to desire. If we could throw into this system a method for transmitting the result to the offspring, we would, indeed, have a method simpler than the mutation method for executing evolution. (In fact, the theory of sexual selection incorporates an element of desire. According to Darwin, the female desires a beautiful mate and therefore eventually produces one.)

In the case of the human brain, in which desire for more and more knowledge, and all the competitive advantages that go with such power, selection may have no limit. It could lead to brains of celestial proportions. As an analogy, Timothy Ferris (1992) sees individual galaxies in the cosmos representing separate segments of a brain. Connecting these parts is a network of channels of electromagnetic communication, just as neuronic filamentous extensions permit communication among various parts of the animal brain. Ferris is a member of a group advocating the more extensive use of radio telescopes for interception of such cosmic messages.

The theory of the inheritance of acquired characteristics is beautifully simple — and it satisfies the first part of the rule of Einstein, "Make everything as simple as possible." Einstein had made a career of applying this rule in physics, especially in the field of energy. But he was keenly aware of the danger of oversimplification — hence the modification of the rule, "but no simpler."

Is the inheritance of acquired characteristics too simple? August Weismann (1834–1914) thought so. The mice from which he had cut off tails for 20 generations had not inherited short tails. He was convinced that hereditary particles are distinct from the rest of the body, insulated from all external influences. The stretching of the neck by the giraffe would not therefore influence the heredity of the offspring.

To apply the principle of the inheritance of acquired characteristics to the case of dragonfly reproduction might simplify the problem a little. At least the development of the reproductive system would be directed by a desire — to reproduce. This direction would eliminate some of the randomness inherent in the natural-selection-of-mutations theory.

A still simpler theory would have been that the entire process had been intellectually conceived by a genetic engineer and put into effect by a single directive. Maybe nature could find a use for human-type intelligence after all. But by the same argument, humans — even given the inorganic world as a starter — would need to possess a type of omniscience to engineer the type of complex ecosystem we see today. It may require an outside cosmic view, a unified field theory encompassing life itself.

This same predicament is faced in the physical sciences. Einstein was unwilling to accept the view that the universe arose by chance, or by the fortuitous concurrence of atoms, as the ancient Greeks put it. Einstein persistently worked under the theory that the universe was put together by a Creator who, Einstein said, did not play with dice.

But paradoxically, in his graduate-school thesis, "On the Motion Required by the Molecular Kinetic Theory of Heat of Particles in Fluids at Rest" (1905), Einstein proved that randomness can lead to direction. He proved statistically that the random impacts of molecules of water bombarding a suspended pollen grain could result in moving that grain a certain direction.

At any rate, in response to Payne's request for a simpler solution to the origin of life forms than a natural-selection-of-mutations explanation, Special Creation, with its inherent implications of conscious directives, would have been the simplest. But this answer would have shifted the entire problem into the department of theology. The trouble with that department is that the personnel there aren't known for testing their theories; they simply believe in them. Such methodology is anathema to the natural sciences. Had the ancient worshippers of Father Sun experimentally withheld their worship to discover whether the object of their devotion would really fail to rise in the east, the theory on which their religion was based would have collapsed, and the entire superstructure would have come crumbling to the earth from which it had sprung.

Three decades ago there was a push to move theology to the scientific stage of intellectual pursuit. One of the proponents, Bishop James Pike (1913–69), lost his life in the effort. His remains were found in the hot, dry, desert sands of the Mideast where he had gone in pursuit of higher theology. The natural science of desert climatology might have saved him.

This entire discourse, of course, was not included in my answer to Payne in the Preliminary Examinations; only a partial sketch was stated at the time. I wondered if I had hit a foul ball down the left-field line. My answer had been neither simple nor direct. But my hitting coach, "Mr. Field Biology," Frank Young, said if it were called a foul he would go to bat for me. The umpire, "Mr. Field Theory," Theodore Torrey (1907–86), called it fair — a home run! I sailed past Mr. Mutation Theory at third base and jumped on home plate.

The prize, the Eigenmann Fellowship, for continuation of studies in sexual selection, was received, but not for study of blind fish. Instead, this project would involve an organism with exceptional visual acuity: the dragonfly. In fact, use of dragonflies — insects in which vision is especially significant in the mating system — would eliminate the persistent problem of smelling and tasting, an especially sticky wicket in studies of animal behavior.

Ideally suited for these studies was a small, dainty dragonfly commonly known as the amber-wing. From the viewpoint of any artist, this one would be hard to beat. The wings of the male are a uniform golden-amber color. Those of the female are clear, but with interesting tan-to-dark-brown spots. Individual dragonflies vary in degree of darkening of the wing spots, which parallels degree of darkening of the general body color. The males also vary in degree of body darkening. The behavior of this dragonfly is strictly related to the amount of sunshine available. In common with many humans, *Perithemis* is a lover of the sun.

CHAPTER 2

LESSONS FROM DRAGONFLIES

PERITHEMIS

HE AMBER-WINGED *PERITHEMIS* MALES DART about under the sun for eminently sensible reasons: to keep warm, to defend territories, to mate, and to lay eggs at the site of their choice. Cold-blooded animals such as insects, which derive only minimal body heat from metabolic sources, are heavily dependent on outside energy for maintaining optimal operating body temperature. Many insects bear dark spots — radiators — that serve as acceptors of radiant heat to be used for warming the blood. For this purpose, some insects have a dark body surface.

The amber-winged dragonfly is a prime example of how a species may adapt to changes in solar radiation by changing the intensity of darkness of its body. It performs this feat by selection of body-color genes during sexual reproduction. The same chemical pathway that produces the dark colors also yields the golden-amber color. The relationship between dark-brown and golden colors is clearly seen in comparing the colors of the wings of dark and light members of an amber-winged population. The intensity of dark-brown pigment appears to diminish as the golden color emerges.

Not only do the dark and golden colors have direct adaptive (physical) value, they have indirect psychological (artistic) value. The colors on the long-wave end of the spectrum — from dark brown through red and yellow — appear as psychologically stimulating (sexual) colors. The color gold is a mixture of these "warm" and "hot" colors, which are appreciated to the point of reverence by animals (at least by humans). Why, otherwise, would the cardinals (the chiefs) wear red robes? The reverence awarded to yellow-red colors may be based on either attractive love or threatening fear — the fear of love and/or the love of fear. The colors at the other end of the spectrum, green and blue, are sedating (vegetative) colors, which are taken for granted as backgrounding.

In line with these observations, the amber-winged dragonfly would represent the yellow-red end of the spectrum. It should therefore be a good species for studies in sexual selection. This species shows all the behaviors called for by Darwinian sexual selection: (1) The males compete among themselves; (2) females are attracted to the males; (3) the males display their beautiful golden wings toward the females during courtship; and (4) the females appear to select certain males in preference to others.

Furthermore, the species is present in statistically significant numbers, and specimens can be individually marked for case-history studies. In contrast to the situation with birds, the mating activity is overt and highly localized, and the specimens can be observed openly with little or no disturbance of their normal activity. Dragonfly studies should help nail down the female-choice dimension of Darwinian sexual selection.

A brown-tinted insect net, held open by wires, was slowly and gently placed over the dragonflies as they perched or laid their eggs. Specimens were marked with small dots of colored paint for individual identification. If they were then laid down gently, they would remain immobile for some time before resuming their normal activities. Over two breeding seasons, 1,392 males and 1,497 females were marked and studied. This should be a statistically significant sample! I observed them daily over their life spans at the pond by continuously circling the small body of water.

Early in my research I learned that *Perithemis* is territorial. This was already quite a find. At that time territorialism (defense of area), though well-documented in vertebrates, was virtually unknown among invertebrates.

I discovered that, upon arrival at the pond, a male flits about the margins while closely approaching potential reproductive sites — be they patches of algae in sunny places, or sticks and logs in shady places. The male appears fastidious in picking his reproductive site. He closely examines a large number of sites before making his selection. In so doing he dips his abdomen to the water after the manner of a female laying eggs. In time he becomes localized to a particular site and at a small spot on the site. He then defends the site against rival males by wing-fluttering and racing with rivals. Each day thereafter, when he returns to the pond, he flies quickly to his previously chosen site with little or no re-examination.

Why does he behave this way? Does he know that what he is doing has anything to do with the mating to follow? Does he have any idea that the female he will invite to that site will lay eggs there? Or is all this behavior simply automatic? This type of question may be asked repeatedly as the reproductive behavior of dragonflies is described.

The female Perithemis *dragonfly follows the male as he leads her to his selected mating site.*

A female Perithemis *dragonfly perches in the feeding area.*

When a *Perithemis* female flies over the water, the male immediately dashes toward her while swaying from side to side. He then turns and flies slowly back to his site with the female following. How does the male recognize that the female belongs to his own species? Does he have self-awareness, as well as species awareness? In these respects is he conscious, or is he innately and simply responding to stimuli? Similar questions may be asked about the mentality of the female.

Upon reaching the site the male hovers above the specific spot he had chosen. He intently flutters his wings there while raising his abdomen toward the female, as in courtship. He treats the female in a most considerate fashion, allowing her every opportunity to make her selection of a reproductive site. The female then dips her abdomen into the water at the spot the male had previously selected and advertised by fluttering thereon. If the female flies away to another site, the male becomes intensely active in re-examining the site. If the female slows down her flight near the reproductive site, the male captures her and gently fastens the claspers on the tip of his abdomen to the back of her head. The coupled pair then lands near or on the site. Mating then ensues, the female cooperating by fastening the tip of her abdomen to the sperm packet on the bottom of his abdomen. This is not a hurried mating, the average duration being 17.5 seconds.

After mating, the pair separates, and the male flies slowly back to the spot where courtship had occurred, again with the female following. The male then hovers low over the site while facing the female, as if reintroducing her to the reproductive spot. After all, he had a lot more opportunity to acquaint himself with the site than she did. The female then begins to lay her eggs there, whereupon the male flies vigorously around her and drives away encroaching males.

Since the number of sites is limited, males sometimes select sites that are clearly unsuitable. Females consistently fly away from courting males at these sites, then mate at other locations. Males that are repeatedly unsuccessful in defending sites flee readily when dashed at by other males, the flight being straight like that of a female, not jerky and erratic like that of a territorial male. This straight flight appears to attract male pursuit.

A female flying over the pond in her steady, deliberate manner is fair game for any male spotting her. This frequently leads to mass chases of the female, until rival males are eliminated from the competition. Each day the first males arrive at the pond 10 to 30 minutes before the first females. The organization is therefore relatively stable by the time the females begin to appear. Both sexes show a remarkable tendency to return to the exact spot where the previous courtship had occurred and where the female had dipped her abdomen.

Throughout the study period, not all reproductive sites were equally used. This inequality did not seem to be due to a special appearance of the males occupying these favored sites. In fact, on one day the male that was most successful in mating was particularly battered and dingy-looking. (Frequent mating may result in wing-battering.) It seemed obvious that it was not male appearance that was determining mating success, but rather the nature of the reproductive site. As further evidence of this, when a male was ousted by a rival and selected another reproductive site, the new site resembled the previous one. If the previous site had been a patch of algae, the newly selected one would also be a patch of algae. If the previous one had been a log, the new one would be a log. The females behaved similarly when they returned to the pond for repeated mating and egg-laying. This behavior was easily documented by virtue of the large number of specimens available for study.

My observations at that southern Indiana pond opened up a view of the causes of male mating success, independent of general appearances of the male. Psychological attachment of a male to specific characteristics of the territory appears to give that male an enormous advantage in male-male competition. This would single out certain males for a competitive advantage. The more his physiological traits match the microniche traits, the more successful will that male be in male-male competition. Consequently, that male will be the one most available for mating with arriving females.

Seven of the marked, localized territorial males were captured and kept under refrigeration for seven days. After that, they were released in a small thicket about a half-mile from the pond where they had previously been observed feeding and resting. Of the seven males that had been released, five returned to their respective territories at the pond from which they had been removed.

Throughout the study the darkness of pigmentation of the adults had been recorded by making comparison with color standards. When a statistical analysis was finally made of the results, a highly significant correlation was found between darkness of body/wings and type of reproductive site selected. Light forms of both sexes tended to select patches of algae (characteristic of sunny places), whereas dark forms tended to select sticks and logs (characteristic of shady places).

The females were indeed making choices, but not according to an abstract aesthetic appreciation of male appearances — beauty for the

sake of beauty. Rather, their choices were based on sound domestic economics. They were selecting sites containing the proper food suitable for
rearing their young, in line with their own ecological and physiological
requirements. What appeared to be choice of a male by a female was
really a mutual selection of reproductive site on the part of both male
and female. Toward this end, a delay in mating — thereby giving the
female the chance to make a choice — was provided by the courtship
ceremony. The result of such a mating system is niche specialization,
providing a species the opportunity to match genotype with specific
environmental conditions.

This finding greatly complicated the conventional approaches to
the study of the female-choice aspect of sexual selection. Are females
choosing males, or are they choosing reproductive sites? Even today, few
(if any) reports of female choice of highly ornamented males have ruled
out the possibility that it is really the territory of the male that the female
is choosing. In the final analysis, the success of a certain male may
depend simply on his success in defending a reproductive site favorable
to both himself and his mate. In territorial competition, male dominance
may be influenced by attractiveness of the reproductive site as well as by
the adornment of the male. The adornment may be directly involved in
male-male competition. Also, the aggressive behavior of a male may be
enhanced by his own adornment and thereby complicate studies in
which the male adornment is artificially manipulated in studies of
female choice. Sorting out all these influences on male mating success is
excruciatingly difficult. It approaches the principle of indeterminacy, a
negative conclusion some physicists reach as they attempt to sort out the
causes for behavior of electrons and photons. The experimental conditions set up influence the behavior of the object being observed.

Helena Cronin in her book, *The Ant and the Peacock* (1991),
reviewing the claims made for female choice, presents this summary:

> But how did the peacock acquire his flamboyant tail or
> the bowerbird, his predilection for decoration? Although

the debate has advanced immensely and very excitedly since Darwin's and Wallace's time, many of their own questions, both theoretical and empirical, are no less pressing today. ... The issues raised by sexual selection, throughout the theory's history, have fallen into two categories. The first is the question of whether sexual selection is required to account for the phenomena at all or whether they [the problems] can be explained instead by the standard forces of natural selection alone. For nearly a century, the majority of Darwinians saw this as a major issue. They sought almost any alternative to sexual selection, and it was on natural selection that they relied above all. The second category of questions concerns mate choice — in particular, the reasons for making a choice and how, or even whether, Darwinian forces could allow them to evolve. These questions were raised from the first, but it is only recently that the role of mate choice has become the main focus of attention. It is now a flourishing line of research — and an enormously fruitful line it has proved to be.

In the *Perithemis* study, to determine whether the beautiful amber color of the wings of the males is attractive to females, an experiment was performed. In each set of three males, the amber wing color of one male was obscured with black shoe dye. The wings of the second male were treated similarly with clear varnish. The wings of the third male were left untreated. The reactions of females to these males were then observed.

The results of this experiment were quite unexpected, but highly revealing. One reason *Perithemis* had been chosen for study was that it appeared likely the females were following the males on the basis of the lovely amber color of the wings of the males. But no evidence in support of this was found. Instead, the females followed the blackened males, were courted at the reproductive sites, and mated normally. The amber color of the wings of the males did not appear to be essential for successful courtship and mating. In fact, the females appeared to mate equally with the blackened and the unblackened males.

The amber color of the wings of the males, however, is clearly involved in territorial defense. A blackened male may begin wing-fluttering near the normal male, as in male-male competition, but the normal male fails to react and perches at his customary lookout. The blackened male then pounces repeatedly on the perching normal male, thereby driving him away temporarily, but the localized normal male returns and perches again. Eventually, the two males may perch near each other in the same territory.

If a female arrives under these conditions, the males fly toward her in the normal fashion. She may follow either of the males to the reproductive site and be courted. She may then mate and lay eggs at the site. Of 19 matings so observed, 10 were with the normal male and 9 with the blackened one. Of course, this is not a significant difference from the 50 percent that would be expected if the chances of mating with a normal and blackened male were equal. Female choice of an amber-winged male in preference to a blackened male was not found in this study.

PLATHEMIS

The study with *Perithemis* was essentially repeated with another dragonfly, the white-tailed skimmer, *Plathemis lydia*. While the behavior of *Perithemis* could be characterized as courtly and refined, the manner of *Plathemis* is just the opposite. Whatever the male does appears abrupt and crude. Whereas the *Perithemis* male courts his female for a long time before she acquiesces, the *Plathemis* male unceremoniously grasps the head of his female shortly after spotting her. The *Plathemis* male is so rough that the neck of the female may become twisted, whereupon she loses equilibrium and falls into the water. After dumping the female onto the reproductive site, the male dashes at encroaching males and some-

Male Plathemis *dragonflies display the white upper surfaces of their abdomens in territorial competition.*

times collides with them, knocking them into the water. Wolf spiders lurking nearby may secure the fate of these downed dragonflies.

In stalking a female, the male hides the white upper surface of his abdomen from her by lowering it. While so doing, he may stealthily hover behind vegetation. In no case was a *Plathemis* female observed to be attracted to a mature *Plathemis* male.

As the male hides behind the vegetation — and lowers his abdomen so the white upper surface is hidden from the female — does he know that the white upper surface of his abdomen may scare the female away? (In fact, when interacting with an intruding male, the defending male elevates the white upper surface of the abdomen toward the rival.) In heading off a female high over the pond, the male does not fly straight toward her. Rather, he calculates her distance and her speed in directing his flight to the place she will be when he gets there. Is all this complicated behavior automatic? We do know that we as human beings can execute very complicated behavior consciously or automatically — for example, when we are in the unconscious state, as when sleepwalking.

The white upper surface of the male's abdomen is effective in territorial spacing, much as the amber wing color in *Perithemis* males is so used. In territorial competition *Plathemis* males display the white upper surface by raising the abdomen toward a rival male. If this activity fails to intimidate the rival, maybe a mad race will do it. In racing, the males fly together like a couple of fighter aircraft. Their wings can be heard buzzing as the males dart overhead. The males attack even inanimate white objects, such as white feathers blown about by the wind.

There is considerable disparity in the number of matings that occur in the territories around the pond. A male may localize at a specific area of the pond for his entire life span, up to 36 days. Also, females returning to lay their eggs generally use the same territory for repeated egg-laying. If all males are removed from the pond, some females perform dual races with other females in the same manner as do two males.

In the interval between emergence and re-entry to the pond, the dragonflies rest and feed in the wooded area surrounding the pond. As the males mature, the upper surface of the abdomen changes from the same brown color as the female to a bluish-white color. Finally, this surface turns brilliant white. This progression toward whiteness is related to maturation of the gonads.

Some of the males come to the pond before they are completely mature. These bluish males offer lessons in animal mentality. They appear to learn in part how to recognize females of their own species. From the outset they make advances toward other dragonflies, such as *Anax junius*. But after several such experiences, they ignore dragonflies of other species. When the proper *Plathemis* females finally arrive (about 40 minutes after the first males arrive), these same immature males recognize them as their own species. Such immature males, without territories, dash at and capture females while making attempts to mate. Such couplings involving the young males are often abortive. Apparently, the female refuses to bend the tip of her abdomen properly, thereby failing to reach the spermatophore on the bottom of the male's abdomen. Eventually, the female is released.

INTERPRETATIONS OF DRAGONFLY BEHAVIOR

Comparison of the reproductive strategies of *Plathemis* and *Perithemis* illustrates specialization in action. *Plathemis* employs the generalized approach to reproduction, investing little time and energy in strategic planning. The males simply and abruptly grasp the females and mate. The eggs are aimed toward the egg-laying area in an indiscriminate, shotgun-like fashion. They pile up there in a haphazard, glistening mass. Other females are attracted to the mass and stack their eggs on top of the ones already present. This may lead to suffocation of the embryonic dragonflies. To make up for the mortality of the developing dragonflies, the females simply produce lots of eggs. Perhaps, out of the glistening profusion of eggs, two dragonflies will mature to replace the two parents.

Perithemis, on the other hand, uses the specialized approach. This species invests considerable time and energy in strategic planning, with careful discrimination. Through careful cooperation of both male and female, the eggs are delicately nestled on the chosen spot at the specific reproductive site. On hitting the water, the jellied package bursts open to spread the eggs, thereby ensuring that the nymphs will have plenty of oxygen for their rapid development. Prior selection of the reproductive site will ensure that food to match the individual physiologies of the nymphs will be there when needed.

The conspicuous adornment of the males, be it *amber* on the wings of *Perithemis* or *white* on the abdomen of *Plathemis*, is important in territorial defense and therefore in enhancing male mating success. This alone would appear adequate for explaining the origin of such exhibitory adornment of the males, without evoking a female-choice explanation. The display features, instrumental in spacing the males, minimize the energy involved in actual physical fighting.

At first the oversupply of males at the pond appears non-adaptive, since the presence of extra males results in interference with egg-laying by the females. The availability of numerous extra males, however, ensures that the spermatophore supply is adequate. (With most of the males removed, the remaining males, though going through the normal coital motions, sometimes do not fertilize the eggs.) Also, interference with egg-laying at certain highly attractive spots helps prevent over-crowding of eggs and young.

It would also be advantageous for the males, who are the pioneer-ing explorers of the reproductive sites, to be conspicuously adorned so as to attract predators. In the case of *Perithemis*, a species in which the males attract females to the sites, elimination of the male through preda-tory activity would serve to save the female from a similar fate. Indeed, males examining reproductive sites are frequently preyed upon by frogs, fish, water bugs, or spiders. Likewise, the conspicuous white upper sur-face of the abdomen of *Plathemis* males exposes them to predators. These males are frequently preyed upon by kingbirds as the dragonflies zig and zag above the pond.

These insects are remarkably space-conscious. A male quickly rec-ognizes his specific reproductive spot with respect to the total layout of the pond and environs. When the *Perithemis* male leads the female to his reproductive site, he commonly evades encounters with other males. This strategy is, of course, important. The other male proprietor might spot the female crossing his own border and, by chasing her, disrupt the normal course of events.

Using the behavior of *Perithemis* as a model, it may be postulated that a randomly mating population, adapted for living in an ecological niche, could be split into two partially segregated groups by choice of microhabitats. In this case darkly pigmented forms of both sexes, mutu-ally attracted to shaded microhabitats, would become at least partially segregated from lightly pigmented forms, adapted for living in sunny microhabitats. A courtship period introduced into the mating system would ensure that the female had opportunity to choose a microhabitat.

Interestingly, the differences in pigmentation of the dragonflies is appropriate for inhabiting different microhabitats. In shaded habitats the dark pigments may assist in absorption of external heat. Also, the pigments may help camouflage the specimens relative to their habitats. A specimen with amber wings is quite inconspicuous when perched on an algae patch growing in the sun, but it's clearly visible among sticks and logs in the shade. On the other hand, darkly pigmented forms of dragonflies are conspicuous on algae but hard to see on logs and sticks.

In variable species the tendency for both male and female to be attracted to specific reproductive sites would promote adaptive specialization to specific niches. Included in the specific niche would be specific types of food found there. In this specialization, mutual choice of a microhabitat on the part of both male and female would bring together males and females of similar tastes, similar biochemistry, and similar physiology — all appropriate for inhabiting that microhabitat.

This mating system of "like with like" has its downside. It may lead to loss of flexible adaptability of the species if the segregation process becomes complete. To lessen this problem, *Perithemis* incorporates a significant amount of cross-mating. Such a mating system would be appropriate for a species inhabiting two different microhabitats, either of which might be temporary (depending on climatic conditions). By simulating egg-laying at the reproductive site, both male and female may be measuring the temperature of the water. This temperature would indicate the amount of solar radiation that site receives. The amount of solar radiation would determine the characteristics of the food at the site, particularly if the food is of a photosynthetic variety.

The habit of male dragonflies closely examining the egg-laying site, and even dipping the tip of the abdomen into the water there, may also have implications for other organisms, such as frogs. A number of studies indicate that female frogs choose larger males with deeper voices. It is conceivable that females are adaptively programmed to be attracted to such males, and these are the ones that succeed in defending the more favorable sites.

The programming may still be evident under laboratory conditions, in which males of larger size and deeper voices are more attractive to females. Assuming there is no environmental influence related to this behavior, certain observers have interpreted the female choice by what is popularly called sensory bias. (Bias in this context is that which slants probability in a particular direction.) This bias explanation assumes that a chance mutation has caused the female to program her sensory system in a certain direction. Then, even if the mutation has no adaptive value, it may become incorporated into the sensory program of the female and be re-enforced by exploitation of other mutations that have arisen by the same method. (See Ryan 1990.) This is all in line with Darwin's original account of sexual selection. But, at least with frogs and dragonflies, an alternate interpretation based on the food-drive theory may be employed to explain at least a portion of the total origin of elaborated male traits. This theory, by assigning an adaptive driving force to the scheme, would minimize a chance non-adaptive explanation.

The dragonfly manuscript, containing the observations and interpretations in line with the food-courtship theory, was submitted to *Ecology*. The editor had trouble finding anyone in the United States qualified to review it. He finally sent it to William Thorpe in England. At the time Thorpe was in the process of releasing his book, *Learning and Instinct in Animals*. Thorpe subsequently hailed the dragonfly manuscript as "of the greatest theoretical importance." The journal's editorial review board declared the manuscript to be "the most remarkable article ever published in *Ecology*." It was published in 1955 in *Ecology*, Vol. 36. It was reprinted in 1972 in *Readings in Entomology*, Barbosa and Peters, Editors.

CHAPTER 3

LESSONS FROM
COURTSHIP-FEEDING

Male cardinals chase females away from food in the winter,
then feed them in the spring.

HY DO MALE CARDINALS, WHO DRIVE female cardinals away from the bird feeder in winter, begin feeding the females as the spring season arrives? The obvious explanation is that during the spring mate-selection season this behavior aids the female in her selection of a mate who will exemplify the feeding habit. This helps ensure that the growing young and incubating female will receive an adequate food supply from their territorial mates.

But there are additional advantages to feeding during the courtship ceremony. The system would balance population density with food supply. If the abundance of food, the staff of life of a species, enhances courtship and mating, it would also enhance reproduction — and thereby provide for natural birth control. Furthermore, this mating system, which involves specific foods, would segregate genotypes to form races and, finally, species for niche specialization.

In the world of nature, how widespread is the phenomenon of courtship-feeding? How close are the relationships between food supply, courtship, and mating? With these questions in mind, I began extensive field excursions. Specific foods were found to be involved in the courtship and mating of many insects. Males defended such foods against rivals. They then waited until females arrived to partake of those same foods. As a female fed, the male captured her. Coitus ensued.

MONARCH BUTTERFLY

Behind our backyard runs a north-south railroad. Along the right of way grow numerous milkweeds. This is just what is needed for the monarch butterfly, *Danaus plexippus*, also known as the milkweed butterfly. The railroad, with its hot thermals resulting from solar radiation, forms an ideal energy-saving glide path for the butterflies in their north-south migrations, and the milkweed flowers serve as a continuous supply of high-energy snacks as they travel.

Over two seasons the territorial behavior of the males was studied. As the butterflies fed on flowers, they were marked with small drops of paint. In summer the adult males established their territories around patches of milkweed, driving away rival males by extended chases. Winning males maintained their territories for up to 22 days.

The color of the monarch butterfly, especially the underside of the wings (the side exposed when the butterflies are feeding on the flowers), closely resembles the red-orange color of the flowers. When a female

*Monarch butterflies mate while feeding on the monarch's host plant
(the milkweed) in the male's territory.*

monarch arrives and begins to feed, the male perches beside her. After a
few seconds he catches her, and they mate. They may feed together on
the milkweed flowers up to 83 minutes while mating. A day or two
thereafter, the female flits around numerous young milkweed plants.
Occasionally, she lays an egg on the underside of a leaf. (This story is
continued in Chapter 7.)

DOGBANE BEETLE

The dogbane plant, having milky juice like that of the milkweed, is
not widely used as food by insects. But there is one picturesque, multi-
colored, gold-and-green beetle, the dogbane beetle, *Chrysochus auratus*,
which uses the dogbane plant for food. The male beetle becomes localized to a certain plant on which it feeds. Later, the female visits and
begins feeding, whereupon the waiting male captures her, and mating
ensues. After mating, the female continues feeding on the leaves of the
dogbane plant.

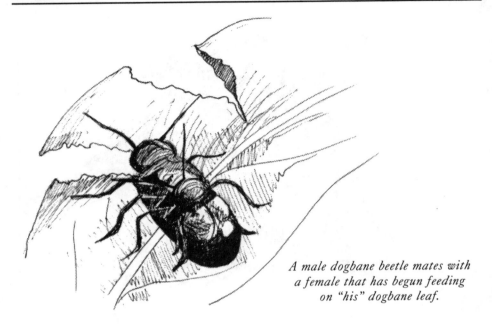

*A male dogbane beetle mates with
a female that has begun feeding
on "his" dogbane leaf.*

SOLDIER BEETLE

A male soldier beetle, *Chauliognathus pennsylvanicus*, was seen feeding on the blooming head of a sunflower. The colored markings of the insect closely matched the color of the flower. Presently, a female arrived and began feeding on the sunflower's head. The male, upon encountering her, felt her body with his antennae and coitus followed.

TIGER BEETLE

An insect that shows the connection between animal food and mating is the tiger beetle, *Cicendela sexguttata*. The males establish territories along woodland paths from which they repel intruding males by charging. They feed on ants and other small insects entering their territories. If a female enters, catches prey, and begins to feed, the male immediately takes advantage of the situation by pouncing on her — and mating takes place. Another male may rush in and attack the mating male, whereupon the female departs. The two males then engage in a vigorous wrestling match, which can last nearly four minutes. The contest usually results in the departure of the intruding male.

HANGINGFLY

(1976) describes a remarkable example of courtship-feeding among hangingflies, *Bittacus apicalis*. Males present gifts of food to their potential mates. The female allows the male mating time in proportion to the size of his food gift.

HAWFLY

That isolated food supplies may lead to species formation is also dramatically demonstrated by the American hawfly, *Rhagoletis pomonella*. In primeval America this fly fed and reproduced on the small, red, apple-like fruits of hawthorn bushes. When European immigrants colonized America they introduced their apple trees into the hawthorn area. Part of the hawfly population then became adapted to feeding and reproducing on the apples. This led to segregation of *pomonella* into two races. Males of the apple race defend apples against rival males, then mate with females attracted to the apples. Flies of the hawthorn race behave similarly on hawthorn fruits. Will the two races eventually end up as two distinct species? The case has been well-researched by Feder et al. (1990).

MOURNING DOVE

Near a garden pool in our backyard, a male mourning dove performed nesting behavior on the ground! While sitting there he reached

A male mourning dove places sticks around himself as a kind of false-nest "bower," then he "coos" loudly.

out and gathered sticks, which he tucked around himself. Intermittently, he swelled up his throat, adorned with iridescent golden feather tips, and cooed loudly. This behavior simulates the behavior of bowerbirds, in which the male makes a nest away from the female's nest.

Shortly thereafter, a female flew down and landed about six feet away. The male approached her, and the two fed together on the ground for about five minutes. Suddenly, the female flew to a spruce tree directly behind the pool, and the male followed. As they perched on the limb, the female moved close to the male and pecked at his throat. The male then fed the female by regurgitation. Immediately thereafter, they mated on the limb.

They built a nest in that tree. The male furnished the sticks, which he carefully selected from the ground near the pool. He rejected many sticks before choosing one. He took the chosen stick to the nest where the female was sitting. He landed on her back and placed the stick before her. She then tucked the stick around herself in the nest. They raised two chicks. Both parents fed them. The baby birds pecked at the throats of their parents before being fed.

COOPER'S HAWK

In the summer of 1996, a male Cooper's hawk established a nesting territory on the campus of Goshen College. He fed on chipmunks, starlings, grackles, blue jays, mourning doves, and robins found about the campus. A female arrived, and nest construction was begun in an oak tree on campus. On April 4, 1997, nest construction was resumed. On May 2 he was observed leaving a freshly killed bird on a tree limb in the presence of the female. While the female was feeding on the bird, he mated with her. In due course they raised four offspring.

GALAPAGOS FINCHES

From the first accounts of Charles Darwin, it has been known that certain finches on the Galapagos Islands off the coast of South America have become specialized, relative to bill structure, to use particular kinds of foods present in very limited supply on the islands. It is thought that, by this specialization process, certain species pioneering onto the islands split into splinter species.

Now if distinctive foods are responsible for splitting the species, then supplying an abundant supply of a common food should lead to merging the splinter back into one species. This appears to be precisely what happened when bird feeders were introduced onto the Galapagos Islands. A hybrid swarm resulted from crossing the two species.

There is evidence that, even in the absence of bird feeders, an abundant food supply, brought about by a rainy period in the weather cycle, enhances hybridization of the birds as they become less discriminating of food while feeding on the overflowing common supply. In drought periods, when food becomes scarcer and the birds compete for the scant isolated supplies, the groups of birds become more segregated. See Weiner (1994) for an interesting account of research on these finches.

ARENA BIRDS

Among some birds in which males are not involved in helping rear the young, the males station themselves within an arena where they defend small stages. As distinguished from an ordinary wide ranging territorial system, nesting does not occur in the actual arena but in the surrounding vicinity. Otherwise, the arena system maintains the general characteristics of ordinary territorial systems. The females mate there with the male proprietors of the small territories. It is sometimes said that on the arena the females receive no benefits from the males' activities except genes received from the males. It is presumed that food is not involved in this mating system.

It may well be that the arena form of courtship and mating grew out of compression of formerly traditional territories into small stages. Memory of certain territories, in which the favorite food of the species had been found in rich abundance (and where courtship and mating had occurred), became fixed into the arena mating system of the bird. Even today, arena birds tend to be firmly attached to these places where they return to mate, much as salmon return to their specific mating grounds.

Early support for Darwin's theory of female choice came from study of an arena bird, a small European sandpiper called the ruff because of the ruffled collar. The males strut and fight on a small arena. Finally, they settle down some and, since the ruffs differ in coloration, the birds resemble flowers staked out on a flower bed. The plain-colored females, the reeves, then arrive, and some are seen picking at the ruffs of certain males. Mating sometimes ensues.

Selous (1907), who studied sexual selection among the ruffs, observed that males with light colored ruffs appear discriminated against, and those with ruffs colored shades of brown are favored by the reeves. Both sexes are customarily observed pecking at the substratum in the arenas, as though finding something to eat there.

A problem perennially bothersome to students of arena behavior is the problem of genetic fixation which would naturally result if the females of the species kept choosing the same type of male year after year. Polymorphism regarding the trait being selected would gradually disappear from the population, leaving only one type of male on the arena. However, the variegated male ruffs are still out there studding the arena with their strikingly different plumages, black, brown, gray, white, and others. There seems to be a gigantic paradox here.

This paradox would be resolved if it were shown that not all females choose the same type of male. This would lead to a measure of assortative mating to perpetuate the observed polymorphism in the species. If food tastes are involved in the selective mating, such a mating system would serve to adapt the species to a variety of niches.

Do the small stages in the arena bear a unique attraction for individual birds according to the popular "hotspot" theory? If so, does the attractiveness of a small territory reflect a sample of the food situation of the general area? The better the food supply, the more vigorously would the territory be defended by a particular male. The physical prowess of the male along with his physical condition would cue to the female good reproductive conditions including food availability in the general nesting area. The female might respond by mating and rearing young in the vicinity, otherwise she might go elsewhere. Male and female genotypes would, by this process, be matched with specific food niches. In some cases specific plumage color may aid the female in identification of the male relative to the niche requirements.

It appears that this would be a fertile field for environmentally minded students to explore. In this connection, it is to be realized that a male may defend a territory on the basis of a food that is not there presently, but which will be there when the proper maturation time arrives. A male as well as the female he will later attract to the territory may recognize — either by instinct or by memory former experiences — that the desired food, though at the present time not yet matured, will be available in the reproductive area in due course.

Though the stages on the arena may appear equal to a human observer — whose awareness of the source of food hardly goes farther than the grocery store — certain places on the arena may be especially attractive to a "discriminating and place-conscious" wild animal or bird. I spent some time studying various arena birds with the intention of determining whether the birds do indeed feed in the arena during the courtship period.

PRAIRIE CHICKEN

It has long been known that male prairie chickens gather in arenas called "booming grounds" in the spring. It is also well-documented that females, visiting these booming grounds, appear to show a preference for certain males over others when they visit such arenas and mate. Male mating success appears to depend on the stationing of the successful males on certain spots in the arena. Is there any relationship between mating and feeding among these birds?

A male prairie chicken courts a female while she feeds in his territory just before they mate.

On April 20, 1993, my wife, Liz, and I visited the field station of the University of Wisconsin at Stevens Point to observe the arena display of the greater prairie chicken. The aim was to pay particular attention as to whether or not the birds found anything to eat in the arena. We were assigned a blind for the next morning. We had a professional video camera with a maximal magnification of 109X. We placed the ED Beta audio-video recorder in an insulated box to keep it warm. A short candle within assisted in this. It was a cold morning, but there was little wind, and the sun would soon be up. We crawled into the blind in the dark. Just before dawn, the shadows of the male birds became visible as the prairie chickens stealthily approached the booming ground. We blew out the short candle so as not to disturb the birds.

> Out, out, brief candle!
> Life's but a walking shadow,
> a [fowl] player
> That struts and frets his hour upon the stage
> And then is seen no more.

> —after William Shakespeare

As the sunlight became adequate, we videotaped the entire production. By 5:20 AM, two of the males could be seen feeding at certain spots within the arena boundary. Even on video at about 100X, it was not evident what the males were eating.

By 5:46 feeding by any male ceased. There was more important business at hand. Males began to approach each other head on. They gave each other "greetings." Part of the ceremony was to extend toward the "greetee" the black, pencil-shaped pinnae of feathers, one on each side of the head just above the big orange drums. To a human these look merely like cute decorations, but to a male prairie chicken (pinnated grouse) they are probably much more significant. They may be important signals to other individuals. In addition to these visual signals, the tense male prairie chicken stamps the ground and bellows his drums for all to hear.

I first heard this sound in 1943 while studying marsh hawks at the Jasper Pulaski Game Preserve in Indiana. At a far distance it sounded like the cooing of mourning doves. After creeping slowly toward the sound, I finally saw the delightful spectacle, a group of prairie chickens on the booming ground. The birds have long since disappeared from that game preserve. Like many other highly specialized life forms, the prairie chickens became victims of their own success. Apparently they were overspecialized. If their booming grounds and environs were suddenly changed by the advent of human civilization, the species would be hard put to adapt.

At the Wisconsin study area, early in the day, there were many cock fights. The physical fighting gradually diminished as the males came to make their points in their individual spaces in the arena. By the time the hens began to arrive around 6:00 AM, the scene had become somewhat tranquil.

At this time a hen started feeding at the same spot where a certain male had been observed feeding. She fed much more persistently and voraciously than the male had fed. By then, bouts of male-male display encounters were frequent. If the hens showed any interest in these displaying males, it was not evident. They continued behaving as though feeding were their sole interest. However, the females were not above competing among themselves. One feeding female chased other encroaching females far from her feeding ground.

After the scene had quieted down (by 6:18 AM), the proprietary male lowered his wing toward the feeding female. She immediately crouched and the male mated with her. She then shook her feathers a little and continued feeding for 14 additional minutes before flying away. No other matings were recorded, though a total of 8 hens and 16 cocks had been observed.

The behavior of the prairie chickens resembles that of the domestic chickens I grew up with at home in southwestern Pennsylvania. The rooster finds food, defends the area against rival males, attracts the female to the food with vocalizations, and lowers his wing toward the female. The female then crouches, and mating ensues there. The call of the male prairie chicken closely resembles the one we used for calling the chickens at home: "Heeere, chicky, chicky, chicky!"

Motion pictures of the behavior of prairie chickens broadcast on television are intriguing — and a bit frustrating. Just as it seems the appropriate time for the female prairie chicken to start feeding, the camera zooms to the ostentatious male strutting nearby. Is there something improper about showing prairie chickens feeding in the arena? Has the female received her due from observers of wildlife?

Were we just lucky in being there at the appropriate time to observe this prenuptial feeding behavior? We were told that we had come at a particularly good time for observing the birds. The previous weather for that spring had been unusually inclement, and prior observers had not reported any matings.

Regarding another arena grouse, the black grouse, Alexander Skutch (1992) reports that the females feed at the arenas. In *Through Our Eyes Only, The Search for Animal Consciousness* (1993), Marian Dawkins claims that black grouse females show ingenious ability to determine the potential longevity of their potential mates. Walking through the arena, the females select these long-lived males on the basis of subtle cues independent of male appearances. These results, based on the work of Alatalo et al. (1991), are capable of a simple territorial explanation. Perhaps the selected males are the ones stationed in the most attractive territories, and successful defense of these territories is correlated with longevity.

Skutch gives a description of the feeding behavior of the female of another grouse, the sage grouse, in its arena:

> Hens first appear on the strutting ground two or three
> weeks after the cocks take up their stations and begin to

perform there in March. After they begin to attend, they arrive in the morning from ten to thirty minutes later than the cocks. Many walk into the lek: Those who come seldom alight in its center. As they stroll throughout the assembled males, they appear unmoved by all the displays that they incite. They may wander about the lek, stopping here and there to pick up food, to rest, or to look around.

MANAKINS

Another arena bird we had read much about in connection with the issue of territorial behavior is the manakin of Central America, especially the white-collared manakin. We spent some time observing these birds. On February 28, 1992, we visited Michael Snow in his home on the Caribbean slope near the town of Squirres in Costa Rica. Snow had told us there were some white-collared manakins near his home. Indeed there were. At that time, the place had only a very small human population. We went part way up the slope, following a pack horse with our luggage.

Male manakins were busy in their small territories in a grove of *Melastoma* trees. Berries of these trees form an important part of the diet of the birds. A male had established a territory about 3 feet in diameter from which he was seen removing litter to leave a rather bare stage with a sapling on each side. Near the larger of the two saplings appeared a densely packed pile of small pink flowers. It is not known whether the male had placed these flowers there, but at least he had not removed them (though he was seen removing the leaf litter around them). In this connection, it is of interest that the orange-collared manakin — which closely resembles the white-collared species, except for the orange color — allows to remain in his court liberal amounts of wild *Jallinoza* beans in their pods. This species was studied at the Carara Biological Reserve in the Pacific region of Costa Rica. Its arena habits closely resemble those of the white-collared species.

The male made cracking sounds, much like those from a cap pistol. Video photography of a perched male showed he would gradually accelerate the beating of his wings until they reached a point at which the cracking sound exploded. The cracking of an actual whip illustrates this principle: The tip of the whip, exceeding the speed of sound, makes a sharp crack. Perhaps the crack, which would require great physical effort on the part of the bird, announces the physical prowess of the male manakin in his small territory. (Males of species with large territories — mallard ducks, for example — achieve the same goal by racing with rivals.)

As I watched the orange-collared manakins, a female of this species flew in and landed in the arena. She flew from one of the two saplings to the other and back again. The male did the same, sometimes crossing the female's path. Finally, the female perched on the larger of the two saplings. The male immediately pounced on her as she perched there, and they mated for only an instant. The female hopped back and forth again between the two saplings before leaving.

BOWERBIRDS

Finally, we come to the zenith of our investigations into courtship-feeding behavior of birds. We managed a trip to Australia to study the fabulous bowerbirds. These birds are sometimes called "the other birds," just as humans are called "the other mammals." These birds are alleged to exhibit a human-like aesthetic sense.

Bowerbirds were first discovered in 1872 by the explorer Odoard Beccari in New Guinea. He found little huts constructed by male gardener bowerbirds, the surrounding yards having been decorated with flowers arranged in color groups. Among other items on display in these courtyards were fruits, mushrooms, and beetle skeletons. A century later, Europeans became regular visitors to the area. The decorations then came to include colored man-made objects such as shotgun cartridges and yellow, cardboard Kodak film cartons.

The feat of grouping objects according to color may be observed among parrots trained to place colored rings on similarly colored posts, be they red or yellow. Such orderly arrangements of objects may be the equivalent of grouping together jars of cherries, peaches, pickles, etc. Such grouping may facilitate inventory appraisal. After all the produce merchandiser does not scatter the fruit displays hodgepodge.

A pioneering student of bowerbirds, E. Thomas Gilliard (1958), notes:

> Each species decorates the bower with ornaments of particular kinds and colors, sometimes extremely gaudy. The Satin and Regent mix a muddy grayish blue or pea green kind of saliva paint in their mouths and apply it generously to the inner walls of their avenues. The Satin uses a wad of bark and the Regent sometimes uses a wad of greenish leaves to assist in spreading the paint.

This behavior has been abundantly reported in the literature as a work of fine art in the bird world.

SATIN BOWERBIRD

The satin bowerbird male has often been described as preferring the color "blue" in its choice of objects for display in his court. We videotaped the behavior of these birds near Cairns, Australia. On October 12, 1993, I observed a male satin bowerbird at his bower near a road going up Mount Lewis. He had placed a mat of sticks on the ground for the floor of his bower. Into this mat he was in the process of inserting two rows of vertical sticks. This created an avenue just about as wide as his body. He had placed a neat nest of fresh moss within the avenue. In the yard on

The male satin bowerbird nips at the sticks on the wall of his bower.

the northwest side of the bower were pieces of blue plastic; some four-angled plant-seed capsules; brown cicada casings; and partly chewed-up, dark, grayish-brown snail shells.

Just after sunrise, the male arrived and flew back and forth among the shrubs southeast of the bower. While perching, he gave harsh calls. He then flew down to the southeast side of the bower and began working on it. He picked up sticks and inserted them into the mat, adding them to the vertical walls of his avenue. He did considerable nipping at the sticks in the walls as if finding something tasty there. He then proceeded to the northwest side of the bower and fed a little on some of the materials in the courtyard. Shortly thereafter, he walked through the avenue, at which point he appeared to have a small wad of debris in his bill. Onto this wad he exuded from his throat some light-colored semi-fluid. With his bill he then smeared this material onto the inside sticks of the avenue.

Soon two females arrived on the southeast side of the bower. Almost immediately, one of the females began feeding on materials in the court-yard. As that female came within viewing range of the male, he actively and openly began lifting up the materials on the court, particularly blue objects and snail shells. As the female watched, he chewed up the contents of snail shells while occasionally lifting his head and looking toward her. He subsequently coughed up some semiliquid material that resembled the stuff the male goldfinch regurgitates when feeding his mate or his young. While performing this regurgitation, the bowerbird male made loud coughing sounds. At this point, the female closely approached him. The male then made a sudden dash toward her, whereupon she darted behind the bower. The male now stood stiffly in front of the bower, holding a snail shell in his bill and displaying it through the avenue of the bower. Next he did the same with a blue plastic bottle cap. The female, stationed at the other end of the avenue, came closer and almost entered. Now the male rushed around the bower and charged her. She departed, only to return twice shortly thereafter, with essentially the same results. She then left the area. Perhaps she was not yet ready to mate. Presently, the male flew to some low shrubs overhanging the bower and pounced from branch to branch while uttering loud, harsh calls.

This appeared to be a case of courtship-feeding waiting to happen. In fact, the female did feed at the court. The habit of smearing the bower may simply represent an additional, and permanent, display of otherwise perishable food used in courtship. Similar smearing behavior is reported by Pruett-Jones (1988) among birds-of-paradise, *Parotia lawsii*. In this case, materials the male places in his court, including snakeskins and chalk from a chalk cliff, are rubbed over the display perch. Females pick up the snakeskins from the courts and use them as nesting material. The females eat the chalk, which is rich in calcium.

The North American white-breasted nuthatch performs similar food-smearing behavior at the nesting hole. At the home of Dwight Jacobs, near North Lima, Ohio, a pair of white-breasted nuthatches were maintaining two cavities about 20 feet up in a large linden tree. The holes to the cavities were 2.5 inches apart. In the top cavity, the birds stored food. The pair nested in the bottom cavity.

On May 24, 1996, the parent birds were observed rubbing what appeared to be insects and seeds into crevices of the tree bark around the two holes. They did this by vigorously sweeping their bills against the bark while holding the items in their bills. Examination of the bark around the holes revealed parts of insects, such as pieces of beetle wings. There was one specimen of a dried, but nearly intact, long-legged spider. There were also a few tufts of hair stuck around the hole. At one point the female, prior to nesting, emerged from the top cavity with an insect pupa in her bill. Later, the birds built their nest in the bottom cavity and raised young there.

Similar behavior of the white-breasted nuthatch has been described by Kilham (1968). He noted that in some cases the birds hold crushed insects in their bills, which they then wipe onto the bark around the nesting hole. He also noted appreciable amounts of hair stuffed in the bark crevices all around the nest hole. Both birds come to the nesting tree and store bits of food in bark crevices near the nest. According to Kilham, some of these materials are retrieved later and used in mate-feeding or feeding of the young. Foreign nuthatches sometimes steal some of the stored food.

Since food is so important to a species, it is little wonder that food supplies are so vigorously defended. The white-breasted nuthatch raises its wings and sways back and forth and makes loud clicking sounds with its bill while defending its food cache. This behavior closely resembles that of the Victorian riflebird of Australia, who elevates his wings high over his head as he defends his food supply at bird feeders. He performs similar display to members of his own species. This bird feeds on fruits as well as seeds and insects. Many other birds expand their wings in defending food sources. The expansion emphasizes size in a threat display. In this connection, it is interesting that the wings of many birds are colored with flashing white undersides.

Blue jays expand their strikingly marked blue and white tails toward competitors at their food supplies. The slate-colored junco displays its white outer tail feathers toward rivals. A certain individual of this species at Goshen, Indiana, possibly a mutant, bore a cap of white feathers in place of the normal slate-gray color. If such a white cap were to become advantageous in competition, it might eventually become incorporated into the plumage of the species. Birds in general, including the junco, lower their heads, presenting a top view to competitors. Among many species of birds, the males have conspicuous white, yellow, or red patches or stripes on the top of the head.

Though bill-sweeping behavior, probably related to food storage, appears to be a rather remarkable invention by the nuthatches, the habit may have been discovered by accident. After the nuthatches have picked grains out of sunflower seeds, they frequently clean their bills by sweeping them over the bark.

The *red*-breasted nuthatches also show some of this type of bill-sweeping behavior. A pair nested in a dead snag of a wild black-cherry tree in our backyard in Goshen, Indiana, in 1970. The male carried in his bill sticky sap from a nearby spruce tree. He spread the sap around the hole until the environs of the hole were visibly coated with the sticky material.

In the Chiricahua Mountains of Arizona, the Mexican chickadee repeatedly anoints the area below the entrance to its nest with the juices of small insects, which appear to be beetles (Fricken and Fricken 1987).

Just as the satin bowerbird spreads blue-berry pulp onto the inner walls of his bower, as reported by numerous observers, other species spread red-berry pulp. Does this habit represent display of these foods in a non-perishable (dried) form? The extensive observations of Borgia (1986) indicate that the female satin bowerbird nips at the twigs inside the bower: "The female's initial response is to enter the bower and 'taste,' or nip, at a few sticks. Then she intently watches the courtship. If she is ready to copulate, she crouches and tilts forward."

When the female nips at the twigs, is she tasting fruit pulp pasted thereon? To a bird whose survival is precariously dependent on a continuous supply of food, particularly food for the young, who live constantly on the verge of starvation, the use of food in courtship could well be of paramount importance. Nuptial gifts may serve as indicators of the availability of appropriate foods for rearing the young.

Since proper nutrition enhances physiological conditioning, the availability of an abundant supply of the species' food may be indicated by the resplendence of the plumage of the male and the vigor of his behavior. In line with this, color and appearance of that food may likewise be reflected in the plumage of the male.

For some reason, there appear to be no reports that bowerbirds eat any of the food items displayed in their courts. Yet we recorded both sexes of the satin bowerbird doing this. The lack of reports of feeding at the courts of the bowerbirds has resulted in the most exotic of interpretations. No less an ethologist than Karl von Frisch (1974), reviewing the behavior of Lauterbach's bowerbird, negates the idea that the articles displayed by bowerbirds represent foods:

> It is important that their display with berries should not be looked on as an offer of food. It has never been observed, either with this or with any other species, that the courted female has eaten any berries. Like the bleached bones of kangaroos, like flowers and other ornaments, they are simply a means of signaling to the female that a male is waiting for them in the bower.

GOLDEN BOWERBIRD

Another bowerbird found in Australia is the golden bowerbird. We studied this species higher on Mount Lewis than the satin, in an area of big rocks on which beard lichens were growing. The bower of this species included a horizontal perch, a branch of a *Syzygium* tree that had been pinned onto the top of a rock by a nearby fallen tree. On the side of the perch still fastened to the *Syzygium* tree, the male was observed piling up large sticks, one of them 17 inches long, adding to the pile

A male golden bowerbird places a fresh orchid flower at the end of the perch in his bower.

already about 6 feet high up the trunk of the tree. On the other end of the horizontal perch, around a branch extending vertically from the perch, another group of twigs was piled up.

In addition to adding to the pile of sticks, the male was observed strewing grayish-green beard lichen over the sticks, as sort of a background for the decorations to come. On this background he studded seed capsules and, finally, a fresh, white orchid flower. He placed this flower near the end of the perch away from the tree. Later, he picked up the orchid with his bill and rearranged it to the side of the perch near the tree.

He then emitted a quiet, melodious song as he perched between the displays. Subsequently, he flew to nearby trees and sang the melodious song, along with a loud rattling noise like that of a woodpecker's staccato assault on a tree. At one point, a female landed on the golden bowerbird's perch between the two piles of sticks on which the seed capsules and the orchid were on display. The male flew swiftly down from the tall trees toward the female on the perch, and the two birds immediately flew together up into the nearby trees, vanishing among the foliage.

Apparently, the food items displayed by the golden bowerbirds differ from bower to bower. A bower located at Crater National Park, some 60 miles south of Mount Lewis, was decorated with an abundance of yellow-red seed capsules.

TOOTH-BILLED BOWERBIRD

Near Lake Eacham we observed a colony of tooth-billed bowerbirds. In this species, which feeds on leaves, both sexes are streaked brown. The male uses his toothed bill, which acts as a pruning scissors, to clip off large, elliptical leaves from trees. He places these, shiny side up, inside a circular-shaped area 9 feet in diameter, around a small sapling. Do these leaves advertise the fact that there is a plentiful supply of such fresh leaves available in his territory? At any rate, he keeps adding fresh leaves to the court, while tossing away those that become deteriorated.

He then perches on an overarching limb about 7 feet above the ground and sings loudly and continually. He starts out the day with a

The orchid is now ready for visitor viewing.

basic harsh call. Later, he picks up the calls of other birds around him and incorporates some of these into his own song. Throughout the day, his repertoire thereby becomes more and more complicated. Occasionally, he ceases singing and appears to be listening to the surrounding songs. Soon thereafter, he adds certain extraneous calls to his own harsh call. The added calls are easier on the ear than the initial harsh call. Consequently, the entire song becomes much more melodious as the day progresses.

What is the adaptive function of this mimicry? Various explanations have been offered. Skutch (1992), speaking in general of mimicking birds, offers this anthropomorphic theory:

> Perhaps, in the long hours while they await the females' visit, they amuse themselves by reproducing all the diverse sounds they hear — or can invent. ... I would go so far as to assert that, if birds take no pleasure in singing, they are incapable of enjoyment, and that, if they find no joys or satisfactions in their lives, all their efforts to survive and reproduce are barren. They might as well be dead.

But if the entire sequence of events in the daily routine of a bird is followed, as when the behavior is being videotaped, it soon becomes obvious that what appears to be recreational singing on the part of a male bird is simply his method of constant communicative vigil, performed primarily when the female is on the nest. The male, familiar with the territory from the beginning, modulates his song as a method of painting a picture of environmental safety. The incubating female has, of course, little such occasion for observational opportunities. A male rose-breasted grosbeak or song sparrow, sitting on the nest, will, upon leaving the nest, sing its song. Shortly thereafter, the female will come to the nest. Singing of males also is involved in male-male competition and in attracting females to the territory.

The following interpretation of sound mimicry among birds seems obvious: If it is advantageous for a bird to look like its environment, why should it not be similarly advantageous for a bird to sound like its environment? Perhaps mimicry amounts to little more than sound camouflage. In line with this, the tooth-billed bowerbird is also an accomplished ventriloquist. Calls used for communication within a species can be more safely used if mixed with the calls of other species, thereby inhibiting a predator from focusing on a species with a distinguishing call.

The leaves displayed by the tooth-billed bowerbird represent those of plant species that are an important food source for these birds. The flowers strewn about by other bowerbirds may similarly represent food. In Australia many birds feed extensively on flowers and their buds. The colors of the displayed fruits may indicate not only ripeness but also fruit specificity. In addition, the color makes the fruit conspicuous against the green foliage and thereby attracts seed-disseminating birds.

Displayed inanimate objects may be substitutes for the real thing. Blue plastic objects may, for instance, represent blue berries or blue flowers and therefore elicit from the bird a common, innate, food-attraction response. One satin bowerbird we observed placed a manmade ornamental blue pendant (with small, central, red markings) in a prominent place in his court. The pendant was the facsimile of a flower. The male tore off and discarded the red, plastic, holding ring before placing the pendant in his court. Another male satin bowerbird stole this pendant. Next day, the former owner brought it back and placed it near its former position.

In regard to artificial representations of flowers and fruits as substitutes for the real thing in the courtship ceremony, it is of interest that the blue plumage of the male satin bowerbird correlates with blue objects in his court. The irises of the eyes of males are reported to vary between brown and blue at various times during reproductive activities.

Other species of bowerbirds favor objects of other colors to display in their courts. We were fortunate to find the bower of the great bowerbird in a low, dry area near a creek. In the court of the male were pieces of green glass. In addition, there were green seed capsules. The male was working on his tunnel-like bower through which were strewn whitish snail shells. Also, in the front yard of the bower was a huge patch of such shells. In the yard of another male great bowerbird were numerous bones.

REPRESENTATIONS OF FOOD OR NESTING MATERIALS

These observations of bowerbirds lead to the interpretation that at least some of the objects the bowerbirds place in their courts represent foods, perhaps the favorite foods or nesting materials of the species. This applies even to the use of feathers, as with the satin bowerbird. On one courtyard of this species we observed the male placing blue quill feathers, along which the serially arranged blue segments resembled flowers or fruits distributed linearly. This is of interest with respect to the observation of Frith and Frith (1990), who discovered plumes of the King of Saxony bird-of-paradise in the courtyard of Archibold's bowerbird. These plumes extend backward from the head of this bird-of-paradise far beyond the length of the bird. The plumes resemble a thin stem along which are linearly arranged small, blue, berry-like patches. Some of the bowerbird courts contained up to six of these plumes.

Jared Diamond (1991), a pioneering student of bowerbirds, anthropomorphically interpreted the presence of King of Saxony bird-of-paradise (*Pteridophora*) plumes in the bower of *Archiboldia* as follows: "[A] female *Archiboldia* finding a bower with several *Pteridophora* plumes knows at once that she has located a dominant male who is terrific at finding or stealing rare objects and at defeating would-be thieves."

But a theory based on the interpretation that the female is attracted to these feathers on the same basis as she is attracted to food or nesting material would seem more appropriate — certainly more simple. Furthermore, it is reasonable that the rarity of the feathers renders them even more attractive. The phenomenon of noticing the novel is characteristic of many animals — from insects through fish to birds. Many female birds — including catbirds, wood thrushes, and cactus wrens — place distinguishing and sometimes brightly colored objects on the outside perimeter of their nests.

Birds commonly display nesting materials during the courtship ceremony. Use of these materials would serve the same function as use of food, bringing together male and female of the same niche requirements. The bowerbirds, of course, are prime examples of this. The bower itself is composed of nesting materials. Each species (and even each geographical variety) of bowerbird demonstrates its own distinctive bower construction.

The satin bowerbird displays mosses as nesting material within the bower. The golden bowerbird displays sticks interlaced with beard lichen, typical nest materials used by the species. MacGregor's gardener bowerbird displays, in his tower-shaped bower, tassels of insect silk attached to the ends of sticks.

The striped gardener packs moss onto the sticks of his tower to make a central cone. He then brings many additional sticks to form a dome-shaped pavilion, or hut, with a wide opening in the front. Beneath it, he builds a flat nest composed of blackish fibers that he extracts from the central stems of tree ferns (Skutch 1992).

The brown gardener bowerbird, *Amblyornis inornatus*, found in the mountains of the Vogelkop Peninsula of western New Guinea, builds his central cone of mosses. On top of the cone, twigs are arranged in a radiating manner. Stems of the orchid, *Dendrobium*, are freely used in this construction. In the court, he places a "meadow" of moss. On this moss, the male places rose-colored flowers, apple-like fruits, fungi, and insects. Ripley (1942), studying this species four decades later, found the gardens in front of the bowers decorated with flowers and fruits, segregated by color. Ripley dropped into the garden a pink begonia, small yellow flowers, and a pretty red orchid. The male bowerbird threw aside the yellow flowers and, later, the begonia. He gave the red orchid special treatment.

He took it from one pile of fruit and flowers to another, finally laying it on a pile of pink flowers. (There were also some black pebbles in the courtyard.)

The habitat of the brown gardener bowerbird, being difficult to reach by humans, is still relatively wild. Within the range of this bird in New Guinea are five sub-ranges. Diamond (1986) describes the variation in the "animal art" of the species: The birds on different mountains of New Guinea build bowers that differ greatly in construction and decorations.

On the Kumawa Mountains, the male gardener bowerbird separated the following into neat piles: black wing coverts of beetles; dark brown, brown, or gray snail shells; dark-brown stones; and black twigs from small trees or tree ferns. The male then smeared a black oily substance over some of the objects. He had also dragged into the bower sword-shaped pandanus leaves up to 6 feet long, propping them against a supporting pillar or laying them flat. The males demonstrated their preference for dark objects in their choice of variously colored plastic poker chips that Diamond placed beside their bowers or on the moss of the court. The male discarded chips of bright colors and chose the dark ones.

In the Wandamen Mountains, the males construct their bowers after the pattern described by Beccari for the species in the mountains on Vogelkop Peninsula. These males show their liking for brightly colored decorations by eagerly accepting the chips offered to them, with a decided preference for blue, followed by purple and orange. White chips are neglected by the males.

Among male bowerbirds, the importance of the bowers is indicated by the vigor the males display in defense of their "castles." Just as male ring-necked pheasants use their spurs to damage the plumage of rivals, so bowerbird males destroy the nests of rivals and take ornaments from their bowers. These actions may be a form of male-male competition for a territory attractive to certain females.

As remarkable and exotic as the nest-building prowess of the male bowerbird might seem, it hardly outdoes that of the house wren. Having spent an enormous amount of time and energy hoisting huge sticks up to the wren house, into which a female was soon situated, the male turned around and constructed an even bigger nest in Liz's clothespin bag on our back porch.

The behavior of the male bowerbird is equivalent to the male *Perithemis* dragonfly's activity taken to its logical conclusion. From the dragonfly's simple examination of the reproductive site, which the female is later invited to inspect, we see actual manipulation of the reproductive site on the part of the male bowerbird. What could be more appropriate and adaptive than for the male to present to the female a comprehensive picture of the environs of the reproductive site — for the female to view at a quick, imprinting glance? A more mobile version of the same idea would be to represent special aspects of the environment as male adornment carried on his body.

Colored floral designs on the plumage of birds, especially of fruit-eating birds, may simply represent simulations of the favorite food of the species. The spherical-looking "eyespots" in the plumage of the peacock and the serially arranged, spherically shaded spottings on the wing plumage of the argus pheasant and peacock pheasants may be representations of such fruits or flowers.

It is well-documented that birds are attracted to pictorial representations of food and will peck at such pictures. Birds may very easily confuse imitations of food for the real thing. For example, in California, two scrub jays were seen carrying off and burying marbles — as many as 50 in a half-hour — in much the same way they do acorns. (See Dennis 1981.)

The peacock was studied by Petrie et al. (1991) at Whipsnade Park, England. Females usually visit a number of males before returning to one of them for mating. The number of matings of males increased as related to the larger number of "eyespots" on the tail.

These results are usually attributed to female attraction to the colorful spheres on the basis of an aesthetic sense as proposed by Darwin.

However, if the females are indeed attracted to these "eyespots" they may see in this "artwork" mere representations of colorful foods. Also, it should be pointed out that advantages of the spotted tails as displayed by males in competition for reproductive spaces has not been ruled out in these studies, as noted also by Andersson (1994).

However, eyespots may be generally attractive. Butterfly students in Costa Rica maintain that such spots on the wings of butterflies attract predators looking for a meal. The idea is that the spots — instead of the body — of the butterfly being the attractive focus will allow for the escape of the butterfly. As discussed in the OVERVIEW of the present book, the Zahavis (1997) suggest that the "eyespots" of peacocks enable the peahen to determine the physiological fitness of the male.

The males of not only peacocks, but also some pheasants, show pictorial representations of fruits. (For excellent color photographs of some of these pheasants, see Johnsgard 1994.) The display of such adornment is described for *Tragopan temmincki* by Rimlinger (1984), as well as Johnsgard (1986). The male displays a horseshoe-shaped breastplate studded with a row of serially arranged red markings. Underlying the breastplate is a reddish background studded with bluish-green, serially arranged markings. This adornment looks remarkably like an artistic display of fruit.

During courtship, the male pheasant crouches behind a rock, peeking out toward an area the females traverse. When a female appears, the hiding male makes a prolonged sequence of chick-like calls. He then intermittently exposes his fruit-like, ornamented breast to the female. At the proper moment, he pounces toward the female. Coition may ensue.

Among the peacock pheasants of the genus *Polyplectron*, the males' tail and wing plumage have serially arranged, elliptical, greenish markings so shaded as to resemble spherical fruits. During courtship, the male stands sidewise in front of the female, displaying these markings to conspicuous advantage. Among the Malay peacock pheasants, *malacense*, the display sites are kept clean by the males and may be used for up to two months per year. One male may maintain several display sites. Males

Male and female scarlet macaws groom each other.

known to receive visits from females are birds in adult plumage that show high rates of display (Davison 1983).

In the Monteverde area of Costa Rica I observed the resplendent quetzal feeding on its favorite fruit, the wild avocado (a member of the laurel family). The fruit closely matches the green color of the bird, while the bright-red swollen receptacle of the fruit resembles his red breast.

This is the cloud-forest area in the highlands between the Caribbean Sea on one side and the Pacific Ocean on the other. The warm, moisture-laden winds blow up the mountain to condense as clouds; these mists supply the cloud forest with constant wetness. The quetzal is well-suited for all this dripping moisture. His upper tail coverts are greatly extended beyond the flight feathers of his tail. Likewise, his wing coverts, extending well over the flight feathers of his wings, end in drip points. He can sit in the rain, assured that his flight feathers will be kept dry for instant flying when necessary.

Lower on the Caribbean slope of Costa Rica is the rain forest. Here dwells the great green macaw, which also has a long, pointed tail. This bird's favorite foods are greenish legumes and greenish almonds. The counterpart of the great green macaw is the scarlet macaw, which may be seen feeding on bright-red wild cashews and breeding at the Carara Biological Reserve on the Pacific side of Costa Rica. The scarlet plumage of the bird closely matches the red berries.

When not feeding, the macaws spend extensive periods preening the long tails of one another and carrying on nesting activities. It would be difficult for the birds to groom their long tails by themselves. Elongated tail feathers may play an important signaling role. When the birds are inside the nest cavity, the tips of their extremely long tails extend out through the hole. This could help the parent bird determine whether its mate is inside. Woodpeckers achieve this same objective by code-pecking on the tree — outside or inside, as the situation requires.

Among other birds showing similarity of colors of plumage and foods are the toucans. Near La Selva Biological Station on the Caribbean slope may be seen the keel-billed toucan feeding on the fruits of the palm the natives call "heart of palm." The hearts of the young trees are dissected out for making gourmet salad, hence the common name of the tree. The small, red, spherical berries of this tree are also used by the natives for food. They have a sweet, nutty flavor. The hard, round seed contains meat much like that of a coconut. The fruits are voraciously consumed by birds.

The tip of the bill of the keel-billed toucan appears to be a perfect instrument for picking and holding fruit. The tip of the bill curves around the palm fruits and closely matches their color. Furthermore, additional yellow color of the bill, as well as parts of the plumage, match the yellow pulp of the fruit. There is also a little patch of red under the tail that bears a striking resemblance to the coat of the fruit. When the male is cavorting over a bunch of the red berries, his undertail patch adds attracting motion to the fruity display. Any female of the species might find the scene to be downright stimulating.

Other birds (such as the Montezuma oropendola) observed feeding there showed similar close matching of: fruit colors, the red-tipped bills, and yellow facial and tail markings of the birds. When one of the oropendolas picked at the bill of another, as in courtship-feeding, it was not clear whether it was picking at the red bill, or fruit pulp carried on the bill. Crested guans were also feeding on the palm fruits. This large brown bird has a round red throat pouch which closely resembles a red palm fruit.

Leaving the Caribbean slope and entering the Monteverde cloud forest I observed the *black* guan feeding on tree leaves. This counterpart of the crested guan has a bluish bill and no red throat pouch.

In Peru, in the vicinity of the Pueblo Hotel near the town of Aguas Calientes in the South American Andes Mountains, I observed the breeding behavior of the silver-billed tanager. The male has a silvery-white bill with a black border. During courtship the male carries in his bill a butterfly, which is similarly marked with white wings bearing a black border.

The three-wattled bellbird of Costa Rica has fastened near the base of its bill three worm-like structures. Although presently these birds are said to feed exclusively on fruit (Snow 1976), it's possible that worms may be included on the menu, especially the diet of the nestlings. Since the young are fed regurgitated materials from the food pouch of the parent, it would take a microscopic examination to reveal worm content. It is also possible that the wattles represent not worms, but nesting material. The crested grebe displays nesting materials held in its beak during the courtship ceremony.

The male bearded bellbird of the Rio de Janeiro area wears a group of wattles in a beard-like cluster extending down over his green-skinned throat. David Snow (1976), reporting the observations of his wife, Barbara, gives the following account of courtship behavior of this bird:

> When a female visits the male at one of the low perches
> an elaborate ritualized ceremony is enacted, which cul-

> minates — if the female is receptive — in mating on the
> special perch. ... His upper breast feathers are puffed out,
> so the beard of wattles is pushed prominently forward. ...
> He then begins a sort of stereotyped preening, raising one
> wing and preening the feathers beneath it, and stretching
> one leg forward so that a curious patch of deeply colored
> bare skin is exposed on the thigh. Between preening
> movements he stares fixedly at the visitor.

The male white bellbird of the Kanuku Mountains of Guyana near the Brazilian border has only a single wattle. The male bare-throated bellbird of southeastern Brazil has no wattles, only a naked patch of green skin on his throat. It remains for ecologically sensitive students to solve the problem of the relationship between the wattle number of the different species and the niche requirements of each species.

The male black grouse, *Tetrao tetrix*, in displaying to the female, inflates his red eye combs. Red berries form part of the diet of these arena birds (Skutch 1992). Various species of birds have red combs or wattles, which may be involved in the mating systems. Male king vultures have the upper base of their beak overgrown with large, fleshy, red clumps that look like pieces of meat. During male-male competition, these structures are picked by rival males. Male turkeys have red, fleshy appendages on the bill and throat area. These, along with body feathers, are attacked during male-male competition. This may be the equivalent of food-stealing or ornament destruction during male-male competition, as observed among bowerbirds.

David Snow, a student of tropical American birds, in his book, *The Web of Adaptation* (1976), was one of the first to link colorful plumage of certain birds with the fruit-eating habit. He speculated that the ready availability of fruit as food made it possible for the males of fruit-eating birds to spend their time displaying their brilliant plumage. Snow maintains that under conditions of readily available food the males are not needed for helping feed the young. The idle males could therefore prance and preen to their heart's content in the mating arena, showing off their ornamented plumage to females of the species. It was this leisure-time activity, related to giving female a choice of beauty, that supposedly gave male arena birds their ornamented plumage. Along these lines, Snow favors Darwin's view that females select males on the basis of beauty. He criticizes the explanation of Wallace that highly adorned males are more successful in mating simply because the adornment is connected to a physiological superiority that affords an advantage in male-male competition. Writes Snow:

> Why, in fact, if the male's vigor were all that is important, need it be linked with any adornment at all? We are on much stronger ground if we stick to the original idea that the females do actively select the males on the basis of their individual adornments and performance, even if we cannot prove that they do so. ... Another puzzling fact, which one encounters again and again, is that whenever a species with well-developed male plumage and adornments is split into isolated populations, each separate population tends to evolve along its own line, differentiating in ways that seem quite arbitrary.

Since Snow had been so fortunate as to see the female cock-of-the-rock pick at the orange-colored feathers of the male, it's puzzling that he doesn't mention the possibility that females choose males partly on the basis of drives for differently colored fruits — and that differences in tastes might explain why each separate population tends to evolve along its own line.

Steven Hilty (1994), an avid student of tropical birds of the Americas, agrees with Snow that adornment of male birds is related to a fruity diet. He gives the following interpretation:

By almost any measure, the most colorful tropical birds are usually fruit-eating and nectar-feeding species. These are followed in colorfulness ranking by partly fruit-eating birds, while the legions of dull-colored species are drawn mostly from the ranks of insect-eating birds. But why are fruit-eating and nectar-feeding birds so often colorful while their hard-working, insect-eating counterparts are so rarely dressed in finery? ... Bright colors further increase the risk, probably to unacceptable levels, among insect eaters. It is this difference in foraging behavior between fruit-eating and insect-eating birds that seems to explain why bright colors evolve much less frequently in birds that are forced to search in places where their backs are turned and their vision obscured — just the places where insects are likely to hide.

There is considerable merit in Hilty's theory for explaining the concealing colors of the plumage of insect eaters. The streaked, brown plumage of birds is highly useful in camouflaging. This is beautifully illustrated by the song sparrow sitting on its nest of brown, curved grasses. The lines of the grasses and those on the curved body of the bird blend remarkably.

While acknowledging the validity of this explanation for the concealing coloration among the insect eaters, we still need an explanation for the striking coloration of the fruit eaters. The theory presented in this book should help explain the adaptive value of the florid, fruity display of the fruit eaters. Not only food itself, but even the sight of food, may play an important role in reproduction. In regard to this, the reddish throat pouch of the male lizard, *Anolis carolinensis*, has been experimentally shown to stimulate ovarian activity in the female (Crews 1975). Insofar as the pouch may resemble the red-brown colors of the outer surface of many insects, this experiment may show a connection between a visual food stimulus and reproduction.

Not only tropical birds, but those of temperate regions, demonstrate a connection between colorful plumage and the fruit-eating habit. Among the finch-like birds in our local area, those bedecked in red are frequently seen eating red berries, such as sumac, scarlet elder, and hawthorn fruits. These birds include the cardinal, scarlet tanager, rose-breasted grosbeak, purple finch, and house finch. On the other hand, black-brown-streaked finch-like birds, such as common sparrows, are seldom if ever seen feeding on red berries. In Costa Rica, the scarlet-rumped tanager feeds extensively on red berries of a spiny plant called "poison ivy" there.

SEXUAL SELECTION AND VITAMIN A

Among fruit-eating species, the highly conspicuous yellow-red colors indicate ripeness and specificity of fruits, as well as the abundance of carotenes (named after the carrot, from which carotene was extracted by biochemists). When animals eat these plants, they can convert the carotene to vitamin A, which is stored in the liver for future use. Fish-liver oils are especially rich in this vitamin. (There is also some vitamin A in green plants, but the yellow-red color is obscured by green chlorophyll.)

From 1913 on, it has been abundantly documented that dietary carotenes play a crucial role in animal nutrition. The results of deficiency of this vitamin in developing young animals are dramatic. The animal literally falls apart. Cell walls become scaled, connective tissues and bones disintegrate, glands fail, and kidney stones develop. An early symptom of beta-carotene deficiency is night blindness. Vitamin A is directly involved in synthesis of retinene, a carotenoid used by rod-shaped cells in the retina to make them highly sensitive to light.

A consideration of the involvement of carotenoids in both behavior and physiology relates, of course, to the problem of sexual selection.

HOUSE FINCHES

The house finch, *Carpodacus mexicanus*, provides a good example of the role of dietary carotenoids in sexual selection. These birds feed extensively on the red buds of maple trees. They also pick red, ripe cherries. They are commonly called "cherry birds." The red plumage of the mature males closely resembles the color of these favorite foods. The red color of the plumage of the male may be enhanced by eating food rich in carotenoids. According to Hill (1990), the red coloration is related to enhanced foraging behavior of the males — and the rate at which they feed their young. A high-carotenoid diet is also related to improved survival and mating success of the males.

Claiming that the males do not compete for territories in the mating season, Hill (1991) attributes the enhanced red coloration of the males to female choice of the brighter-colored males. However, Hill admits that the males do show male-male mating rivalry. It is conceivable therefore that the enhanced mating success of the redder males is at least partly due to an advantage these males have over less-red rivals.

Given the fact that diet enhances the red color of the males, the females may innately associate the high degree of red color of the resident male as indicating corresponding high quantity of dietary carotenoids in his territory.

Historically in the United States, the house finch was a Southwestern species. Since the males of the species are attractively reddish and have beautiful songs, a pet dealer caged some and took them back to New York in the 1940s. It was found that the males in captivity were less colorful than they were in the West. Furthermore, the pet dealer found that such interstate commerce of wild birds is illegal. He therefore released his pets.

This original small population of house finches found the East hospitable. When bird feeders became popular, the finches could survive the winters. Within 30 years, this population had spread. The birds reached Ohio in the early 1980s. In Goshen, Indiana, we saw our first one at a bird feeder in June 1984. They are now very common. They are preyed on by sparrow hawks (kestrels) and sharp-shinned hawks. Sparrow hawks perch on utility wires stretched over cornfields where house finches feed on the tassels of the cornstalks. Occasionally, the sparrow hawk flies toward them and catches the less swift as they fly away.

As might be expected, a population arising from only a few caged birds may not possess all of the immunity genes of the wild population. The entire population, carrying the genes from so few ancestors, may therefore be more susceptible to disease. In the winter of 1994, house finches with runny, crusty eyes were noted at feeders in New York. By 1995 the same condition was noted in house finches as far south as South Carolina and as far west as Illinois. Veterinarians suspect that the condition stems from a bacterium, *Mycoplasma gallisepticum*, which causes poultry diseases. The house finches may have originally become infected by foraging in poultry yards — and the marked tendency for house finches to flock and bathe together may have helped spread the disease.

At our bird feeder a female was observed pecking at the reddish, inflamed, infected eye of another female. Also, in the courtship period a female was seen pecking at the red rump patch of a male. Shortly thereafter, the two flew to a nearby tree where the male fed the female.

In this connection the observations of David Snow (1976) in his studies of the cock-of-the-rock are of interest. Snow's records are from the mating arena of these bright-orange birds inhabiting the Kanuku Mountains of the Guiana range of northern Brazil:

> This was about midday on March 4. There was an obvious increase in excitement among the males, and the two males whose courts were in view dropped down onto them at the same moment, and crouched. Shortly afterwards a female landed on the nearer of the two courts. She alighted behind the crouching male, hopped up to him, and then, leaning forward, began to nibble at the long silky fringes of his modified wing feathers. She was

nervous, apparently of the hide, and moved away a couple of feet after about ten seconds; then she approached
him again, and again began to nibble at the golden fringe
of the motionless male. ... I decided to take one picture
and slowly withdraw the camera. I could have cursed the
Exacta's loud shutter; it alarmed the female and she flew
off — and the photograph later turned out to be hope-
lessly underexposed. ... Almost certainly, the remarkable
behavior of the female, which I had been lucky enough to
see, is the immediate prelude to mating. [The feathers] are
presumably sexually stimulating to the female.

Continuing our story of the house finches, on February 10, 1996,
among 14 male and 23 female house finches feeding at our bird feeder,
eight males and seven females were observed with the infection. Not
only is the eye itself affected, the area surrounding the eye is as well. The
feathers surrounding the infected eye may become disheveled and dis-
colored to black or white.

Richard Hostetler, observing house finches at his feeding station
about a half-mile from ours, found three of five males with the eye infection. One of these males had both eyes seriously infected. Among eight
females, only one showed the infection. This female had the infection in
the right eye, with almost total closure of the eye.

As the breeding season approached early in June, the male that succeeded in breeding in the area was a non-infected male. On the other
hand, the female that succeeded in mating with him was the one with
the infected eye. The nest site chosen was a nearby hanging pot with
blooming red impatiens plants. The female built the nest in this pot
among the bases of the stems of the plant. On one occasion the male
brought nesting material and presented it to the female on a nearby tree.
While she was inside the pot constructing the nest, the male perched
briefly on the flowers, then flew to a tree and sang incessantly.

Two weeks after the first egg was laid, the first egg hatched, followed by a second hatching the next day. The remaining two eggs did not hatch. The female did most of the feeding of the young, but the male occasionally helped. Eleven days after the first egg hatched, one young was found dead. The next day the other young bird died. No infection around the eyes of the young was apparent. Though the parents were present, they were not observed feeding the young on the days when the hatchling died. During the nesting period, the tissues around the eye of the female had become increasingly swollen, and the eye itself appeared to degenerate progressively.

A house-finch male with both eyes affected was found on the ground in another yard near the Hostetler's. The bird could be picked up with ease. He appeared still sensitive to light, for when taken indoors, he would fly toward the light.

It's easy to understand why the male with the normal eyes would be the one successful in mating in the face of competition with males having infected eyes. But why, conversely, was the female with the seriously infected eye more successful in mating than females with normal eyes? Early in the season, when the nest site was first established, both the female with the infected eye and those with normal eyes were observed entering the flower pot at the same time. The females tolerated each other's presence, showing no evidence of competition. When the male dashed at the females, the normal ones flew while the infected one remained at the nest site.

Is it possible that a female, as a result of a debilitating infection, may mate more readily than normal? On this general point, perhaps fruit flies have lessons to teach. In the studies of *Drosophila melanogaster*, it was found that females of the mutant "ebony," which show retarded behavior and visual deficiencies, mated earlier, and with higher frequencies, than normal females. It appeared that the mating acceleration exhibited by the ebony females was due to inability of these ebony females to repel the advances of the males. (See Chapter 5.)

At our bird-feeding station, two female house finches, one with the left eye closed due to the infection and the other with the right eye closed, apparently resorted to using male cardinals as leaders. Each was observed perched with her cardinal consort in a nearby spruce tree for extended periods. When the male flew to the feeder, his house-finch partner would follow. This happened repeatedly.

Red flowers may be highly attractive to house finches. At the Hostetler pot of red impatiens, numerous male and female house finches were observed flitting around these flowers. Even after four eggs had been laid, and the female was incubating, several females visited the pot of red flowers.

To get an idea of whether the house finches are especially attracted to red, an experimental feeding station was set up at our home. Two 12 x 18 x 2-inch plastic trays were bought. One was bright red, the other bright green. The trays were placed the long way, 6 inches apart on a board atop the bird feeder. Black sunflower seeds were placed at the end of each of the feeders. Uneaten seeds were replaced with fresh seeds each day, after which the positioning of the colored trays was reversed. When a house finch entered a tray with no other bird of any species in either of the trays, it was recorded as an entry. Other species of birds were similarly observed and counted. The present report is based only on those species represented by a flock of at least 20 different individual birds (as determined by the total number seen at one time in the vicinity of the trays).

The results revealed that house finches prefer the red tray. Among the 660 entries recorded for males, 70 percent preferred the red tray. Of 464 female entries, 58 percent were at the red tray. Slate-colored juncos markedly preferred the green tray. Of 630 entries for these birds that usually feed on the ground, only 35 percent were at the red tray.

In his interesting analysis of the feeding habits of birds, John Dennis (1981) reviews the results of various investigators who have studied color preferences of birds in their selection of foods:

> Birds, like ourselves, are guided to a large degree by color
> when it comes to food selection. ... Red, poorly represent-

ed at the bird feeder, is almost certainly the most important advertising color in the plant kingdom wherever the services of birds are needed. ... Red appears in the ripe fruits and berries of plants that need the assistance of birds as an aid to dissemination. ... Experiments by S. Davis and colleagues, reported in a 1973 issue of *The Condor*, showed that sunflower seeds dyed red were even more popular at the feeder than natural undyed sunflower, while sunflower dyed yellow, green, or blue were less well received. Birds coming to the seeds in this experiment were plain titmice, western cousins of the well-known tufted titmouse.

Experiments with a variety of birds indicate that they prefer colors on the red end of the spectrum. Among male zebra finches, *Poephila guttata*, their orange-red beaks enhance mating success (Burley and Coopersmith 1987). Red leg bands placed onto the males also enhance mating success, whereas green bands do not (Burley 1988). Conversely with another species, *Poephila bichenovii*, which has a blue beak, the opposite was found: Not red, but blue, leg bands enhance male mating success (Burley 1986).

Similar results were obtained by Brodsky (1988) with the rock ptarmigan, *Lagopus mutus*. Cocks marked with leg rings of the same color as the red combs above his eyes had higher mating success than unringed males. In this case, at least part of the enhanced male mating success was interpreted by Brodsky as stemming from the red rings.

The cedar waxwing has, on the tips of the secondary wing feathers, red waxy ornaments that look like red berries. These ornaments become more extensively developed as the birds mature. In common with other birds, the older, more mature cedar waxwings mate earlier and have larger clutches than the younger, less mature, birds. In addition to the waxy red ornaments on the wings, there is a yellow band on the tip of the tail. Apparently, the yellow band becomes more reddish as the birds feed on the more reddish form of carotene (rhodoxanthin).

The waxwings feed extensively on berries and may be seen in spring presenting berries to each other. Included in the menu of berries are the red-yellow ones produced by honeysuckles. Recently introduced into the American environment is the Morrow's honeysuckle, which has particularly red berries rich in rhodoxanthin. Within the past 30 years, as this honeysuckle has spread throughout northeastern states, the yellow band on the tip of the tail of some of the cedar waxwings has become redder. On the basis of berry color as correlated with tail-band color, the bird population is gradually becoming segregated into two groups: those with red tail bands and those with yellow tail bands. (See M. Witmer 1996.)

If all this is true, the yellow band on the tail of the cedar waxwing is an excellent example of how the plumage of a bird represents the food on which it feeds. If the specific color of the tail band reflects some genetic difference in tastes of the birds and is involved in mate choice, this would provide a prime example of the role of courtship-feeding in genetic isolation and niche specialization.

The greater flamingo, *Phoenicopterus ruber*, which feeds primarily on yellow-red invertebrates found in mud, has a red body. On the other hand, the lesser flamingo, *Phoeniconaias minor*, which feeds mostly on blue-green algae, has just a touch of red in its plumage.

On the plumage of the male great argus pheasant, *Argusianus argus*, are long, linear rows of ball-in-socket-looking spheres that create a fruity display. The males make loud calls from their courts, then posture to emphasize the wing and tail markings. The body is almost hidden behind the outstretched, fanned-out wings (Davison 1981, 1982; Johnsgard 1986). It was these "ornaments" that helped convince Charles Darwin that the female argus pheasant possesses a human-like aesthetic sense. He remarked that the adornment was more like a work of art than of nature.

Paradoxically, this same example led Wallace (1891) to *reject* the Darwinian idea that the adornment was instigating female choice. He questioned whether so fine a pattern could be appreciated by a mere bird — in fact, whether any animal other than the human could discriminate so minutely as to appreciate the detail and intricacy of such adornment.

Wallace (1889) also maintained that it is unlikely that all the females of a species, or the great majority of them, over a wide area of country and for many successive generations could be expected to prefer exactly the same type of color and adornment. Above all, he maintained that nature would not tolerate a human-like aesthetic sense, devoid of utilitarian adaptive value. He attempted to interpret all such cases in terms of natural (not sexual) selection.

This matter of human-like aesthetics sparked considerable controversy among students involved in studies of evolution — from Darwin's time to the present. After reviewing the long series of contorted debates about female choice among the adaptationists versus the non-adaptationists, Cronin (1991) presents the following summary:

> In Darwin's theory of sexual selection there is a major premise that cries out to be explained. What is missing is any explanation of how female choice itself evolved. ... Darwin's theory of sexual selection stops short at this crucial point. It simply assumes female choice as a "given." It doesn't explain what adaptive advantages there are in such choice — what selective pressures have given rise to these preferences and how they are maintained. ... With the "sensible" selective pressures of natural selection such problems don't arise. It is obvious why the need for efficient foraging exerts a selection pressure — and a demanding, precise pressure — on the woodpecker's beak. It is not at all obvious, however, what selective forces are involved in aesthetic choice. After all, the

females are choosing characteristics that are of no use and indeed very likely downright disadvantageous, and they are doing so consistently and exactingly. But if there are no adaptive advantages in choice, then there is no reason why it occurs at all. And if there is no more "rational" reason for any particular choice than mere taste, what is there to keep it so very constant and precise? Unless there are selection pressures directing it, what is there to prevent it from changing pretty well arbitrarily?

This is a good question! If a trait is developed beyond the pale of natural selection, what would prevent the trait from developing arbitrarily (without rules). David Snow (1976) expresses similar sentiments:

> [H]as she [the female bird] in fact any innate preference for the adornments and displays of the males of her own species? May she not be attracted by any striking display? ... If there is no strong innate preference, there would be nothing to check or guide the further evolution of male adornments in any isolated population. Whatever might be the extravagances of males, in appearance or behavior, the female might simply prefer those that were the most extravagant.

But if the food-courtship theory is applied to the mating system, much of the "arbitrariness" of the system disappears. The selective process is ruled by food-niche specialization, according to the steadfast law of conservation of solar energy (the driving force of life). What could be more appropriate than a selective mating system involving the use of food, or a reasonable facsimile thereof? At last, aesthetics, dietetics, and genetics come together. In fact, David Lack in his book, *Ecological Adaptations for Breeding in Birds* (1968), notes that birds living in similar ecological conditions tend to have similar decoration. Similar ecological conditions would, of course, include similar foods of similar coloration.

This principle might even apply to human societies. One need only remember the decorations of specific favorite foods employed at a wedding feast to realize that humans possess an urge to use ethnic foods in courtship and mating ceremonies. Why does a civilized suitor present "goodies" to his potential mate instead of a bowl of dead grasshoppers? After once posing this question, I promptly received an answer from a prominent local conservationist. She maintained that she fell in love with her future husband when he treated her to a bowl of strawberry shortcake and cream. We might consider the couple "strawberry lovers." They had common chemistries (tastes).

Much of community artwork represents common human tastes. At home we grew up with a bowl of colored wax fruit as an ornament on a side table in the dining room. Though the artificial fruit was inedible, it stirred up psychological stimuli of the real thing, and it was permanent! All this demonstrates the close connection between foods and emotions.

How similar this is to the blue, flower-like pendant and fruit-like colored objects in the court of the satin bowerbird! In a cafe in Australia, we were served with plates of food decorated with ornamental flowers and fruits. The atmosphere made us feel at home with the rainbow lorikeets (love birds), which were feeding on the buds and flowers of nearby trees. Some of them even entered the open cafe to join the primate society. A human couple was sipping fruit juice from a cup through separate plastic straws. The lady left momentarily, as the gentleman continued sipping the juice. Suddenly, to everyone's amazement, a rainbow lorikeet flew down and perched on the cup. The lorikeet put the end of the vacated straw into its bill and appeared to be enjoying the juice along with the gentleman. Guests gathered around and took pictures of the pair of fruit-juice aficionados.

Volumes could be written on the role of special foods and drinks in maintaining group identity. There is Chinese food, Mexican food, Dutch food, etc. This presents a problem for cooks in public institutions. It is this phenomenon that provokes perennial protests in boarding schools in which students from various traditions are brought together. Students miss their foods of home.

In *Newsweek* (Oct. 2, 1995, p. 29) appears a comment by French Minister of Agriculture Phillippe Vasseur: "Bread is part of our national identity. ... If there isn't any left, we won't know who we really are." What kind of bread did Vasseur have in mind? French toast, perhaps. There are as many different kinds of menus as there are cultural groups. What is more Pennsylvania Dutch than shoo-fly cake? Two members of this community, Phyllis Pellman Good and Louise Stoltzfus, have compiled a compendium of *The Best of Mennonite Fellowship Meals* (1991).

Be it kingdom, phylum, class, family, genus, species, subspecies, etc., the story is the same. The drive toward identification, a sense of belonging, is one of our strongest psychological impulses. Some might call this drive "selfish," and so it may be. After all, whether a particular innate push is selfish or unselfish is not at all simple to determine. Whether the innate push is good or bad depends on viewpoint. Nature has made a value judgment on this. The impulse toward niche specialization appears to be a vital drive, selfish or not, and specific foods are involved in the process.

In a recent public television program, "Nomads of the Wind: Crossroads of the Pacific" (Part 2), red-breasted parrots native to the Fiji Islands are shown feeding voraciously on bright-red flowers closely matching the red breasts of the parrots. In connection with this, male Polynesian humans on these islands present specimens of these red flowers as prenuptial gifts to their prospective mates. Perhaps these natives, living close to nature, know more about food-courtship phenomena than their highly citified counterparts.

The importance of the role of distinctive foods in courtship and mating involves not only the *sight* of food but also the *smell*. The visual display of food, either directly or as a representation on the body, may be matched by olfactory display. We are well aware of this as we remember the aromas of our foods from home.

Relationships between food and body aromas may be readily demonstrated by eating the delectable vegetable, asparagus. Also, traces of ingested garlic are quickly detectable in body odors. Indeed, the entire perfume and cologne industries make use of the amorous effects of fruit essences applied to the body.

As detailed in Chapter 5, essences of the food excreted at territorial spots are important in mating systems of fruit flies (Jacobs 1978). When males court females, they wave their wings in such a way as to force their body odors toward the courted females. Averhoff and Richardson (1976) have demonstrated a male airborne substance that influences fruit fly females.

During courtship, the male *Utetheisa ornatrix* moth excretes a chemical that is the same as that found in the specific food plant of the species. The authors suggest that the females might benefit from preferring males with a high defense vigor, as reflected by high levels of secretion of the chemical (Conner et al. 1981, 1990).

Males of the fruit moth, *Grapholita molesta*, emit the scent of ethyltranscinnamate, which they normally ingest with their fruit diet. The scent is specifically attractive to females of that species (Löfstedt et al. 1989).

The behavior of males in attracting females by use of specific food chemicals closely simulates the behavior of bowerbirds in which the males spread fruit pulp over the walls of their bowers. The same phenomenon may be illustrated by other animals, including mammals, which leave territorial scents within the mating area. The attractants may be in the form of excreted materials — or actual scents as derived from the prey. This may help explain why predatory animals rub their fur over that of the prey. Then, just as the peacock carries a picture of the food of the clan on his feathers, so the coyote carries the scent of the food on his fur. The pictures and scents may indicate to the female the abundance of desirable food available in the territory of the male.

FEMALE CHOICE OR MALE-MALE COMPETITION?

In studies of sexual selection, investigators have tried a variety of methods to determine whether enhanced male mating success is due to his being selected by females on the basis of his appearance — or whether his success is due to his prowess in winning during male-male competition. Various attempts have been made to rule out the importance of territory in male mating success. Mats Grahn et al. (1993) performed experiments involving the mating system of the ring-necked pheasant, *Phasionus colchicus*. Males with large fighting spurs on the legs are more successful in mating than males with smaller spurs. Is this mating advantage a result of success in territorial competition or is it a result of female choice? The investigators reasoned that if it could be shown that the females are not influenced by territory in selection of male mates, it could be concluded that the differences in male mating success may be attributed alone to female attraction to the males with the larger spurs.

The investigators then set out to show that mating success among the males is not influenced by territorial quality. They worked with the premise that those males released first into an area would acquire better territories than males released later. However, when males with all about equal-sized spurs were used, early and late males had about equal mating success. From this they concluded that territorial differences do not influence mating success among the males. They therefore felt sure that in those experiments showing males with long spurs being more successful in mating than those with short spurs, the results must have been due not to differences in territories but to female choice of the males with longer spurs.

But is it safe to assume that males released early in the season will have better territories than those released later? What if an early male had eaten much of the food out of his territory before the females arrived? The late males might by then have territories as rich in food as the early males have. Consequently, females would just as readily mate with the late males as with the early males. If so, the conclusion that differences in territory make no difference in mating success would be invalid.

Beyond this, even if territorial quality were to be proved unimportant in determining male mating success in these pheasants, the enhanced success of the males with the larger spurs need not be interpreted as a result of female choice of the larger-spurred males. The males with larger spurs may be more physically fit and psychologically "spurred on" to gain a competitive advantage for access to females in contests with males not so endowed.

Furthermore, the females may be simply intimidated into submission to mate in view of the large spurs of the courting male. This could hardly be interpreted as choice on the part of the female, but simply submission to force. In studies in which it is claimed that females choose males on the basis of magnificent horns or antlers, this same critique applies. Also, in studies of such birds as swallows, in which it is claimed that females choose males on the basis of tail symmetry, it must be asked whether the improved aerodynamic ability of the symmetrical males gives such males an advantage in male-male competitive flights, with no female-choice hypothesis needed to explain the mating advantage of the male.

In a more direct attempt to rule out the importance of territory in the mating system of a species, Clutton-Brock (1989) performed an experiment in the mating arena of the fallow deer. The males defend small territories in a larger arena. Females visit these territories where they find tender grass to their liking. Clutton-Brock covered the territory of a dominant male with a black tarp. This deer was found to be still dominant and eminently successful in mating in another territory. This result was purported to show that it was not choice of the territory, but choice of the male himself that enhanced the mating success of that male.

But it's obvious that this conclusion does not necessarily follow. Elimination of the most desirable territory may simply have resulted in the male substituting the next most desirable territory.

Malte Andersson (1982) performed experiments with the long-tailed widowbird, *Euplectes progne* of Africa, in attempts to prove female choice of a male ornament, the long tail. The males jump up in their territories while calling. Andersson maintained that, since the tail is not displayed during male-male competition for territories, it is not involved in contests among males. On the other hand, the males expand their tails when performing their advertisement flights performed when females arrive. When the tails of the males were experimentally trimmed down, the number of females nesting in the territories of these short-tailed males was *reduced*. Conversely, if the tails of the males were experimentally elongated, by gluing on tail pieces, the number of females nesting in the territories of these long-tailed males was *increased*. The enhanced mating success of the males was attributed to female choice of males with elongated tails.

In reviewing the case for female choice of long tails among widowbirds, James and Carol Gould in their Scientific American Library book, *Sexual Selection* (1989, as reprinted in the 1997 version), were not convinced that male-male interactions had been satisfactorily ruled out in the conclusion that female choice had been responsible for the enhanced mating success of male widowbirds having longer tails. The Goulds evaluated the tail-lengthening experiments as follows: "This widowbird demonstration does have its shortcomings: first, it is a mixed system in which both male-male contests and female choice operate successively; second, the choice behavior is inferred later by the distribution of new nests."

The Goulds apparently realized that the tricky problem of determining whether differences in male mating success are due to female choice, rather than male-male competition, would be much easier if a species were found in which the males do not interact or defend territories. So, after some study, they selected guppy fish, maintaining that: "The males do not interact with one another — that is, they do not fight or defend territories." Of course, if the males *do* interact with each other, the origin of any male adornment may be attributed to an advantage it confers in male-male competition for access to females.

The Goulds studied fancy-male varieties of guppies. To demonstrate that guppy females are attracted to males with red tails, they placed a female into the central glassed-in compartment of an aquarium. A male was placed in compartments adjacent to the central compartment containing the female. It was discovered that the female spent most time on the side containing a male with the largest red tail.

Furthermore, when males with large red tails and males with small red tails were placed together with females, those males with the larger red tails were more successful in mating than were those with smaller red tails. Also, the offspring produced in this experiment showed a greater proportion of males with larger red tails than smaller red tails. (For details of these studies, see Bischoff et al. 1985.) Accepting the negative premise that male guppies do not compete for access to females, the students attributed the results to female choice of males with larger red tails.

I was highly skeptical of the premise that fancy-male guppy fish do not fight or defend territories, particularly since the same book shows a picture of a displaying male ring-necked pheasant with the caption: "Male pheasants do not fight nor do they provide females with any tangible resources or aid; instead, females apparently decide whether to mate with males on the basis of their courtship displays."

This "fact" comes as a great surprise to any observer of these pheasants. An expert on pheasants, Johnsgard (1994) says of male ring-necked pheasants that the sharp tarsal spurs are used for male-male fighting.

To resolve this problem of whether fancy-male guppy fish do or do not engage in male-male competition or defend territories, I undertook a study of guppy fish and some other members of the family Poeciliidae, which give birth to swimming young. An attempt was made to provide the fish with a variety of territorial choices within a simulated stream.

Since Chapter 4 contains much previously unpublished — and detailed — information that some casual readers may find tedious, they may choose to read only the CONCLUSIONS FROM THE FISH STUDY at the end of the chapter.

CHAPTER 4

LESSONS FROM GUPPIES AND SWORDTAIL FISH

Whales have calves,
Cats have kittens;
Bears have cubs,
Bats have bittens.
Swans have cygnets,
Seals have puppies;
But guppies just have little guppies.

—Ogden Nash

GUPPIES

GUPPIES DO, INDEED, HAVE LITTLE GUPPIES — but not *just* little guppies. Each little guppy is an individual. Guppy fish are so variable that early students had a hard time finding a specimen that could be used to describe *the* species (a type specimen in the conventional sense). In aquariums each fish can be identified by its distinctive markings. These colored markings are created by blue-green light diffraction — or by red-yellow carotenoid pigments. It has been well-documented by J.A. Endler (1980) and others that when the wild-type guppies are pursued by predatory fish, those guppies most nearly matching their backgrounds are most likely to survive the predators.

From wild populations collected in Trinidad, a large number of fancy-male varieties have been selected by breeders. Some of these varieties have larger-than-normal tails, which may be conspicuously colored with solid-red or blue-green colors — or black and yellow stripes.

To investigate whether it's true that fancy-male guppies do not interact or defend territories, I used a large (4-foot) aquarium and a 10-foot eaves trough. These enclosures were supplied with a bed of red gravel and plastic red vegetation at one end, and a bed of green gravel and plastic green vegetation at the other. To provide additional cover and food, I planted living Elodea and algae among the plastic vegetation. The fish food included Wardley tropical-fish food, which contains animal and vegetable ingredients and essential vitamins, including carotenes that enhance red colors. Each day about 10 percent of the water was removed from the trough and the aquarium, to be replaced promptly with fresh water.

The aquarium was maintained with four males of each fancy-male variety having red, blue, or black-and-yellow-striped tails. Plainer wild-type guppies were also studied. Females of each variety were included. The trough was maintained with two red-tailed males.

Observations totaling more than 2,500 hours were continued for about 11 months. I also have about 24 hours of "guppy video."

The guppy studies showed that the two red-tailed males in the trough wander the extent of the trough, eventually becoming localized, one in each of the two territories. When they swim out to feed, and encounter each other, skirmishes result, each male darting toward the tail of the other in a type of "dogfight." Sometimes one of the two fish enters the actual nest site of the other. This results in a vigorous fracas with quick departure of the intruder. The same scenario was repeated at regular intervals throughout the seven-week period of study. (The sole purpose of the trough study was to investigate territorialism.)

The males in the large aquarium also do a lot of skirmishing. In this, the color red is of paramount importance. Red-tailed males make sudden direct charges at the tail of the opponent, who may then flee, while his tail is being pursued by the victorious male. Direct fighting among males is diminished by the use of the tails in threat displays, each male bending his tail and waving it toward his rival. This mutual display appears to hold the males in a temporary standoff.

Yellow and black alternating (tiger-like) stripes on the tails are also effective in male-male competition, though less so than the red color of the red-tailed males. On the other hand, blue colors appear not to be effective at all. Blue-tailed males perform mutual tail displays, but standoffs do not result, as the color blue does not appear to threaten the males. Consequently, blue-tailed males vent their aggressive interactions by persistent chases throughout the aquarium. Blue-tailed males, however, lacking the advantage of red or black-and-yellow-striped tails, may still induce temporary standoffs by performing head-to-head displays with their yellow-red foreparts. Such head-to-head displays appear much less effective in alleviating physical chases than the mutual tail displays of the red-tailed males. Chases among blue-tailed males appear to be performed side by side, with the pursuing male only a little behind the other. It is not the blue tail that is being chased. Rather, in dogfights between red-tailed and blue-tailed males, the red-tailed male attacks the yellow-red *foreparts* of the blue-tailed male, whereas the blue-tailed male attacks the red *tail* of his rival. Plainer wild-type males, with transparent, almost colorless, tails (but brilliantly colored body markings), compete by pecking at the bodies of rivals. The ocellus spots on the sides of the plain males are particular targets for pecking.

Males appear particularly attracted to new males put into the aquarium as replacements for males that died. This leads to aggressive interaction between the resident males and the newly entered male. (Attraction to the novel is a common characteristic of animals, including fish.)

Males vigorously attack the red tails — or black-and-yellow-striped tails — of other males, while ignoring blue tails. They seem able to recognize specific rivals, for they pass up other males in keeping up with their rivals. If the rival gets lost, the charging male renews the chase upon finding him. Various color markings on the males might aid individual identification. However, many of the observations are also capable of a chemical-reception interpretation. Such chemoreception on the part of guppies appears remarkably sensitive. When food is placed at one end of the aquarium, it attracts fish from the other end, even when the lights are off.

As indicated, the aquarium had green gravel and green plastic vegetation at one end, and red gravel and red plastic vegetation at the other. Occasionally, a male would localize above the green or red gravel under the vegetation where fish of both sexes are inclined to feed and rest. Such a male vigorously charges and drives out other males entering his private domain. In the green end of the aquarium, one blue-tailed male held his "ground" for 26 days. In the red end, a red-tailed male controlled his territory for 12 days. Other males behaved similarly for shorter periods of time.

Certain females suddenly appear to become highly attractive to males that recognize and pursue them throughout the aquarium. Some such females seek refuge from pursuing males by hiding in the vegetation, from whence they chase away intruders.

A male, spotting a female feeding in his territory, may back away from her some 8 inches and intently observe her for a minute or more. He then approaches her while bending and vibrating his tail toward her head. If she moves away from the territory, he heads her off and herds her back into the territory, while displaying his tail toward her head. Both red-tailed and blue-tailed males perform this display. If the female makes a departure, the male follows her tail and pursues her wherever she goes.

The fish, be they male or female (or young fish only a few weeks after birth), are attracted to their own images reflected from the inside of the glass of the aquarium. They intently go up and down in front of the glass, following their own images.

The young are born in the recesses of the vegetation, where the pregnant females customarily rest when about to give birth. The young form a school in front of the vegetation during the daylight. Toward evening, or when the lights are turned off, they immediately return to the recesses of the vegetation and hide until the light returns. Surprisingly, this retreat of the young to the vegetation is quickly made when the lights are suddenly turned off. The young fish appear to be able to return home in the dark. Ordinarily, these young fish are quickly gobbled up by other fish.

Guppies spend a lot of time feeding on the algae growing on the bottom of the aquarium. The practice of feeding on the algae appears to be initiated by a single fish. Others soon imitate the practice, and it becomes widespread as the fish feed as a group. They then feed in this manner continuously over the entire period of observation. When so engaged in the feeding area, there is little interaction among the fish. However, when a female departs, a male frequently chases her. She then becomes the object of pursuit by other males.

This imitation of feeding on *plant* food is even more dramatically shown as the fish feed on *animal* food. Males and females frequently bite at tips of the red tail fins, the black-and-yellow-striped tail fins, or the reddish spots on the bodies of their fellows. If the bite is effective in nicking out some of the tissues, the biter may soon develop a habit of taking repeated nibbles. Such biters, if not removed from the aquarium, may eventually kill the victim. After the wound has been created, other fish imitate the feeding style of the biter, often leading to a feeding frenzy.

One red-tailed male, who had spent his best days vigorously chasing females, finally approached his "golden" years. He frequently languished on the algae growing in the feeding area on the bottom of the aquarium. At last he became immobile there, though his tail continued to wave. Soon thereafter, four females gathered around. One female actually brushed against him with her tail. It could not be determined whether the females were weeping, for the water would have swept away any tears.

At that point I was tempted to make an anthropomorphic interpretation of guppy behavior, but a moment later was spared the temptation when a female turned and took a bite out of the tip of the male's red tail. Soon other females followed her example. The scene was reminiscent of that reported by David Snow (1976) who saw a female cock-of-the-rock nibble at the bright-orange plumage of a male squatting on the floor of his arena.

A major aim of this study was to determine whether the attraction of female guppies to red tail fins or to black-and-yellow-striped tail fins may represent, at least in part, a response to a food drive. Or does the attraction have merely a sexual basis? The fact that fish actually *feed* on the colored tails points toward the likelihood of a food-drive interpretation.

SWORDTAIL AND PLATYFISH

Just as investigators had studied the role of female choice in the origin of red tails of male guppy fish, *Poecilia reticulata*, they studied the origin of swords on the tails of male swordtail fish, *Xiphophorus helleri*, another member of the family of tropical fish, Poeciliidae. The method employed was the compartmentalized-aquarium method used in guppy studies. Using this approach, Alexandra Basolo (1990) found that female swordtails, placed in the center compartment of the aquarium, were attracted to males in adjacent compartments. Furthermore, the longer the sword of the male, the greater the attraction by the female to that male.

Given this result, Basolo naturally wondered whether females of closely related species of *Xiphophorus*, in which the males are swordless, would also be attracted to males with swords. There was a species available for such studies, *Xiphophorus maculatus*, called a platyfish. Platyfish often cross with swordtail fish to produce fertile hybrids. In fact, many fancy-male varieties of swordtail fish are products of such hybridization. The ancestral variety of swordtail has a green sword with black borders.

Basolo cut a plastic sword and painted it to resemble the sword of a swordtail fish, but with the center stripe yellowish instead of green. The idea was that this might represent a sword of a color expected to grow out of the yellowish tail of a platyfish. Basolo surgically attached this sword to the tail of a male platyfish. The female platyfish now had a choice of swords or no swords among the males placed in compartments near her. Basolo found that the females indeed preferred males with the added swords. This experiment raised the question of whether the swords of male swordtail fish (of the species, *helleri*) arose in response to a built-in desire of females of that species for swords in their males, a desire held in common with platyfish females. If so, this might indicate that certain features of males in nature emerge in response to a predisposed desire in females. In evaluating this experiment, Stephen Gould (1993) remarked:

> The title of Basolo's article says it all — "Female preference predates the evolution of the sword in swordtail fish." ... Something in the sensory system of ancestral fishes evidently predisposed females of the *X. helleri* line to prefer males with swords. ... This sensory cognitive bias ... must be regarded as fortuitous with respect to the evolution of swords.

Though this "fortuitous," or chance, explanation says something, it does not say it all. The mutation might have arisen by a chance process, but it was then subjected to the food drive, the most basic selective force in nature. The colored tails of swordtails — yellowish bordered with black, in the case of Basolo's experimental *maculatus* males — might be attractive to the females in the same way females are attracted to colored foods. The same interpretation could be applied to the results of Rowland (1989), who performed experiments with stickleback fish,

Gasterosteus aculeatus. Females are attracted to red models of males, particularly to those models of larger size.

Red-yellow colors, being characteristic of food containing the important vitamin beta-carotene, may be especially attractive from a nutritional point of view. This interpretation can be extended to include other organisms that use display of colors in courtship. The female might be naturally programmed to be attracted to the colorful displaying male. If the vigorous display of the male and the color of his adornment are correlated with the quality and quantity of the food, this choice by the female, representing a choice of a favorable reproductive territory, would enhance reproduction of the species.

Are female platyfish indeed attracted to swords colored at the red end of the spectrum and, if so, can at least part of this attraction be attributed to a food-response stimulus? The same questions may also be asked about attraction of female swordtail fish to swords colored at the green end of the spectrum — and about the black borders on the swords. It is conceivable that the green stripes resemble strands of algae, while the yellow-red or black stripes on the undulating swords resemble wiggling worms.

When the guppy studies were terminated, studies of swordtail and platyfish were begun, also in my living room, using the same equipment and methods used for the guppies. Both sexes of wild-type swordtail fish (called "greenswords") are pale olive green about 2 inches long. On each side they have a dark, violet band extending from the snout to the base of the tail. In the male this band assumes a black hue as it emerges from the stem of the tail, then continues as a black line along the top side of the sword. There is also a small, black spot on the middle of each side of the body of the male. The intensity of this spot strengthens with increasing aggressiveness of the male. The middle of the sword is the continuation of an iridescent green-blue band that starts above the anal fin area on the body of the fish and extends to the tip of the sword. Along the bottom side of the sword is another black line extending from the base of the tail to the tip of the sword. The rest of the tail-fin area is a faint, blue-green color. The sword is more conspicuously colored than is the rest of the fish. To humans, the sword is strikingly beautiful, and swordtails are popular aquarium fish. The females have no swords. It is of interest that the brightly colored central stripe of the sword is conspicuous against a dark background, whereas a black border stripe stands out against a light background.

From these wild-type (greensword) fish, fancy-male redsword and blacksword varieties have been produced by fish breeders. Both sexes of the redsword variety have red bodies, and the swords of the males are even more intensely red than the body. There is a black band on the bottom of the sword. The blacksword variety is similar, but the fins and swords are black.

The platyfish studied included the common, bluish-green variety with yellowish fins and a large, reddish spot on the base from which the tail arises. The red variety is intensely red with yellowish fins. The red-black variety has a red body and black fins.

For what purpose are the swords of swordtail fish used? Certainly not for stabbing; they are far too flexible for that. Development of the swords parallels advance in sexual maturation of the males, and the swords are obviously employed in male-male competition. Competing males dash swiftly toward the swords of other males and whip their swords toward the heads of rivals. This activity may create intimidating "sound" waves in the water. This use of swords appears equivalent to the use of a whip as a directing instrument, just as whips are used in directing horses.

The swords may also have a display function. Addition of the sword to the body of the fish gives the impression that the fish is twice its actual size. Extension of the entire tail fin of a male to create an impression of larger size would have serious drawbacks, however, in the case of swordtail fish. The huge wide fin would resist fast swimming. Swordtail fish swim exceptionally swiftly, and streamlining in water is particularly important.

Males display their swords toward rivals, as well as toward females. They also display them toward their own images reflected from the glass of the aquarium. Males appear especially sensitive about having other fish approach their swords, jerking them quickly away. Males with well-developed swords generally dominate less-well-endowed males.

The swords are also employed in courtship. When a female is feeding among the pebbles in the territory of a male, that male may join her and feed briefly, then characteristically back away about 8 inches and stiffly hold his position while facing the female. Suddenly, he dashes toward her. If she begins to leave, he heads her off by making quick darts back and forth in front of her path while whipping his tail back and forth. If she goes back into the territory, he may corner her there and, by backing toward her, thrust his long sword toward her head. In doing this, is the male using his long, worm-like tail as a type of "fishing" lure?

Greensword females are, indeed, attracted to black swords, and the motivation appears to be food-stimulated. They bite the tips of the swords of slow-moving blacksword males. Females are also attracted to thin, black, *inanimate* objects and peck along their linear surfaces.

Redsword males court and herd their females after the manner of their greensword counterparts. The males vigorously attack the red swords of their rivals, while ignoring the greensword males. Redsword males frequently localize to certain feeding and resting areas from which they drive away redsword rivals. One such male became localized to, and defended, a territory above the red gravel even before his sword had shown itself beyond a mere small bump at the bottom of the tail. As the sword developed, a black line began to appear on its bottom. As the black line developed, the male became increasingly aggressive in driving away his rivals.

Not only swordtail females but also platy females are attracted to the red swords of redsword males with an apparent food-stimulus motivation. On numerous occasions, platy females bit the tip of such swords. One consumed a dark thread of fecal material streaming from the male near the sword.

These observations may help explain Basolo's findings that female swordtail fish are attracted to swords, especially larger swords, of males — and that female platyfish are attracted to artificial swords attached to swordless males. The attraction may, at least in part, be in response to a food stimulus — and the larger the display, the greater the attraction.

In a brief article in *Nature* (1994), Sarah Haines and James Gould present some data that, on the surface, appear to militate against a view that female fish are attracted to swords in response to a food stimulus. Using the three-chamber technique used in their guppy studies, they found that a female platyfish, *Xiphophorus variatus* (a species with reddish tails), placed in the middle compartment was attracted to models of males of the species placed in an adjacent compartment, especially if those models had red swords attached. Furthermore, the attraction was greatest if the swords were placed in the position that is normal in swordtail fish, on the underside of the tail. Now, if the fish were attracted to the swords merely on the basis of a food attraction, why should this positioning influence the attractiveness?

Some observations made in the present investigation may help solve the riddle of why a sword located on the bottom side is more attractive than one located on the top side of the model's tails. There is a marked tendency for a fish to approach another from the bottom side and peck at the anal fin or the gonopodium (a stiffened rod that develops on the bottom surface of the anal fin used by the male for inseminating purposes). This usually leads to rapid departure of the "peckee." This is true for all fish tested: guppies, swordtails, and platyfish, including the species *variatus*. Pecking at this worm-like structure may be interpreted as a response to a food stimulus.

CONCLUSIONS FROM THE FISH STUDY

Regarding fancy-male varieties of guppies, the ones studied here showed conventional territorial behavior, including localization to specific areas and aggressive repulsion of intruding fish. The oft-quoted opinion that guppies do not interact or defend territories may have originated on the basis of observations of non-fancy guppies studied in small aquariums.

Anne Houde, who has published a comprehensive analysis of the origin of coloration in wild-type guppies, *Sex, Color, and Mate Choice in Guppies* (1997), presents the following assessment:

> From first principles, the guppy system seemed promising for studies of female choice. Male guppies court one female after another and rarely interact or compete with other males. Generally, if a male is to be successful in mating, females must respond to his displays and cooperate in copulations. ... Male-male competition could involve the use of color patterns in intimidation displays between males ... but displays between male guppies are rare.

It may well be that, along with the artificial selection that has produced the fancy-male varieties used in some studies of sexual selection, has gone selection for male-male aggressive interaction. At least under my conditions, using a large aquarium or trough offering a variety of territories, males with fancy red tails persistently display them by bending and waving them toward rival males.

Guppies show dramatically how adornment can be an energy-saving device. Blue-green-tailed fish (lacking the red display feature useful in distance threat) compensate for this lack by accelerating expenditure of physical energy in chasing rivals. Blue-green-tailed males do display the broad sides of their tails toward other males, but the display appears ineffective in repelling those males.

The behavior of fancy-male guppies in the trough would indicate that territorial behavior may be characteristic of wild guppies. Not much is known about the behavior of guppies in their natural streams. They are said to be difficult to observe there, as they show a marked tendency to hide under the vegetation. But there are a few studies indicating that male guppies show male-male display competition in the wilds. (See Reznik and Endler 1982.)

The red-yellow colors, though stimulating a threatening response, may also stimulate a food-procurement response. This should come as no surprise to manufacturers of fishing equipment. These inventors go to great pains to make strikingly colorful lures for attracting hungry fish. Pecking of fish at the red (but not green) small spheres of gravel placed in the feeding area may represent an attraction to reddish foods. Small invertebrates on which the fish prey often have cuticles colored at the yellow-red (orange) end of the spectrum (including brown and tan colors). Red-tailed males were frequently attracted to a small piece of yellow-brown (tan) rubber tubing used as a connector to the glass tube of the aerator.

The conventional method of studying female attraction to males among guppies is to place females in an aquarium where they have opportunity to be attracted to either males strikingly marked with bright-orange colors — or duller males. The females are entered as virgins that have never before seen a male, or as those that have not seen a male after having given birth.

At the start of the mate-choice tests, the newly entered females dash toward the males and, in the mad melee, show little or no discrimination among the males. To quiet down the females, the investigators wait a day before starting to keep records. By that time some of the females have mated and lost much of their interest in males.

The females' lack of interest is conventionally ascribed to having their sex drive depleted after mating. However, the females may (at least in part) lose interest in the colored markings of the males upon discovering they are not an available food source. When a fancy male is newly entered into an aquarium, it is particularly attractive to resident fish.

The yellow-red coloration, which apparently attracts females and is involved in male-male aggressive interactions, may be enhanced by carotenoid feeding. Therefore, presence of a bright yellow-red male would attract a female to a territory rich in a long-term supply of nutritious food. The male had been there long enough to assimilate, onto his body, a sample of the carotenoids found there.

But there is also a *downside* to becoming brightly colored. The color attracts predators. Guppies may strike a balance between being bright-yellow-red or duller colored. Houde (1988) demonstrated this with fish collected from streams with different concentrations of guppy predators. Guppies from *low*-predator streams are found to be brighter yellow-red than those from *high*-predator streams. Appropriately, females from the brighter yellow-red population are more attracted to bright-yellow-red males than are females from the duller population. Such differences in attraction would genetically preserve the bright and dull populations in their respective streams.

In emphasizing the yellow-red end of the color spectrum, we must not lose sight of the other end, the blue-green one. In some instances, even certain blue-green foods may not be uniformly distributed in the aquatic environment. These chlorophyll-equipped plants, being directly dependent on sunshine, are concentrated in sunny niches. A male with a bright-blue-green tail, maintaining a territory rich in blue-green foods, may attract a female with a similar taste for such delicacies. On the other hand, males with yellow-red tails would maintain territories in the shady niches, which are comparatively rich in yellow-red animal foods.

It should be pointed out here that food drives and sex drives are not mutually exclusive. In line with the theories presented in this book, a sex drive would provide the genetic variability on which selection for the food drive would operate. Food-niche specialization, not sex for sex itself, would be the ultimate aim of the selection process.

The findings from the studies of guppy fish may help explain some curious results obtained by Lee Alan Dugatkin and Jean-Guy J. Godin as outlined in the April 1998 issue of *Scientific American*. These investigators — studying predator-prey relationships in guppies — found that when a predatory fish enters an area frequented by a group of male guppies, a certain male, usually the brightest orange one, swims toward the predator as though daring him. A watching female then chooses him for a mate in preference to less daring males in the area.

The investigators interpret these results in line with the handicap principle. That is, females choose those males that display the most bravery in the face of danger. This is in keeping with Darwin's original idea of sexual selection. The females are presumed to conclude that such males are endowed with the best "fitness genes."

A less convoluted explanation of these results is that the male most successful in mating is the one most aggressive in driving away from his territory potential predators, including fish of his own species. The breeding area defended by that male would then be the one safest for the rearing of young guppies. Female guppies would select such males for mating in response to the males' bright-orange color — in line with the interpretations presented in this book.

CHAPTER 5

LESSONS FROM FRUIT FLIES

*T*HE DRAGONFLY STUDY HAD RAISED SEVERAL problems regarding: possible relationships between sexual selection and niche specialization, the role of food in courtship behavior, and particularly how dark body color relates to these questions. These were further pursued with the fruit fly, *Drosophila melanogaster*. First, precisely what, if any, is the adaptive value of dark pigmentation relative to population genetics? Second, is the spectrum of pigments varying from black though brown to light tan simply of adornment value? If so, the origin of the pigmentation may be explained on the basis of sexual selection alone, as Charles Darwin postulated for the origin for skin pigmentation of humans.

However, if the pigments reflect underlying biochemical and physiological conditions that are expressed in basic differences in behavior, the origin of the pigmentation differences may be explained on the basis of natural selection alone.

This is the question raised by Wallace. Is there a relationship between adornment of a male and his underlying biochemistry and physiology? If so, any apparent female choice of a male based on his adornment may rather be explained as a result of his physiological superiority, enabling him to win male-male contests for access to females.

But there is still a third alternative, considered by neither Darwin nor Wallace. If adornment is connected with basic physiology, the origin of the pigmentation may be explained on the basis of both sexual and natural selection in the same package! This would be an integrated explanation of the pigmentation differences. It would take a combined study of sexual selection, biochemistry, and physiology to confirm this integrated explanation.

During the dragonfly study it had been noted that museum specimens of the amber-winged dragonfly, *Perithemis tenera*, from North Carolina showed differences in degree of dark pigmentation, even more pronounced than those shown in the Indiana population. The path led to Duke University, from which field studies of the behavior of these darker forms could be studied. The aim was also to study the biochemical genetics of dark and tan pigmentation relative to mating systems and adaptation to ecological niches. There was a large cement pool with a screened enclosure next to the biology building. This seemed just right for rearing dragonflies. The aim was to raise *Perithemis* there and study the genetics of dark body pigmentation.

I drove to Florida and swam around in ponds in the dark collecting a large number of newly emerged specimens of *Perithemis*. The adults were allowed to fly freely within the car. Several gas station attendants stared at this as somewhat of a spectacle — pet dragonflies! But back at Duke the dragonflies made themselves at home in the "pond" decorated with algae, sticks, and emergent vegetation. Small flying insects were entered as food for the adults. The idea was to cross the dark and light forms for genetical studies.

Shortly thereafter, Theodosius Dobzhansky (1900–1975), a population geneticist from Columbia University, passed through Duke on the way to Raleigh for a speaking engagement. The Columbia group studied various species of *Drosophila*, particularly with reference to mechanisms of sexual isolation between species. However, they were not studying a possible process of sexual selection within a species.

Dobzhansky was particularly interested in the evolution of chromosomal alterations as involved in the origin of species. His book, *Genetics and the Origin of Species* (1937), was widely read. He studied relationships between survival of the fittest and rearrangements of parts among the chromosomes. In connection with this, he was also interested in "hybrid vigor." This is a type of super vitality alleged to result from crossing different strains of plants or animals. For example, it had been reported that when the mutant ebony of *Drosophila melanogaster* is crossed with normal flies, the normal X ebony hybrids show enhanced survival in competition with normal flies in population cages (L'Heritier et al. 1937). Hermann Muller thought that this result was best explained on the basis that the normal gene and the ebony mutant gene make different products. Since two different products are better than one, the normal X ebony hybrid should be better than either the normal or ebony true-breeding flies.

It turned out, however, that the normal gene and the ebony gene do not make different products. The normal gene makes the product (an enzyme that combines beta-alanine with dopamine), but when this gene mutates to ebony it loses its ability to make this enzyme. The reason the hybrid flies show a hybrid advantage is because under certain conditions one normal gene (as in the hybrid) is better than two normal genes (as in the true-breeding normal flies). The advantage to be gained by having only one gene operating is that an intermediate condition is better than the more extreme conditions.

In the meeting at Raleigh, Dobzhansky was lecturing on his flies that showed super survival-fitness. The chairman of the genetics group asked him if he had any biochemical evidence for why the flies were super. Dobzhansky replied, "I am completely ignorant of biochemistry and hope to remain so." Perhaps "hope" is translated from "expect" in Dobzhansky's native Russian. However, at that time very little attention was paid to biochemical genetics. In fact, my first report on the biochemistry of pigmentation in *Drosophila* ended up in the very first volume of *Biochemical Genetics*.

In consideration of the possibility of hybrid vigor in humans, Dobzhansky was somewhat at odds with Muller's concerns about the dire consequences resulting from the continuous "load" of recessive mutations accumulating in the human gene pool. Since these mutations are, for all practical purposes, harmful, Muller feared that humans are genetically doomed unless they practice artificial selection (eugenics). A "sperm bank" was his solution. Save a sperm supply frozen for future generations. The pedigree of the donor would be on file for inspection for those females seeking artificial insemination. This was the female-choice aspect of sexual selection taken to its logical conclusion.

Some thought this was a dangerous solution to the problem of mate selection. But Muller was simply proposing what he considered a much-needed service. After all, it was realized at the time that an atomic holocaust was not only possible, but had actually been recently executed in Japan. Anticipating exposure to radiation, males at that time were apprehensive about the safety of their genes. (For example, Jim Watson usually ducked out of the laboratory when Muller was demonstrating how he irradiated fruit flies with X-rays. Muller had used outdated dental radiation equipment in his early radiation experiments.) In view of all this, some males at the time were anxious to have their sperm frozen before they might be exposed to mutational radiation. It is reported that Muller once had a nightmare in which there was a power failure resulting in the thawing of his sperm bank. In his dream, the precious gene pool of the ages leaked out over the floor and was lost forever, down the drain.

Dobzhansky thought Muller was overdoing his emphasis on eugenics. He insisted that if some mutant genes that are harmful by themselves confer superior fitness in the hybrid condition, elimination of such harmful genes by a program of eugenics may be ultimately non-beneficial to the overall human gene pool. Muller countered that if hybrid vigor plays an important role in nature, true-breeding systems that incorporate the advantages of the hybrid conditions could be arranged by nature. (Some such systems actually are found in nature.) A eugenics program might include this type of system, in which case it would not be necessary to maintain inferior strains for crossing to get the hybrid condition. But the true-breeding strains would, by being genetically fixed, be incapable of varying to fit into changing environmental conditions. The *Drosophila* studies described in this book deal with these problems in reference to variation in pigmentation.

In his visit to Duke, Dobzhansky showed considerable interest in my dragonfly project, for he had done some work on dark-pigmentation differences among ladybird beetles. But he expressed skepticism about the possibility of getting dragonflies to mate in captivity. Genetic studies did not therefore appear feasible. He had a good point there. Furthermore, upon discovering that the same spectrum of dark-pigmentation variation exhibited by the dragonfly, *Perithemis tenera*, was also shown by the fruit fly, *Drosophila melanogaster*, I turned to *Drosophila* for continuation of studies involving pigmentation variation in insects.

For biochemical genetical studies, *Drosophila melanogaster* would be hard to beat. The genetic system is simple, with only four pairs of chromosomes on which many genes have been located. Standardized stocks of mutants are available in culture centers at various laboratories, and there is an impressive amount of genetical literature. To collect wild specimens, all you need to do is set out culture bottles: In a couple of weeks, you will have all the specimens you need.

Questions pursued were: (1) What is the role of food in courtship and mating? (2) Is dark pigmentation related to selection of habitats varying in degree of illumination and, if so, does this result in mating of like-pigmentation phenotypes? (3) Are these pigments merely of adornment value, originating solely from a process of sexual selection? Or are they related directly to natural adaptation, originating from a process of natural selection? Or are both types of selection involved? (4) Do wild *melanogaster* collected from sunny and shady places in nature show differences in degree of dark pigmentation? (5) Do dark and tan body pigmentation differences reflect differences in underlying biochemical and physiological conditions?

To collect wild fruit flies, bottles with standard laboratory *Drosophila* food were exposed in various sunny and shaded places, including burrows of wild animals. The search was successful: A whole spectrum of true-breeding cultures of light tan, dark, and intermediately pigmented flies was selected and raised in the laboratory. Some very dark (black) flies were found in an animal burrow. Even darker (ebony) flies were also located. Studies were begun with these flies immediately after they were discovered to be true-breeding in the laboratory.

An attempt was made to simulate field conditions in the laboratory, particularly with reference to differently illuminated territories. In an air-conditioned laboratory, the variously pigmented flies were studied within large enclosures, containing food dishes placed under illumination-graded conditions, including nearly dark conditions created with red optical filters. (To a fruit fly, living under red light is like living in the dark.) The illumination levels in the various stations in the observation chamber were determined. The flies were marked with tiny dots of aluminum paint for identification and were entered into the enclosure.

Territorial behavior in *Drosophila* was soon revealed. When adults (newly emerged from their pupal cases) are placed in the large observation chamber the flies explore their new environment and gather on the food dishes. As the males mature sexually, some become strictly localized to particular food dishes, which they defend against other males by charging with their wings extended. This sometimes leads to tussling in which a male pounces on another from any angle and tugs at the body and wings of the other male while flexing his abdomen. Such tussles may become mutual, whereupon males face and tug at each other and sometimes tumble about as in wrestling. After such fighting, one of the males may depart, flicking his wings. Many males fight with, and subsequently depart from, the same male on a dish. Usually males are successful in eliminating rivals by simply charging. Ebony males, on the other hand, being deficient in effective charging technique, resort more frequently to wrestling than do normal flies. Females were not observed to tussle, but they sometimes briefly charge other flies that get in their way as they're feeding (Jacobs 1960).

Food appears essential for bringing the sexes together and for stimulating mating. If no food (only water) is available, very few matings are observed. By far, most matings occur on or very close to the food dishes.

As the female passively feeds on the male's dish, the male faces her, making sidewise movements while buzzing his wings toward her head. During this courtship the female still appears quite passive. She may flee from the male's advances and pass to the territory of another male. Finally, she may spread her wings and allow a male to settle on her back with his front feet clasping her spread wings. On the average, mating lasts 17.4 minutes. The time is greatly increased, however, in matings involving ebony flies (which show numerous behavioral abnormalities). The average mating time of ebony flies is 25.4 minutes. This extension of mating duration is due primarily to the males.

Although very few matings occur away from the food dishes, some coital activity also occurs on patches of excrement deposited by the fruit flies in spots away from the food dishes where the flies frequently rest. Some males defend these spots against rivals. The flies are also attracted to small pieces of filter paper infiltrated with fly excrement. Perhaps the excrement contains traces of the food eaten by the flies (Jacobs 1978).

This is interesting with respect to the origin of arena behavior. In certain Hawaiian *Drosophila*, males traditionally defend spots of excreted materials deposited on leaves (Spieth 1968).

It was soon discovered that the ebony flies are more photonegative than the rest. This resulted in some sexual segregation of ebony flies from normal flies. Males and females of the dark flies were mutually attracted to the darker areas, whereas those of the light flies were mutually attracted to the lighter areas. This relates to similar findings with *Perithemis* dragonflies. In addition, ebony flies exhibit marked abnormalities in behavior. Their vision is defective and their movements are retarded and uncoordinated. The ebony males fail in normal posturing and circling of the female. Instead, they make immediate contact with the female and lick her body. If they do extend and vibrate the wing toward the female, the extension is slow and weak and not directed toward the head of the female in the normal fashion. Ebony flies, being defective in vision, appear to accentuate use of taste instead of vision in mating. Black flies also show some behavioral abnormalities, but less extreme than ebony.

There appeared to be a relationship between the dark body pigments and the general behavior (and possibly physiology) of the fruit flies. This called for biochemical studies.

PIGMENTATION RELATIVE TO BIOCHEMISTRY, PHYSIOLOGY, AND ECOLOGICAL ADAPTATION

(Rated 'T' for Technical — From Here Through Some of the Remaining Portions of This Chapter!)

Dark (melanistic) pigment variation is observed from here to the horizon. The reason for the widespread use of melanoid pigments in nature is based mainly on the fact that these pigments aid in protecting creatures from the damaging effects of light, especially ultraviolet light. The outside coatings of insects are often mottled or solid black. The black pigments not only protect from light damage, they also aid in temperature regulation. In light of this, it is little wonder that the *Perithemis* dragonfly, which inhabits a variety of habitats varying from sunny to shaded, shows variation in the amount of dark pigmentation. The tendency for the dark males to mate preferentially with dark females in dark areas, while the lighter forms are behaving likewise in sunny areas, makes sense here.

Not all melanoid pigments are black. They show a spectrum of colors from black through brown to light tan. At the beginning of the dragonfly investigation, in the 1950s, it was known that the melanin responsible for black pigmentation of animals is produced from the amino acid tyrosine. The tan and brown "melanins" were called "pheomelanins." Little was known about how these were formed. It was known also that tyrosine could be shunted from melanin products to produce important physiologically active products including adrenaline (the fight-or-flight hormone), dopamine (the pleasure-producing hormone), and thyroxine (the metabolic-enhancing hormone). It was also known that melanin effectively absorbs ultraviolet light, protecting the underlying tissues from damage. In addition, it absorbs infrared and other heating rays. It may therefore act as a collector of solar heat. If so, dark-pigment variation may be directly related to niche adaptation as influenced by climatic conditions.

While this study of pigmentation in *Drosophila* was progressing, radio chemists were discovering that radioactive carbon-14 could be useful in tracing metabolic pathways. Individual carbon atoms in organic carbon compounds could be radio-labeled, and the metabolic fate of these carbons could be analyzed. By use of these methods the metabolism of intact living organisms could be studied. This is just what was needed for the fruit-fly project.

First, precise, small amounts of the radioactive chemicals must be injected without harm to the fruit flies. This was achieved by drawing a small capillary tube to a fine tip, then breaking the tip at an angle to leave a sharp point. The tube was then fitted to the tip of a syringe that had a spring inside. The syringe was clamped to the barrel of a microscope for lowering the sharp point of the tube onto the surface of the fly. The cuticle was gently pierced and the injection into the circulatory cavity (hemocoel) of the fly was performed expeditiously by means of a screw mechanism that put pressure on the stem of the syringe.

Sixteen different radio-labeled amino acids were injected. Those compounds involved in the tyrosine-to-melanin pathway were the prime targets of investigation. Perhaps the dark flies would show excessive deposition of products from these compounds bound up in cuticular melanins. Surprisingly, these compounds involved in production of melanin showed no appreciable differences in incorporation rates among the differently pigmented cuticles.

But, completely unexpectedly, another compound not at all known at the time to be related to melanin production, beta-alanine, showed drastic differences in incorporation rates among the differently pigmented flies. During the tanning process beta-alanine was incorporated into cuticles of normal tan flies at very high levels — but little, if any, was incorporated into the cuticles of ebony flies. The normal X ebony hybrid showed intermediate incorporation rates. This finding led to an explanation for the phenomenon of hybrid vigor among the flies.

The rates of beta-alanine incorporation were at first determined by exposing cuticles of the injected flies to X-ray film. The radio label from the injected compounds registered itself on the film. This method of study of the radio-labeled compounds was admittedly not very quantitative. More discriminating methods of study were imperative. Kenton Brubaker, a friend at Eastern Mennonite College in Harrisonburg, Virginia, offered use of some Geiger radiation-counting equipment he had recently secured with a federal educational grant. By use of this equipment, the essential quantitative verification of the discovery was made. We sat in awe as the first counts came from the Geiger counter, with its red eyes that lit up when a beta ray passed through the detector. Soon thereafter, the results were published in *Science* (Jacobs and Brubaker 1963).

It was quickly realized that the numerous questions raised by this discovery could be pursued only with the aid of much more expensive equipment, which would far exceed the budget of a liberal-arts college. At that time liberal-arts colleges were reluctant to accept federal funds in support of research. Some of the faculty and constituency had their roots too close to European church-state tyranny to feel comfortable with the influence such support might have on the independent atmosphere of these liberal-arts colleges. But others argued that undergraduate students would be left with a big hole in their educational package if they had no opportunity to engage in costly frontier research. This debate became particularly divisive after the atom was split. Atomic research, for example, required federal aid in copious amounts. Some then argued that the students could be sent to big-research institutions to further their education in these expensive sciences. Others countered that the students should remain at their alma maters, where they would not be splattered against the wall as pancakes. After all, focusing too narrowly violates the very essence of a liberal education. The outcome of the debate was that limited research funds could be sought for support of research in liberal-arts colleges. It was recognized that, with respect to scientific discovery, federal funding is justified. If properly administered, such funding would allow for freedom in investigations.

In fact, the philosophy of the National Institutes of Health at the time was to encourage freedom to explore. The NIH administrators had received numerous complaints that the peer review system, being very cumbersome, greatly impeded novelty research into new vistas. In response to these complaints, special grants were set up in support of pioneering projects. These Biomedical Research Support Grants were awarded to those investigators who already had substantial support for their standard research. The special awards bypass the peer-review system, thereby greatly speeding up the funding process. When it comes to exceptionally original research, peer reviewers often fail miserably in understanding the thrust of a novel proposal. This is highly frustrating to the originators of the research, who must face the fact that they really have no peers. This problem is faced also by creators of music. The awful critiques some such artists give to the work of other artists they do not appreciate are of scandalous proportions.

In spite of attempts to remedy the potential downside of government funds, there is still a concern that federal dollars could have an unwholesome influence on scientific inquiry. How many graduate students have become disillusioned with the fact that researchers too often seem to be under the pressure of bread-and-butter issues rather than issues of free and unencumbered investigation. It is the old argument of economic dependency versus individual initiative and freedom.

Above all, the history of science abundantly shows the grave dangers of mixing politics with science. On the other hand, research grants actually favor independence of researchers. It is said that Thomas Morgan needed to fight the administration at Columbia University for an allocation to buy bananas for culturing his fruit flies. Federal grants liberated many such investigators.

ANTHROPOMORPHIC MACHINES

Modern scientists are supposed to gather information as spewed forth from the bowels of objective machines. Such data are said to be "sophisticated," sometimes even more so than what the ancient Greek philosophers spun off the tops of their hoary heads.

While sitting in the laboratory at Goshen College studying the behavior of fruit flies deporting themselves in an illumination-graded observation chamber, with the federally purchased sophisticated machines whirring merrily around the room, it occurred to me that the behavior of these machines could be interpreted anthropomorphically.

First, there was the low-background, gas-flow Geiger counter. I called it Frankenstein (Frank, for short) after the fabled robot that got the upper hand on humans. With his simple binary brain, Frank could tell whether a particular carbon labeled with carbon-14 had been excreted as carbon-14-labeled carbon dioxide, or whether it had ended up in another molecule in the fly. After precisely and tirelessly counting the radioactivity in each sample pan, Frank would change the pan for another from the stack. He registered meticulous notes on a long strip of paper. Frank was a smart idiot. He might sit all day counting empty sample pans and recording the results. But Frank was utterly dependable. All his knowledge was programmed. He had nothing to do with creativity. If anything went wrong with him, he could not repair the damage.

Then there was Jezebel, the high-performance liquid chromatographer. Jezebel's brain was more intuitive, less certain, more inferential, than Frank's. She was also cantankerous, but necessary. She could determine the metabolic fate of the carbon atoms. She worked closely with Frank. Jezebel liked to study not organisms, but fluids extracted from ground-up organisms. She was a traditional biochemist. To her, the only good cell was a dead cell.

Jezebel was obsessed with metabolic pathways. Examining the cellular juices, she could detect the most minuscule quantities of molecules. She could tell you if there was something unusual there, but she never told you exactly what it was. She could, however, inform you if what she found was like something else. It required a lot of speculating and analogizing into the realm of the unknown to deduce what the new compound was. Jezebel worked with the motto, "If this is true, that must also be true." Chemists, lacking the luxury of direct observation, live on the precipice of uncertainty. Most enjoy their uncertain life; it keeps them guessing — though some of their guesses are way off the mark.

Elsie, the electron microscope, liked cells with their internal structure left as intact as possible, though petrified with toxic chemicals. Hardly anyone could outdo Elsie when it came to meticulous observation. She made human bean counters look positively slipshod by comparison. Elsie could see where a particular carbon-14 atom ended up in the ultrastructure of the cell. In addition, she could determine whether beta-alanine injected into the fruit fly had any influence on the fine structure of the fly's cuticle. She made detailed observations of the actual internal skeletons of individual cells.

Finally, there was King George the First, the calculator. George was the final authority. He was in charge of Frankenstein and all the other mechanical monsters. He was the mathematician. Any results not signed by George were invalid results, "by George!" King George himself was not beyond improvement; he rapidly matured during the course of the study. He started out as a cranky bucket of bolts and ended up with an electronic chip on his shoulder. King George was the original slave driver. He wouldn't take "no" for an answer, realizing, of course, that a double negative is a positive. George had a "bigger is better" mentality. Recognizing that variability is an essential component of vital systems, George had an obsession with analyzing variability. He had little use for a single specimen that yielded merely anecdotal evidence. He based his conclusions on a broadly based consensus.

His head was full of probability theory. The mathematicians from Gauss to Gosset would have loved King George. Calculations that once went oh so slowly and laboriously through the collective heads of mathematicians, zipped effortlessly through George's chips. But then, if

George ever had any fun, any ecstatic experiences when a revolutionary discovery was made, it was not evident. George was completely set in his objective traditional beliefs. Any set of data qualified as a discovery.

George passed judgment on everything that went on in the lab or field. He was an armchair theorizer who depended on the observations of others. George liked results that showed differences between experimental and control groups large enough so that the results could be explained as mere sampling errors a mere 1 percent of the time, though he would settle for 5 percent. This was the percentage of times a difference in averages as great as that between the experimental group and the control group could be explained on the basis of chance alone. The smaller the percentage, the more confidence the observer could have that the difference was real — and not simply due to chance. King George determined whether the results could be celebrated with abandon (at the 1 percent significance level) or simply with exuberance (at the 5 percent level) or with no celebration at all (at a level of 20 percent or greater). At a level of 50 percent the whole experiment was abandoned and the data simply stored in notebooks not published, or better, published as a note with significant published data, sparing someone else the trouble. The negative results had been worth the effort nonetheless.

King George had a long line of progeny, all much smarter than he. This led to a struggle for dominance. Some humans predicted that these smart machines would someday outdo the human, not only in making calculations but in actually doing some of the creative programming. Under these conditions, the investigator could be out in the field doing interesting things, while the machines were back in the lab doing the tedious work. The calculators were already performing many of the ordinary tasks of making calculations. It finally came to the point that these machines wrote up reports in a form with so few errors that editors would give their blessing. How did Darwin ever write his big *Origin* book without a computer? He didn't have George looking over his shoulder, immediately correcting all the mistakes to which we humans are notoriously prone.

In a manner of speaking, we became slaves to these machines. When the machines were up, we were up. When the machines were down, we were down. At their beck and call, we hopped and skipped to keep the machines running properly. But the machines never complained. They never tired. They just kept doing what they were supposed to do. But they were expensive to obtain and operate. The maintenance contract for Elsie alone took a big bite out of the research budget. The machines ran on solar energy bound up in fossil fuels to be distributed throughout the various academic niches. Only the most efficient would survive this competitive struggle. No funds were to be wasted. We were dealing here with not only natural, but also artificial, laws of economics.

MELANIN PIGMENTATION AND ADAPTATION

It is one of the ironies of life that specialization leads at once both to greater independence and dependence. Nowhere is this more dramatically illustrated than in comparing the essential food requirements of the relatively unspecialized micro-organisms with those of highly specialized animals, such as fruit flies and human beings.

The only ingredients some little green creatures require for living are solar energy, rocks, and air. We call these green creatures "plants." Animals are a step up the dependence ladder. They depend on the green plants which possess the unique crucial ability to line up six carbons in a row to make sugar, a fuel for running the "creatures great and small."

Sugar for fuel is just the beginning. Without the availability of the six-carbon sugar skeleton erected by plants, no creatures could create their own skeletons or any other part of their bodies. They need this six-carbon chain to make the amino acids of which their proteins are composed. From these proteins, in turn, are erected the skeletons, muscles, and other organs of the body. Without plants for food, the animals we know would not exist. After all, if plants supply the essential ingredients for life, why should animals go to the trouble of making these ingredients themselves? Simply eat the plants, then specialize to do other things, such as farming or hunting. This is the story of the origin of species: Save energy by specializing.

There are many who argue that specialized complexity violates the natural law of energy conservation. They state that to organize is to spend energy. Therefore, organization should not occur in nature. For example, the psychologist M. Scott Peck in *The Road Less Traveled* (1978) says:

> The process of evolution can be diagrammed by a pyramid, with man, the most complex but least numerous organism, at the apex, and viruses, the most numerous but least complex organisms, at the base. The apex is thrusting out, up, forward against the force of entropy. Inside the pyramid I have placed an arrow to symbolize this thrusting evolutionary force, the "something" that has so successfully and consistently defied "natural law" over millions upon millions of generations and that must in itself represent natural law as yet undefined.

Lacking in this argument is the fact that the organization may save more energy than it uses. The driving force of life on earth, solar energy, is not uniformly distributed. To utilize dark spaces, an organism might need to travel to the dark spaces after feeding in the light. For this, nervous organization might be advantageous. The intelligent directions received from the nerve center would certainly be more energy-conserving than would be dependence on random motions (called Brownian movements) for transportation. The nerve center tells the animal when, where, and how to go to the illuminated areas on earth to feed on the photosynthetic organisms there. It also plans the return trip to the dark caves for rest, protection, and reproduction.

In creating their body structures, plants use their six-carbon sugars to erect amino-acid molecules the way many of us boys used pieces of erector sets to build huge, complicated structures. The six-carbon chain may also be employed to create a hexagonal ring. This ring is called a "phenyl" ring. It is used in building many other structures, such as phenol. To the phenyl ring may be hooked a three-carbon amino acid, "alanine," to build the compound called "phenylalanine." This is one of the amino acids essential in our diet. Animals cannot make it themselves; they depend on plants for it. This (along with other amino acids) is used for making the proteins incorporated into our own body structures.

A human deprived of phenylalanine in the diet would cease to exist. Not only would the proteins waste away, there would be no melanin pigments in the skin. To live at all, such a human would need to be shielded from ultraviolet light. Otherwise, the tissues underlying the skin would be damaged. The pigments in the skin could be restored by substituting tyrosine for phenylalanine in the diet, because phenylalanine normally produces the melanin pigments by first being converted to tyrosine. Tyrosine has the same structure as phenylalanine, except there is an oxygen atom attached to the ring. (Tyrosine might as well be called oxy-phenylalanine.) The next step is to add another oxygen atom to the ring; this makes dioxy-phenylalanine, "dopa." Dopa is an amino acid in that it contains an amino group (NH_2) and an acid group (COOH). If the acid group is removed, what remains is simply an amine compound, "dopamine." This removal of the acid group allows the amino group of dopamine to express its astounding physiological properties. A special term, "biogenic amine" (life-giving amine), is used to describe such molecules. What are some of these life-giving properties?

If dopamine is deficient in a human, Parkinson's disease results. Muscular coordination is abnormal and uncontrolled, and the patient is "shaky." The place at the base of the brain where dopamine acts has black stripes due to dopamine deposition. The blackening results from the conversion of some of the dopamine to the black pigment "melanin."

Melanin is found not only in the brain, but also in the eyes of vertebrate animals. There is a black, thin layer of melanin (the choroid layer) underlying the retina of the eyes. If a flashlight beam is aimed at a deer in the dark, the light reflected from this smooth melanin layer causes the eyes to shine back at the source of the light. The nerve cells are positioned with their tips directed toward the melanin layer. This positioning necessitates that the nerve fibers leading from these cells must spread over that surface of the retina nearest the light source. Light entering the eye must pass through this coat of nerve fibrils and accompanying blood vessels and surrounding fluids. Some of the ultraviolet light is thereby filtered out before it reaches the nerve-cell bodies. This not only prevents cell damage by ultraviolet light, but may also improve the image by filtering out these bluish image-blurring rays. This is readily understandable to photographers who use yellow-red filters to screen these undesirable rays.

Though this "upside down" arrangement of the retinal cells appears ingenious, George Williams, in his book, *The Pony Fish's Glow and Other Clues to Plan and Purpose in Nature* (1997), uses this arrangement as a prime example of the many poorly engineered features of some animals, including the human. He does not consider *advantages* arising from radiation filtering. He sees only *disadvantages* arising from the fact that a blind spot is associated with the area in the retina where the nerve fibrils coming from the retinal nerve cells collect to form the large optic-nerve fiber (though he does admit that this blind spot is compensated by the other eye). He also complains that the "upside-down" arrangement leads to an easily detachable retina. He has a point there. With some advantages may come disadvantages. Nature continuously makes value judgments in such cases.

Melanin pigments play many other important roles in adaptation to the environment. Such black and tan pigments of the skins and other outer coverings of animals help protect the underlying tissues from ultraviolet light damage. At the same time these pigments help control the temperature of the body. In the fruit fly, tan varieties of melanin result when the three-carbon amino acid (beta-alanine) reacts with dopamine and thereby prevents formation of black melanin. Instead, a tan form of melanin results (Jacobs 1980).

As might be expected from this description, the cuticle of a fruit fly lacking beta-alanine would be blacker than normal, for there would be no beta-alanine available for preventing formation of the indole. The lack of beta-alanine might be due either to failure of the fly to produce beta-alanine or failure in transport of beta-alanine from the underlying cells into the cuticle. Actually, both of these abnormalities are respectively exhibited by black and ebony mutants of fruit flies. The black mutant is deficient in beta-alanine production, and the ebony mutant is deficient in the transport of beta-alanine into the cuticle. As might be expected, if the black mutant is injected with beta-alanine, it is turned from a black fly into a normal tan fly.

Flies with black cuticles warm up more quickly under solar illumination than do flies with tan cuticles (Jacobs 1985). Appropriately, flies grown in the laboratory under colder conditions are much darker than those grown under warmer conditions. In line with this, studies of wild populations of *Drosophila melanogaster* show that flies inhabiting colder regions are darker than those inhabiting warmer regions (David et al. 1985).

Given the wide range of niches inhabited by the species, it is little wonder that *melanogaster* shows a wide spectrum of body-color types, from light tan through brown to black. Which type will be selected for adaptation to a specific niche will depend on environmental conditions of the niche to which it is adapting. In shaded conditions, where radiation is scarce, dark body-color variants would be selected for maximizing use of the meager radiant energy. On the other hand, under intense solarized conditions, light varieties will be selected to prevent overheating.

In connection with the studies of fruit flies, some observations were made of the mourning cloak butterfly, *Nymphalis antiopa*, a dark-winged species in which the males establish territories along a partially shaded road in a nearby beech-maple forest. The adults become active early in spring when the air temperature is still low. As the males perch in their territories on cool days, they spread their wings when shadows fall, thereby maximizing use of the meager radiation, and close them when the sun returns, thereby preventing overheating.

In the same forest, males of the net-winged beetle, *Calopteron terminale*, establish their territories under the deeply shaded litter of the forest floor. The wings are bright orange, with jet-black, tar-like spots on the tips. In territorial defense, the males display their bright-orange wing markings toward rivals. When resting, they hide under leaves near the ground, exposing only the black tips of the wings to the rays of the sun. The black tips serve as radiators to help warm the insects as they rest, hidden under the leaf litter.

To meet varying environmental conditions, an insect species may employ a mating system that would produce a dark race in a shady microhabitat and a light race in a sunny habitat. Another strategy would be for the species to select for an intermediately pigmented, true-breeding type that would strike the middle of the environmental range. In the fruit fly, *Drosophila melanogaster*, as well as the dragonfly, *Perithemis tenera*, such types are found in nature.

In insects, as the body wall heats up under radiation, the heat is conducted directly to the small mass of body fluids directly underlying the body wall. The insect, which we call cold-blooded, is dependent on this outside radiation for keeping itself adequately warm.

In warm-blooded animals, such as primates, the body wall is remote from the deep, massive body fluids. Under these conditions a black body wall has, in addition to a heating effect from outside radiation, an appreciable cooling (shading) effect on the deep body fluids. To determine the total average result if both the heating and cooling effect were operating at the same time, an experiment would be required.

With this aim in mind, I prepared the equivalent of mammal skins from gelatin (a protein extracted from connective tissues of mammals). The gelatin preparations were poured into petri dishes to create a "skin."

The dishes were placed in contact with artificial "blood" (water) in Styrofoam cups. This system served as an artificial test mammal. Thermometers inserted through the cups into the water just over the bottoms of the cups were used to determine the temperature of the "blood."

Among these three "mammals," the first had a "skin" of clear gelatin. The second had a black "skin" in which the gelatin was stained with dopamine-derived melanin. The third had a tan "skin" in which the gelatin was stained with dopamine converted to a tan color by reacting with beta-alanine. The three "mammals" (clear, black, and tan) were exposed to the heating rays of the sun.

The results were dramatic — and just the opposite of the results obtained with fruit flies. The temperature of the "blood" of the black "mammal" was the coolest. The cooling (shading) effect of the black "skin" was great enough to overcome the warming effect due to absorption of solar radiation. Among the three "mammals," the blood of the clear one was the warmest. Finally, that of the tan one was intermediate (Jacobs 1982).

Among mammals, especially hairless primates, the black skin, by its shading influence, would help prevent overheating of the blood under solar radiation. This would be useful in hot climates. In colder climates, where a benefit from the warming effects of the meager radiation is useful, a clear skin would be recommended. But such a clear skin would allow for damage of the cells by sunshine. To provide for some penetration of sunshine while at the same time providing some protection from irradiation damage, light-tan melanoid pigments are employed. Ingeniously, the tan pigment fades or intensifies automatically in response to the ultraviolet-light intensity.

Of course, maximal effectiveness of this heating and cooling system in mammals would require lack of hair. A hairy mammal might reap the benefits of this heating and cooling system by removal of hair. Conversely, covering the body with clothing, as with civilized humans, including those who have migrated into frigid regions, would overshadow the effectiveness of the pigments. This interpretation would appear adequate to explain the loss of hair on the basis of *natural* selection alone. A system of sexual selection for body pigmentation, as postulated by Darwin, would not be required to explain the origin of the pigmentation among hairless mammals.

Overall, animals make trade-off arrangements between the advantages of hairiness versus hairlessness. Toward this end, hairy mammals shed their heavy coats after the cold season just as humans can quickly shed their coats (and other clothing!) and enjoy the warmth of sunshine. The mourning cloak butterfly, which (as mentioned earlier) is active in the cool days of spring, has its body coated with hair-like scales, but the dark wings that serve as solar panels are devoid of such scales.

How could the hairless condition of some mammals originate? True to form, Charles Darwin attributed the loss of hair to sexual selection. He elaborated on this in the second edition of *The Descent of Man and Selection in Relation to Sex* (1874). To this edition, he added an article, "Sexual Selection in Relation to Monkeys." Darwin explained that the loss of hair would allow skin pigments to be on display. For this purpose, potential mates might remove hair. The resulting hairless areas would exaggerate the coloration and thus facilitate the attraction of mates.

According to the then-popular theory of the inheritance of acquired characteristics, this resulting hairless condition would be inherited by the offspring. Darwin (1868) had proposed a theory as to how this mode of inheritance could work. He called it "pangenesis." Throughout the body are located little particles he called "pangenes." These particles determine the characteristics of the part of the body in which they are located. During the lifetime of an organism, the number of pangenes present in a body part multiplies as the size of that part increases due to use. For example, when the giraffe stretches its neck to reach leaves high in the trees, the elongated neck multiplies extra neck-pangenes. Conversely, if a part of the body were not used, pangene development would be reversed ("use it or lose it"). The offspring would then inherit the higher or lower number of pangenes characteristic of the parents at the time of reproduction. As the saying goes, "Like father, like son." This is close to the theory of use and disuse advocated before Darwin by Jean Baptiste Lamarck (1744–1829).

Regarding the loss of hair in primates, Darwin said:

> It is also possible that the long-continued habit of eradicating the hair may have produced an inherited effect. Dr. Brown Séquard has shown that if certain animals are operated on in a particular manner their offspring are affected. ... Motmots, which are known habitually to bite off the barbs of the two central tail feathers, have the barbs of these feathers naturally somewhat reduced.

Darwin's grandfather, Erasmus Darwin, had supported this view — a simple explanation for evolution. In those days, there was some evidence that even mental traits could be modified by use and disuse, and the modification would be inherited. It was reported that rats, having been trained to run mazes, would give birth to offspring that could run the maze increasingly well generation after generation. (However, other factors, such as traces of odors left in the maze, may have been involved.)

Regarding the tennis-racket shape of the tail of the motmot, these birds show a marked tendency to wave their tails in pendulum-like fashion while perched. The small bunch of terminal feathers that are separate from the body may well serve to attract predators, who see this potential meal moving. The predator may make a pass at this group of feathers, missing the body entirely. A natural-selection explanation for the feather gap in the tail of the motmot is in order here. Considering possible functions of the brightly-colored hairless portions of the anatomy of monkeys, such as the mandrills, these features may be important in male-male competition.

INFLUENCE OF BETA-ALANINE ON INSECT BEHAVIOR

During the course of this investigation, it was discovered that beta-alanine is involved not only in pigmentation, but also in the stiffening, of the insect cuticle. Since cuticles serve as skeletons among insects, stiffening of the cuticle is essential for normal movement. Electron-microscopic examination of *Drosophila* cuticles reveals that "ebony" cuticles, which are deficient in beta-alanine incorporation, are less compacted than normal. This lack of normal compaction could well lead to many of the observed behavioral abnormalities of "ebony" fruit flies, which fail to incorporate beta-alanine into the cuticle.

Also, mutant "black" flies, which are lacking in beta-alanine production, are deficient in compaction of the cuticle. Along with this, black fruit flies exhibit some of the same behavioral abnormalities as ebony flies. Injection of radio-labeled beta-alanine into black flies shows that they are fully capable of incorporating into the cuticle the injected beta-alanine. This being true, injection of beta-alanine into the black fly should compact the cuticle, eliminate the abnormal behavior, and produce a normal tan fly. This was found to be the case.

An extensive study was then made of the behavior of black flies in competition with siblings experimentally tanned by injection with beta-alanine. In the illumination-graded observation chamber, the tanned males were more successful in territorial defense and mating — and were more photopositive than their black siblings. This result essentially agreed with the results of normal tan males as compared with ebony males. In that case, normal tan males mated with significantly greater frequency than did ebony males, and they were more photopositive.

Electron-microscopic examination of the cuticles of the mutants ebony and black, both of which lack beta-alanine in the cuticle (either free or combined with dopamine), show a lack of normal compaction (Jacobs 1978, 1980, 1985). These abnormalities in the mutant black are corrected by beta-alanine injection. They are also corrected genetically by genes that, by enhancing production of beta-alanine, overcome the action of the gene black (Sherald 1981).

These results raised a good question. How could a simple three-carbon amino acid (beta-alanine) be responsible for compaction of the insect cuticle? How could this footnote in general biochemistry suddenly erupt into such a gusher in the field of insect biochemistry, physiology, and behavior? One little gene controlling one little enzyme, which in turn controlled the fate of one little amino acid, became a vast repository of possibility. Along these lines, it wouldn't be too far-fetched to say that sexual selection, sometimes seen as a footnote in the theory of evolution, may itself turn out to be a gusher.

The conventional wisdom of the day had been that the agent responsible for compaction of the insect cuticle is acetyldopamine, which cross-links the protein fibrils in the cuticle. This compound results from combining acetic acid with the amine group of dopamine (Karlson and Sekeris 1962). The actual tan color of the cuticle remained a mystery until it was found that beta-alanine, when incubated with acetyldopamine, produces stable tan colors (Jacobs 1980). But while this helped explain the *tanning* effects of beta-alanine, it did not explain the *stiffening* effects.

Suspecting that the stiffening effects of beta-alanine could result from its taking the place of acetic acid in combining with dopamine, to make *beta-alanyl*dopamine instead of *acetyl*dopamine, I collaborated with several laboratories in attempts to identify beta-alanyldopamine in *Drosophila* extracts, without success. Finally, Hopkins et al. (1982), using newly developed electrochemical methods for detection of such compounds, discovered beta-alanyldopamine as an important and widespread agent involved in stiffening inset cuticles.

What is the source of the beta-alanine during metabolism? *Drosophila* produces beta-alanine from uracil. When carbon-14-labeled uracil is injected into the newly formed puparial stage of the normal tan fly, the carbon-14 is later detected in beta-alanine in the pupal case (Jacobs 1968). Once formed from uracil, the beta-alanine is combined with dopamine (under control of an enzyme) to form N-beta-alanyl-dopamine. The ebony mutant is fully capable of producing beta-alanine, but it is deficient in the enzyme responsible for combining the beta-alanine with dopamine. (See Wright 1987.) The black mutant is not lacking in this enzyme, but it is deficient in producing the beta-alanine in the first place.

The uracil may be derived by disintegration of messenger RNA at a time when it is no longer needed, as at the end of the larval period when larval protein synthesis is no longer required — and also at the end of the pupal period when pupal protein synthesis is no longer necessary. At these times, the uracil from this extra RNA is degraded to produce copious amounts of beta-alanine. The beta-alanine is then used for cuticular compaction and tanning. Were this beta-alanine not quickly eliminated from the hemocoel by transport into the cuticle, it might interfere with normal development and behavior. Humans deficient in urinary elimination of beta-alanine have elevated levels of beta-alanine in the blood (hyper-beta-alanemia), accompanied by nervous convulsions.

MELANIZATION AND HYBRID VIGOR

Thus far we have considered only two roles for beta-alanine: its involvement in insect tanning and structural stiffening of the cuticular exoskeleton. But there are also metabolic uses for beta-alanine. It combines with pentoic acid to produce pentoyl beta-alanine (pantothenic acid, an important B vitamin). This vitamin controls growth and reproduction. The richest source of this vitamin known is royal jelly, the substance that worker bees feed to larvae to convert them into fertile queens. The pantothenic acid is a constituent of coenzyme A, which controls general metabolism. Beta-alanine also forms a peptide link with another amino acid, histidine, to form important peptides involved in muscle physiology.

As evidence for use of beta-alanine for metabolic use in *Drosophila melanogaster*, autoradiographs of sections through specimens injected with carbon-14-labeled beta-alanine show carbon-14 from this amino acid ending up in the egg follicles. This concentration is especially high in the mutant ebony, in which the beta-alanine is shunted from uses in the cuticle to uses in the internal organs.

These findings may help explain the hybrid superiority shown by the hybrid of *Drosophila melanogaster* obtained by crossing the ebony mutant with strains selected for very light-tan body color. This hybrid, which is intermediate in darkness between the parents, may obtain a metabolic advantage over the light flies by shunting less beta-alanine into the cuticle than the light genotype does. It therefore has more of this amino acid available for important metabolic uses. The ebony mutant, on the other hand, overdoes this shunting of beta-alanine from cuticular to metabolic uses. It therefore suffers from a weakened cuticle. The hybrid has achieved an optimal balance by being not too light or too dark. The cuticle is stiff enough for all practical purposes, and there is still enough beta-alanine left in the body for metabolic uses.

A true-breeding genotype intermediate in darkness between light and ebony should also show the superior fitness of the light X ebony hybrid type. But this true-breeding type would lack the niche-adapting variability exhibited by a population of fruit flies with very light cuticles (rich in bound beta-alanine) and very dark types (poor in bound beta-alanine). Considering temperature-regulation advantages of the dark pigment in relation to the variable temperatures of the changing environment inhabited by the species, it is not surprising that there is so much variability in body color among individuals of a species living in the wilds.

When the fruit fly stiffens its adult cuticle by means of beta-alanine incorporation, it leaves portions that are appropriately flexible unstiffened. This applies to those portions close to flexion joints and a spot over the heart region. These unstiffened parts, deficient in beta-alanine incorporation, remain black.

The normal pupal cuticles are uniformly stiffened, tanned, and beta-alanine rich. Those of ebony or black mutants are deficient in both tanning and beta-alanine incorporation. The pupal cuticle of the black mutant becomes the normal tan color when the pupa is injected with beta-alanine. This tanning protects the pupae from damage by ultraviolet light (Jacobs 1974).

Separation of the amino group from the acid group in the special amino acid, beta-alanine, confers not only physiological properties to the molecule but also high polarity. It is therefore readily soluble in water. After its release from RNA, it would diffuse quickly throughout cells. The enzyme for attaching it to dopamine is awaiting its arrival. Its fate is sealed when the combined molecule (beta-alanyldopamine) becomes part of the stiffened and tanned cuticle.

This hardening of the cuticle appears to include also the microtubular structures attaching the muscles to the cuticle. These microtubules pass through the epidermal cells, from the muscle on the inside to the cuticle on the outside. At first the microtubules are long and thin. Later, when the muscles approach the cuticle, the microtubules become shortened. At that point the microtubules acquire thick coatings that appear continuous with the cuticle proper. With its muscle-cuticle junctions completely formed and hardened, the insect is finally ready to walk and fly.

The microtubules are composed of the protein "tubulin." The microtubules may elongate by assembly of the tubulin, or shorten by disassembly of the tubulin. The impression is received that the microtubules are tugging to draw the muscle to the cuticle. However, it may be other microfibrils, associated with the microtubules, that do the actual tugging. Such a process occurs in the contraction of the muscle itself. Myosin fibrils of muscles act together with actin fibrils in such muscle contractions.

In the ebony and black mutants, the cuticle, as well as the associated muscle-cuticle junctions, are less compacted than normal, which may be a result of failure in cross-linking of the cuticular matrix elements. This, then, may help explain the abnormal behavior of these mutants that show deficiencies of cuticular beta-alanine. In the black mutant such structural and behavioral abnormalities are corrected by injection of beta-alanine into the newly forming adult.

The importance of the microtubules in forming these muscle-cuticle junctions in newly emerging *Drosophila* was demonstrated by injecting the flies with colchicine. This substance prevents microtubules from forming. Injection prevents the muscles from attaching to the exoskeleton. The flies then show seriously uncoordinated behavior and soon die. Electron-microscopic examination of their cuticles shows that the indentations from the cuticle that normally form where groups of microtubules attach to the cuticle are no longer formed. This strongly indicates that these indentations are a result of inward traction in these microtubular areas. The colchicine experiment adds support for the observational impression that microtubules appear to be involved in transport of glycoprotein into the cuticle. All this could explain how the long, thin microtubules between the cuticle and muscle are converted to short, thick rods.

THOSE REMARKABLE MICROTUBULES

In addition to their roles in insect movement, microtubules perform many other functions in cell structure and function. They may be involved in wound healing. Connective cells in the wound may extend false feet out in all directions to meet cells on the margins of the wound. After the feet have become securely implanted into the margins, the extensions from the connective tissues cells may contract and pull the margins of the wound together. In this process, microtubules may be involved much as they appear related to the pulling of muscle toward the cuticle in insects.

Microtubules may also play a role in extension and contraction of cellular processes of neurons of the nervous system. These processes play a role in long-term memory. Pictures of the cerebral cells in rats show that extensions from the neuron terminations (axons, for example), are lengthened in rats as they use their cerebrums in exploring their environments. The rats are apparently using their neurons to investigate and memorize the interesting, novel, and challenging objects provided them by the researcher. Extension of the neuronal processes brings the terminations closer together to make the neuronal connections involved in memory.

It is amazing how orderly is the arrangement of the microtubules in a compact lot. They do not intertwine; rather, they lie straight in non-interfering patterns. In this respect the arrangement is as orderly as in a compact group of millions of fibrils in a nerve fiber. Furthermore, after a nerve has been cut, the regenerating nerve fibers appear to be able to find their destination as if guided by an unseen force. Likewise, such an unseen force seems to be involved in directing newly forming micro-tubules as they pass from the muscle into their respective points on the exoskeleton — to which the muscle is ultimately to be attached for prop-er movement. Electron-microscopic examination of groups of such microtubules shows them lined up in an orderly manner like cigars packed neatly in a box. A cross-section through a nerve presents a simi-lar picture. Likewise, groups of microtubules resemble the orderly arrangement of muscle microfibrils.

There is much more to learn about the roles of microtubules in developmental of embryos. Embryologists have long realized that there appear to be fields of force directing the development of the embryo in the fertilized egg cell. Such lines of power are dramatically seen in the dividing cell. They resemble lines of electromagnetic force, observed as particles of iron filings aligned between magnetic poles, or tiny hair par-ticles aligned between electric terminals. In a dividing cell, materials line up to form fibrils that represent similar lines of force between poles of the cell. The small, dense body on the chromosome (called a centromere) is caught up in such lines of force pulling toward the poles of the cell. Finally, the centromere and the chromosome are seen to be duplicated. The duplicates split from each other, and one of them moves to one pole, while the other moves to the other pole. Cell division is then completed, as a membrane develops to separate the two halves of the original cell. These fibrils appear to originate from small, dense bodies at the poles of the cell. In a similar manner, microtubules appear to arise from dense bodies called microtubule organizing centers often associated with cell membranes.

An alumnus of Goshen College, Dr. Orie Eigsti, discovered that colchicine, which inhibits development of microtubules, also prevents chromosomes from migrating toward the poles of cells in onion root tips. By administering colchicine to growing tissues, plants with twice the normal number of chromosomes result. When such plants are crossed with normal plants, triploid hybrids result. These hybrids, being sterile, are called "seedless." This is how seedless watermelons are produced.

What are the forces within a cell that direct the formation of micro-tubules so precisely? We may see the day when all physical and biological phenomena are subsumed under one grand, unifying field theory, integrating electromagnetic, gravitational, and possibly other forces — such as the very strong forces exhibited within atoms themselves. Is the development of the entire cosmos directed by such forces that so mysteriously act at a distance? Scientific discovery is only in its infancy. Untold exciting discoveries lie ahead.

As a starter, what forces are involved in enabling a strand of DNA, swimming around in the nucleus, to attract to itself the specific ring bases: C (cytosine), A (adenine), T (thymine) or G (guanine)? Each attracted base finds its pairing partner on the DNA strand to enable the strand to compose a complement to itself.

But there is much more pairing to come. To prepare the organism for sexual reproduction, the chromosomes swimming in the sea of nucleoplasm performing their vegetative function (directing protein synthesis) suddenly get ready to meet their mates. This is sexual selection at the microscopic level. Each chromosome carries its number. Chromosome #1, which had been contributed to the organism by its father, seeks out its #1 pairing partner which has been contributed by the mother. Pair #2 behaves likewise. This process continues until the entire set of paternal chromosomes has found its partner in the maternal set. What forces act in this pairing process? Consideration of this problem goes beyond the scope of this book.

The chromosomes are something like salmon, swimming in the ocean, embodying the essence of life. Come time to mate, they seek the specific stream of childhood. Here males and females with similar recollections of their home stream meet and mate. Chemical reception (taste and smell) probably bring the sexes together at the mating site. But there may be more to it than this. There may be many forces that have not yet fallen under the scrutinizing stare of researchers.

CHAPTER 6

LESSONS FROM HISTORY

OME 2,500 YEARS AGO, THE ANCIENT GREEKS, who invested much time and effort in pondering such questions, attempted to explain the origin of forms of life in terms of evolution. By 500 BC these philosophers had become increasingly sophisticated. They began to crystallize their thoughts around the problem of origins.

Empedocles (ca. 490–ca. 430 BC) postulated that animals originated from plants. If monsters arose by this process, they were weeded out by survival of the fittest. Anaxagoras (500?–428 BC) viewed the germs of life as originating in a warm primordial slime, with their progeny left to go on with life in their own way. He thought, however, that the world had been designed and created by an intelligent being (or beings), but room was left for chance to play a part in what happened after that.

Aristotle (384–322 BC) proposed a ladder, leading from simple sea creatures to fish, then land animals. "Nature herself seeks to achieve perfection," he stated. "She does nothing without aim. She is always striving after the most beautiful that is possible."

St. Augustine (354–430 AD) thought God created the potential in the heavens and on earth for life, but the details worked themselves out in accordance with the laws laid down by God. It wasn't necessary for God to create each individual species in a process of special creation. Instead, the Creator provided the seeds of the universe and life, then let them develop in their own time.

St. Thomas Aquinas (1225?–74 AD), building on the writings of St. Gregory of Nyssa (ca. 330–95? AD), thought God imparted to matter its fundamental laws and properties, whereupon objects and completed forms of the universe developed gradually, under their own steam, out of primordial chaos.

The Spanish Jesuit, Francisco Suarez (1548–1617), rejected the gradual-development view of Aquinas and instituted fixed creationism as the official view of the Catholic church. This was to be universally believed as coming straight from the Creator's mouth. Fixed creationism soon became normative even in the official creeds of the protesters of church doctrine, the Protestants.

In 1600 the Italian scientist-philosopher Giordano Bruno (1548?–1600) was burned at the stake for declaring that: (1) the earth moves around the sun, (2) nature changes gradually, and (3) the earth is more than a few thousand years old. A contemporary and compatriot of Bruno — Galileo Galilei (1564–1642) — held similar views about the earth moving around the sun, supporting his views with telescopic observations. He fared somewhat better than Bruno, being forced simply to recant and no longer publish his controversial opinions.

By the 17th century, Galileo's discoveries in physics and astronomy, having practical implications for navigation, led a new breed of natural philosophers to appreciate the importance of checking their ideas about the natural world by careful observation and experiment. Fixed doctrines about Divine Revelation, along with Divine Rights of Kings, were beginning to crack. Soon there would be an earthquake.

In the middle of the 19th century, the fault line gave way. Charles Darwin wrote *On the Origin of Species by Means of Natural Selection* (1859). All species, including the human, arose from the earth spontaneously, said Darwin, who did not acknowledge an intelligent creator. The process essentially involved survival of the fittest, with little regard for Christian ethics or beliefs.

This might have been good enough for natural organisms, but not for the human. The human was supposed to be special. If Darwin had not included humankind in the lineage of continuous development, the lava would have been less hot. Darwin had anticipated a strong reaction among the populace and had lined up supporters beforehand, including members of the Royal Society. He had, in fact, reported his evolutionary ideas a year earlier to the Linnean Society, as had Wallace, Darwin's close collaborator. Both agreed on the general idea of the origin of species by natural selection.

One of the critics of particular concern to Darwin was George Douglas Campbell, Duke of Argyll, a prominent politician and naturalist who published *Reign of Law* (1867), an attack on Darwin's *Origin* book. In addition to providing a view that evolution occurred by preordained divine design, leading ultimately to the human species, the book also pointed out that Darwin's views failed to explain why nature developed beautiful-looking creatures such as the hummingbird and the peacock.

Darwin realized that Campbell was right, in that these two problems — the origin of the human species and the origin of male adornment — had not been adequately addressed in his *Origin* book. Subsequently, Darwin published another large book to fill this gap, *The Descent of Man and Selection in Relation to Sex* (1871). According to Darwin, fancy-male varieties in nature are selected the way a breeder of pigeons selects for such varieties, by use of a creative, artistic sense. Assuming common evolution, Darwin deemed it reasonable that insects, birds, and other lower creatures possessed at least rudiments of a human-type aesthetic sense that could be involved in mate selection. He noted that insects and birds seem to be attracted to beautiful flowers. He saw this as evidence of an aesthetic sense.

Perhaps sexual selection could result in the demise of a species. Perhaps also the process, being intellectually driven, could lead to the development of higher intelligence, involving advancement of the arts and sciences. The entire process could lead to a quantitative leap from nature, perhaps a dash over the proverbial fool's hill. How would Mother Nature view this violation of her rules?

This process of mate selection, being mentally contrived, could drastically increase the rate of development of a trait, as compared with the creeping, evolutionary development resulting from blind natural selection. Mate selection of males by females, for example, may take only a few generations to yield a fancy-male variety, whereas natural selection may take ages to develop a new trait. Furthermore, Darwin contended that development of a trait by a process of female choice of a male showing the rudiments of that trait, could, by a feedback process, enhance female appreciation of the trait. Obviously, such a process could get out of hand, as in the case of chemical-feedback reactions known by chemists as vicious-cycle reactions. Such an artificially selective process could produce "an explosion of anomalies."

Development of a trait by this sexual-selection process could proceed by jumps, each jump being sparked by female whimsical fancy. In effect, the species would be designing its own genotype. The extent to which development of the trait could go would be limited only by the mental capacity of the female. Both sexes could be involved in this process of mate selection. Darwin emphasized, however, the role of the *female* in sexual selection, for his theory was evoked primarily to explain the origin of the adornment of the *males* in fancy-male species.

The tendency for organisms to jump as they climb the evolutionary ladder has long intrigued paleontologists. It is such jumping that helps explain the "missing links" so often observed in evolutionary trees. Historically, paleontologists have explained these missing links on the basis of scarcity of the transition forms, which would have filled the evolutionary gaps. Had the transition forms been common enough, they may have been discovered as fossils. Scarcity of such forms has been explained by numerous paleontologists. A sudden change in environmental conditions has caused rapid reassortment of the genotype. In this interim the poorly adapted transitional forms would be scarce. Drastic changes in the niche of a species triggers an emphasis on sexual reproduction, involving mate selection. As in a game of "Speed Scrabble," the genetic components are separated and recombined quickly to produce new species. As a result of rapid sexual selection, numerous mistakes are made. This results in many experimental models unfit to survive in nature.

In some ways it is strange that Darwin connected the subject of the descent of man with the origin of general male "beauty." Even a casual observer would note that if there is any choice of beauty going on in the human mating system, it would be in favor of the female. Darwin did point to the origin of the "ornamental" beard of the male by a process of sexual selection. (Ironically, most males go to great pains to eradicate this ornament.) Darwin also explained the origin of skin pigmentation in humans as stemming from sexual selection for this type of adornment. But strangely, where an excellent case could be made for the role of mate selection in the evolution of the human intellect, this theorist was quiet.

What if mates were to be selected on the basis of superior intelligence? Both female and male might be involved in this selection process, leading to the rapid development of an artificial mentality. The motivation could be for socioeconomic advancement, self-enhancement, or even genetic improvement of the species. This would add superior mentality to even more superior mentality, with incomprehensible results.

Yes, let's keep in mind that every upside has a downside — in keeping with Ralph Waldo Emerson's (1803–1882) law of compensation, as applied to human affairs, or Isaac Newton's law of action balanced by opposite reaction, as applied to physics. Wouldn't elevation of the intellect also elevate perception — not only of joy, but also of pain and misery? There may be something to be said for the sentiment that "Ignorance is bliss." Further, by selecting for intellectual superiority, the total mentality of the species could become so abstract as to lose sight of the real driving forces of life. What would happen then? In his *Letters from the Earth*, Mark Twain has the Devil writing to God that the humans he had created have insidiously placed human intelligence on a precarious pedestal, insinuating that the human mind is a terrible thing.

Superior intelligence would, of course, enable the species to override the laws of natural selection. Since artificial selection is not bound by these laws, a super-intelligent, conscious (but non-adaptive) species might result. What would we name such a species? Perhaps we could define it as having something to do with wisdom. How about ... *sapiens*?

THE ARTIFICIAL AND THE NATURAL: DARWIN AND HIS CRITICS

In Charles Darwin's *Descent* book, the females — be they humans, birds, insects, or other types of creatures — are artists. It is they who adorn their mates according to the whims and fancies of their creative sense. The females use their human-type intellectual endowment in the selection of male mates.

Darwin saw no problem in assigning such a human-like intellectual capacity, including an aesthetic sense, to the females of non-human species, for he saw all of life as a continuum. It is paradoxical that Darwin, hardly an advocate of feminism — at least if we accept the evaluation of Meredith Small who, in her book, *Female Choices* (1993), called Darwin a "Victorian masculinist" — did not hesitate to attribute such majestic intellectual prowess as an aesthetic sense to the female: any female, even a female insect. They preferred beautiful male mates, hence the origin of fancy-male species.

Ironically, Darwin's colleague, Wallace, though a bona fide women's-rights advocate, thought Darwin had gone too far regarding the extraordinary artistic sense of non-human females. Wallace argued that male adornment was adaptive (of practical value) and therefore its origin could be explained in terms of natural selection. He cited the role of poisonous-prey animals' "striking" markings, which would ward off potential predators. He also pointed out that distinctive markings are important in species recognition.

Inconsistently, Wallace did admit that some adornment might be non-adaptive. But in such cases he believed that the origin of the adornment could be explained in terms of special creation. In 1856 he expressed creationist views when discussing non-adaptive traits of animals in general. But by 1871 he was going along with Darwin's idea that non-adaptive adornment might be the result of female choice. Later, Wallace became less enthusiastic about the idea of female choice. By 1889, he had come to reject the idea of female choice entirely.

Wallace's final position was that both sexes have a natural inclination to develop exhibitory adornment. He claimed that the colors are merely linked to physiological reactions of the body and are therefore subject to natural selection. Wallace cited, for example, the humming-birds: The males are brightly colored as a result of increased metabolic activity of their tissues. Being more physiologically intense than the females, they would naturally be the most brilliantly adorned. The female acquires demure colors as a result of natural selection: Her cryptic colors are naturally selected for appropriate concealment during incubation and tending the young — mostly female activities. In short, the female sacrifices physiological intensity for the sake of being inconspicuous.

Wallace pointed out that the female generally pays so little attention to the male's display of finery that there is reason to believe that it's his persistence and energy, rather than his beauty, that win the day. Wallace did not think female choice plays any significant role in evolution.

At many points Wallace's arguments appear self-contradictory, but his basic idea that the resplendent condition of male adornment is associated with enhanced physiological fitness is used by many modern students of sexual selection in their arguments for female choice of "fitness genes." Wallace, however, contended that the connection between physiological intensity and plumage is alone sufficient to account for the exhibitory adornment of fancy males. No female choice is necessary to explain the origin of ornaments.

Hardly had the tornado buffeting the *Origin* book subsided before a tempest over the *Descent* book swirled to life. Students of animal behavior were realizing that the anthropomorphic methods espoused in the theory of sexual selection were leading them astray. Wild animals didn't seem to know anything about the premises involved in the theory. While the males were fighting and displaying, the females appeared to be remarkably inattentive to them. Furthermore, when studied extensively, the behavior of wild animals appeared hereditary, programmed, instinctive. Little evidence was found in support of Darwin's views.

At the time, scientists were busily extricating themselves from the shackles of animism (often described as the practice of ascribing spiritual essence to all of nature). Astronomers were finding that such anthropomorphic interpretations as applied to the heavens are ridiculous. By the early 1900s, so far as many natural scientists were concerned, subjective anthropomorphism was not just out, it was dead! Objective observation, experimentation, and mathematics were considered to be the road to true and certain knowledge. Mechanistic interpretations were in. A revolution was under way, returning to the mechanistic understandings prevalent among academics in the "golden age" of Greek civilization. Science was finding its way back to solid footing.

But as is typical of reactionary revolutions, there was a tendency to go too far. Scientists made a mad dash to machinery in attempts to study the animal mind objectively. Psychologists became so absorbed with studies of animals in their confining mechanical boxes that they overlooked the vast flexibility and quick-learning abilities of animals in their natural environments. Even as early as the 1930s, the author became convinced that it is in the environmental field where the true nature of the animal mind expresses itself. Even in physics, the importance of field studies is today being recognized. Physicists are still attempting to decipher a unified field theory to explain why photons, electrons, and other physical entities behave as they do. It may well turn out that the physical forces that direct the paths of electrons are the same as those that direct vital processes. If so, much of what we conventionally interpret as free will may turn out to be not free at all, but precisely determined.

Darwin had struggled more than 20 years with his model for the origin of species before submitting it, under pressure from his colleagues, for publication. Often in ill health, he used the armchair/theoretical approach, relying mostly on the observations of others. His reports show little, if any, evidence that he intimately observed the behavior of wild animals in their natural environments.

By way of contrast, Wallace published a pioneering report (1856) on primate behavior — the behavior of orangutans in the wilds of Borneo. Wallace risked his health, and even his life, exposing himself to the strenuous elements of the tropics, arduously attempting to ascertain facts (missing links) to fit into the evolutionary theory he was developing and reporting to Darwin. These field experiences of Wallace may be what led him to his strong adaptationist views. Pigeon-breeder Darwin, on the other hand, would have been more inclined to accept an artificial, non-adaptationist view in his explanation of fancy-male species of animals.

Darwin's evolutionary theories were criticized worldwide, both by the academic community and the general populace. At the center of the controversy was his view that life arose and differentiated spontaneously. The Christian hierarchy of Anglican Britain found this hard to swallow. The conventional wisdom of Darwin's day was that life had a divine origin. In fact, one of his main mentors, Richard Owen (who, like Darwin, had mainly geological and paleontological interests), insisted on a Special Creator as the originator of species. On the other hand, Thomas Huxley, another of Darwin's mentors and a staunch supporter of Darwin, attacked Owen as a "pseudo-scientist who wrapped up his ideas in a neat anthropomorphic mysticism."

Darwin's critics were especially vehement concerning his inclusion of humans in the ordinary lineage of the rest of the natural organisms, including apes. (The gorilla had just recently been on display for the first time in Great Britain.) Spontaneous processes involving natural selection might be good enough for a bird, went the argument, but only God could make a human.

Even Charles Lyell (1797–1875), Darwin's foremost mentor, never fully accepted Darwin's model for evolution. Darwin was an avid reader of Lyell's *Principles of Geology* (1830) — noted for the theory of uniformitarianism. Darwin had put a lot of weight on this theory in developing his ideas about evolution. The theory stated that the processes at work in nature today are the same as those that have worked through the geological ages. To understand evolution, then, it is only necessary to study present-day evolutionary processes. After Darwin had published his *Origin* book, Lyell published his own views in *The Antiquity of Man* (1863). Darwin was greatly disappointed in this book, for it was noncommittal over the matter of natural selection, and Lyell had tried hard to avoid applications of natural selection to humans.

Though Darwin's theory of sexual selection speaks to the origin of the adornment of the males, it hardly explains what would be the natural advantages of the ornamental traits. In fact, if there were a natural advantage, sexual selection would merely be a fast form of natural selection. Darwin struggled a great deal with this, without coming to much of a conclusion. That males fight was no mystery. However, it is not self-evident that this impresses females. Likewise, it was less than clear that the grandiose adornment of males is appreciated by the females. To appreciate such "artwork," the females must be sufficiently endowed intellectually to conceptualize which "architectural structures" and colorful embellishments constitute beauty.

Darwin freely used subjective anthropomorphic interpretations of animal behavior, asserting that female wild creatures are capable of making choices of males by virtue of an aesthetic sense. We are quite sure that the human mind is capable of an abstract aesthetic sense. Our fine arts are evidence of this. Even primitive human civilizations have left behind abstract artworks as evidence. Darwin insisted that insects and birds, with which he said humans share a common heredity, also possess an aesthetic sense.

But could nature, a stickler for economy, tolerate such a human-like aesthetic sense? Wallace, ecologist and student of ape behavior, said No! Charles Darwin, paleontologist and biological theorist, said Yes! These two never did get together on this point, though they were both strong advocates of the theory of natural selection, which states that only those animals obeying the economic laws of nature will survive to tell their stories.

Wallace rested assured that male adornment could eventually be explained in terms of natural selection alone. Darwin was not so sure, nor did he rest. After both Wallace and Darwin had reported their views on natural selection to the Linnean Society in 1858, and Darwin had written his *Origin* book in 1859 and his *Descent* book in 1871, Darwin continued agonizing over his idea of sexual selection for the rest of his life, under constant torment from his critics. He even claimed that worrying about the peacock's artistic train actually made him physically ill. It should be noted that Darwin also lost his capacity for art-appreciation in general (including music appreciation) at that stage of his career.

THE MORGAN CRITIQUE OF SEXUAL SELECTION

In his critique of Darwin's evolutionary speculations, especially regarding sexual selection, Thomas Hunt Morgan (1866–1945), an experimental embryologist, concluded in 1903 that:

> [T]he theory meets with fatal objections at every turn. ... Shall we assume that there is still another process of selection going on, ... that those females whose tastes have soared a little higher than that of the average (a variation of this sort having appeared) select males to correspond, and thus the two continue heaping up the ornaments on one side and the appreciation of these ornaments on the other? No doubt an interesting fiction could be built up along these lines, but would anyone believe it, and, if he did, could he prove it?

The words "prove it" were characteristic of Morgan's work. He was a die-hard experimentalist. Morgan was really criticizing Darwin's idea of a rapid uni-directional selection process, a process already amply illustrated by the results of artificial selection as practiced by animal breeders. But could such a process conceivably operate in nature?

If such artificial selection were to occur naturally, the results might become non-adaptive and cataclysmic for a species. Female choice — amplified by male response — may lead to a situation in which the whole population would consist of bizarre forms reminiscent of a modern painting, the product of a modern artist rather than the rendering of classical Mother Nature.

But there is another (more optimistic) side to this coin. On this other side, there might be a chance that the selected trait would be adaptive. In this case, as in the non-adaptive one, female choice might serve to build up the frequency of the genes in the population by the same feedback process as in the former case. Ronald Fisher in his book, *The Genetical Theory of Natural Selection* (1930), emphasized this point. Modern students of sexual selection recognize this duality of utility and non-utility, or "sense" and "nonsense," as results of female choice.

Male choice would have similar effects, but this is practically a moot point in discussions of sexual selection. The female is ruler here, for the problem concerns the fancy *males*, though characteristics developed in one sex may be later transferred to the other sex genetically, as with cardinals and guppy fish.

Darwin's views suffered greatly from lack of knowledge about the principles of heredity. It was not until the early 1900s that T.H. Morgan and his students, studying fruit flies, placed classical genetics on a firm foundation. In these studies, observation, experimentation, and mathematics reigned supreme. But in the midst of all these important laboratory discoveries, biologists lost sight of what originally interested them — evolution of living forms in nature. There was some interest in mechanisms of genetic isolation among species, but little interest in the problem of how such mechanisms originated in the first place. Geneticists paid strict attention to currently operating sexual-isolating mechanisms not within, but between, species. Actually, studies of the origin of species directly involve the process of sexual selection, with strict genetic isolation (speciation) being the endpoint of the selective process.

Early geneticists generally thought that species arose from an ancestral population by geographical isolation. Such isolation was seen to lead to internally generated incompatibilities between the two resulting isolated populations. This process in turn was presumed to lead to such drastic genetical mismatching of chromosomes as to result in hybrid sterility when members of the two populations (now two species) were crossed.

The problem of the possibility that species could arise from a single population, without geographical isolation, was hardly treated by population geneticists. Little attention was paid to the role sexual selection may play in specialization and ecological adapatation. In fact, in those days so much emphasis was placed on the chemical and physical aspects of nature that the entire concept of "ecology" was largely ignored. The early ecologist, Charles Elton lamented in his book, *Animal Ecology* (1927), that there was more ecology in the Bible or the plays of Shakespeare than in all the zoology textbooks ever written.

Regarding female choice of those males which were most highly adorned, many students of evolution thought these colorful markings were important only for the recognition of species as such. However, in 1933 Richard Hingston published his book, *The Meaning of Animal Colour and Adornment,* presenting the idea that male animals, including the human, use adornment, such as structures, colors, and beards, in determination of dominance relationships among males. He also postulated a close connection between aggressive and sexual behavior. His ideas might have been expected to spark a conflagration of interest among students of sexual selection, but since there were very few of these around at that time, the idea went virtually unnoticed. The principle of the use of male display for threatening other males was further elucidated by Julian Huxley in his book, *Evolution, the Modern Synthesis* (1938):

> Many conspicuous characters (bright colors, songs, special structures or modes of behavior), to which Darwin

assigned display function, have now been shown to have
other functions. ... Of these, that of threatening characters
includes a large number, probably the majority, of the
cases adduced by Darwin as subserving display and
therefore evidence of the existence of sexual selection. ...
These effects directly promote effective reproduction and
need no special category of "sexual selection" to explain
their origin.

This idea that colorful adornment of males could be used in male-
male territorial competition had escaped the attention of Darwin and
Wallace. Such a battle of the ornaments would have helped provide an
explanation for the origin of much of the exhibitory adornment of males
of various animal species, independent of female choice. Darwin's
descriptions of highly adorned males bounding around a female and trying to attract her attention can now be seen as a group of males displaying to each other, vying for access to the female.

There are still other ways in which threat display is useful in order-
ing the mating system:

1) Male display of "ornaments" — such as colorful plumage, spurs,
and antlers — may overwhelm the female into an attitude of submission.
It's easy to imagine that a female Jackson's widowbird, *Euplectes jacksoni*,
could be intimidated into a submissive stance when the male, with his
massively spread-out tail, swoops down on her from above. Could a
dashing display of colors be similarly intimidating? After all, as Wallace
pointed out, such striking colors are used as warning signs in the case of
poisonous animals.

2) Flashing colors may also be employed by the males for sex recognition. Display of the colors in threatening gestures toward rival males
would evoke corresponding threats by the other male. Colored designs
on the male, perhaps resembling favorite foods of the species, might
attract females to the territory of the male. When a female comes close,
the territorial male would dash toward her as he does toward a rival

male. If she fails to charge back, the male would recognize her as a female. The threatening, flashing color might then be instrumental in intimidating the female into submission. At that point, the previously hostile behavior of the male may suddenly change to mating behavior. This form of sex recognition may be more fundamental than one based on mere appearances.

In some cases a submissive male may be mistaken for a female. This is dramatically seen in the case of the ebony mutant of *Drosophila melanogaster*. Because of deficiency in wing-flicking ability, the males of this mutant are less able to counter the aggression of normal males. As a result, the normal male may couple his genital apparatus onto the proboscis of the ebony male (Jacobs 1960).

The importance of ornamentation in psychological warfare is, even today, greatly underestimated. The connection between exhibitory ornamentation and competition operates even in human societies in which pompous ceremonial displays play a role in establishing social dominance. Who can overestimate the psychological effects of imposing architecture? The immense impact of fine artwork, along with the daunting architecture, plays an especially important role in the maintenance of politico-religious domination.

Given this background, it's remarkable that adherents of the Judeo-Christian tradition took so long to recognize the close connection between fear and affection. The awesome grandeur of the creation, and therefore the Creator, that had once overpowered the Israelites into a state of fear and submission, overwhelmed the Christians into a spirit of love.

Whether adornment will stimulate a love — or fear — response may be sex-related. The red tail of a guppy fish that may be viewed mostly as a fearsome threat to other males may be viewed mostly as a source of lovely food by a female.

If in the course of male-male competition the more ornate males win, they would be relatively more successful in fathering ornate male progeny. Consequently, fancy-male species would result without female choice of fancy males. Considering this, after the 1930s the whole idea of female choice based on aesthetic factors was finally pronounced dead, and any declarations regarding female choice were summarily dismissed as lacking in rigorous scientific evidence.

Lately, however, a fascination with traditional female choice, based on abstract aesthetics, has been resurrected. Even as we write, anthropomorphic claims for female choice are proliferating, and it is commonly maintained that non-human females select beautiful males on the basis of a human-like aesthetic sense.

Darwin's idea of a universal aesthetic sense had created quite an aftershock, for it equated mentality of humans with that of their non-human ancestors. Were human beings about to lose their last claim at uniqueness? Is there no essential difference between the intellect of a human and the intellect of a bird?

As Wallace, a strict natural selectionist, saw it, the human does not fit into the scheme of nature. In fact, while sitting in his jungle hut in Borneo observing ape behavior, he began to wonder if civilized humans are an *enemy* of nature. At this point he may have wondered whether the human was created by good God or a satanic Devil. As a victim of industrial Britain, and not of the Royal Society, he was among the very earliest of nature conservationists.

Wallace apparently recognized the unnatural tendencies of humans. Histories of human civilizations show a direction of human societies not back to the natural, but ahead toward the artificial (contrived by art, rather than nature). Art that is non-functional we call "fine." Of course, this reflects the artificial drives of the human intellect. What goes beyond faithful reproduction of nature is called creative. Creativity involves imagination. Imagination involves mental symbols. Symbols serve as analogies, simulations of reality. In this, are humans set apart from wildlife? Are non-human animals in any sense capable of making conscious choices or contriving schemes to be executed in the distant future?

Through the ages, mystical powers of consciousness, even superconsciousness, were attributed to animals. Many popular books of fables and romantic novels have been based on this theme, freely attributing human thoughts and emotions to animals. When Charles Darwin made a study on *The Expression of Emotions in Man and Animals* (1872), he tried to decipher the thoughts and emotions of animals by means of their facial expressions. For example, "snarling" indicates anger. Vestiges of this behavior are still evident in humans. In his *Descent* book, Darwin says:

> Man does share with animals the principles of self preser-
> vation, sexual love, maternal affection, and the senses of
> pleasure and pain, jealousy and rage, pride and shame,
> excitement and boredom, wonder and curiosity, imita-
> tion, memory and imagination. Some animals are capable
> of a limited degree of reasoning, and some can use tools.

This is quite a mixed bag of emotions and reasoning, but in the 1800s it was popular to lump this all together in assigning anthropomorphic interpretations to animal behavior. It is known today that emotions and reasoning may be polar opposites. In fact, part of the function of the cerebral cortex is to use reasoning for controlling the emotions.

Regarding reasoning ability of animals, many interpretations are based on observations of the behavior of domesticated animals. Animals living in association with humans often imitate human behavior, especially if this behavior is related to food procurement. In this manner the animal may be the simple beneficiary of the results of human reasoning. Darwin made his observations of animal behavior on domesticated animals, although he frequently referred to observations of field naturalists. His contemporaries, especially his close colleague George Romaines, took few precautions in accepting reports on the higher intelligence of domesticated monkeys. Romaines accepted such reports and interpretations of his sister, who had trained a monkey to crack nuts with a hammer. This was used as an illustration of reasoning in monkeys.

Romaines' *Animal Intelligence* (1882) became very popular. It started with single-celled animals and progressed through the primates. Romaines marshaled evidence that parrots know what they are talking about and experience pride after they utter words of wisdom. Romaines' reports encouraged others to make similar reports of mental affinity between animals and man. They collected other anecdotes of talking parrots, tool-using monkeys, and door-opening cats and dogs that purported to demonstrate that our fellow creatures are capable of flashes of insight and of a consciousness that is human in scope.

Darwin's anthropomorphism had its critics. Douglas Spalding (1872), in his studies of newly hatched chicks and newborn pigs, found that much behavior formerly considered to be a result of learned behavior was already present at birth. Whereas Spalding's contemporaries speculated that consciousness spurred the body into action, Spalding was convinced that behavior, whether of man or beast, was in a sense automatic. Being outside of the predominant Royal Society of Science, Spalding never made much of a dent in the history of science. He was of the "working class."

German-born American physiologist Jacques Loeb (1859–1924), on the other hand, made a big impact on the history of science. Early in life he became intensely interested in the question of free will. Later, he joined Julius Sachs in the physiology department at the University of Würzburg. Sachs was doing research in plant tropisms, which could be defined as an innate tendency to react to stimuli in a definite manner. Loeb eventually pursued similar studies in animal tropisms. In doing physiological work with tube worms, he discovered that these animals behaved much like plant seedlings in that they automatically turned toward a light source. Loeb eventually became disenchanted with the idea of free will among animals, including the human.

Loeb discovered that some moth caterpillars were "slaves to light." He found that barnacle larvae, when released in the beam of two lights, one of which could be dimmed in stages, swam at an angle that could be predicted by mathematical calculations. Their responses appeared robot-like. Loeb maintained that we are all biological machines compelled to react to physical conditions with little room for "voluntary behavior."

Loeb had much to do with delivering a death knoll to the idea that life was controlled by a sort of spiritual essence "vital principle." To Loeb, such ancient animisms were superstitions to be dispelled by a view that all life could be explained by mere physics and chemistry. In his work with artificial parthenogenesis (inducing eggs to develop into organisms without fertilization), he saw no evidence to support the ancient idea that a spirit was involved in reproduction. Even complicated animal behavior required no spiritual explanation; physics and biochemistry would suffice.

A behaviorist in the United States, Edward Thorndike (1874–1949), pioneered in studies of animal learning. He discovered that baby chicks searching for food could learn to memorize mazes created by arranging books. He placed cats in boxes with doors that could be opened by various mechanical devices. By accident, a cat would happen to open a door by pushing a certain lever. The cat, learning from mistakes, thereafter opened the door deftly. In this learning Thorndike saw no evidence of insight or anticipation indicating higher mental processes that might be capable of proof or disproof. If the side of the box were suddenly opened so the cat could simply walk out, it still pulled the lever.

Thorndike's law of effect could explain away much of the myth connected with alleged animal intelligence. What appeared to be insightful reasoning was simply explained as random activity selected by chance trial and error. If the reward is food, that behavior pattern is reinforced; attributing insight to the behavior is spurious and unnecessary. Even the most arresting acts of apparent cleverness could be accounted for by the process of learning through trial and error.

Thorndike's views led directly to the school of "behaviorism" ("mechanism" may have been a more appropriate designation of this method of interpretation). The gauntlet was taken up by John Watson (1878–1958), a behaviorist who studied animals in "black boxes" in which the animals' mechanical responses to stimuli could be analyzed quantitatively. In 1900 Watson began his career in the study of "animal education." Studying maze-learning in rats, he formulated the creed that our environment shapes behavior by reinforcing habits.

Burrhus F. Skinner (1904–90) refined such mazes to include automatic puzzle boxes in which an animal could record its own activities. By pressing a lever, a rat or pigeon obtained a small pellet of food. If it took a number of pressings to obtain the food, the animals would patiently do this, as if contemplating a reward. Furthermore, if a light were set up to flash during the pressings, the animal "knew" that the system was working, and this increased its patience in pressing toward the goal. Such techniques are now used by animal trainers, but instead of training animals to press levers that flash a light while a reward is forthcoming, the trainer teaches the animals to play pianos, ride bicycles, dance, etc. A trained parrot may soon learn that the way to obtain a choice morsel of food is to slam-dunk a ball into a hoop. This is certainly easier than spending the greater part of the day hunting for food.

Skinner maintained we are all born with blank minds. The environment induces the behaviors we observe. The behavior patterns are then reinforced and conditioned. The view that all behavior is shaped by the environment conflicted with that of the zoologists who were by then insisting that much behavior is determined genetically by a process of natural selection, not a process of learning. As is usual in such cases of thesis and antithesis, the truth lies somewhere near the middle in the synthesis, following a law of moderation.

For some 50 years, the behaviorists, with their rigid mechanistic interpretations of animal behavior, were so busy working with their Skinner boxes — and concocting philosophical abstractions from the results — that they paid little attention to where animals live: in nature. Not surprisingly, in light of their favorite research tool, they were victims of compartmentalized thinking. Any naturalist would notice that there's more to natural behavior than animals display in their little black boxes.

The rationale for using Skinner boxes had been precisely to reduce "extraneous" elements in the study of specific behavioral patterns. It was presumed that determination of the individual components of behavior, later taken together with other components, would give a complete picture of what happens in nature. Though to a certain extent this may be true, there is a danger that concentration on individual components may lead to false deductions about the whole picture. In fixating on a tree, one may lose sight of the forest.

The role of mathematical deduction in predicting animal behavior has had a checkered career. Some physiologists, notably Loeb, espoused the view that all of life, if thoroughly understood, could be predicted mathematically. Physicists had already proved the power of mathematics in predicting the behavior of matter and energy. The German mathematician, David Hilbert (1862–1943), who founded a school of mathematics at Göttingen, attracted the interest of physicists who realized that mathematical reasoning could play an essential role in understanding electrical phenomena.

In 1905 Hilbert and Hermann Minkowski (1864–1909) organized a seminar on "The Electrodynamics of Moving Bodies." Strangely enough, this was the very year that Einstein's first articles on the special theory of relativity were published. One of Einstein's articles even had the title, "Towards an Electrodynamics of Moving Bodies." In 1908 Minkowski brought the theory of relativity to mathematical completion. He showed that the principle of the constant velocity of light could stand in purely geometrical terms and created a four-dimensional "world" of space and time, which is now called Minkowskian space. Minkowski's work provided the basis for Einstein's work on a general theory of relativity. Hilbert was fascinated by the developments attending the birth of modern mathematical physics. Talks by theoretical physicists became a tradition in the Göttingen Mathematics Club.

But not all mathematicians and physicists were enamored of the supreme emphasis mathematics was given in physics. One of Hilbert's students wrote: "We mathematicians became uneasy as we listened to the mathematical physicists presenting principle after principle without any supporting evidence, then going on to base all kinds of assertions and consequences on these principles."

Hilbert's favorite pronouncement in this connection was: "Physics is too complicated for physicists. The mathematicians had better have a try." But Hilbert was well aware that mathematics alone, despite all its power and potential, would never manage to bring order out of chaos without knowledge of the laws of physics.

The importance of observation in physics was dramatically demonstrated by the career of Einstein. Though Einstein is known as a theoretical physicist, his early years had been spent in a patent office where his duty was to study the behavior of machines. In fact, it was observations of the behavior of streetcars in which he rode that helped him develop his theory of relativity.

When Hilbert heard about the successful formulation of the theory of relativity by the physicist Einstein — a theory over which the mathematician Minkowski had labored so mightily — he said, "Any schoolboy that you could meet on the streets of this capital of mathematics knows more about four-dimensional geometry than Einstein does. Nevertheless, the credit for this achievement belongs to Einstein, not the mathematicians." (See Ryutova-Kemoklidze 1995.)

This scenario has had its equivalent in biology. Although strict mechanists attempted to predict the behavior of animals, it soon became apparent that in general animals seemed unaware of these mathematical abstractions as they went about their daily activities. I became keenly aware of this problem when an evolutionary biologist with strong mathematical inclinations visited my laboratory and immediately began to predict how long it would take for the ebony gene to become exterminated from my population cages. It was obvious that there was not enough known about the mating behavior of the fruit flies under these conditions to warrant such mathematical predictions.

In the early 1900s, as the strict mechanists were attempting to dissect and mathematically formulate the elements of animal behavior by use of compartmentalized methods, Oskar Heinroth (1871–1945), director of the aquarium at the Berlin Zoo, laid the foundation for the science of comparative behavior, which mirrored and complemented the discipline of comparative anatomy. He called his discipline "Comparative study of gesture." Heinroth described the results of his bird studies between 1926 and 1933 in four illustrated volumes: *The Birds of Central Europe.* Soon thereafter, Konrad Lorenz (1903–) took the study of animal behavior farther afield.

Lorenz was reared in the Vienna woods, along with a little girl, Marguerite, who was later to become his wife. They played with ducks, which became imprinted with the images of the children. Lorenz went on to study the way bird displays had evolved. He aimed to study ducks under the most natural conditions possible. However, this presented a problem. Wild ducks are shy and elusive and panic even at the glint of binoculars. He settled for second best. Between 1935 and 1938 he reared goslings from eggs collected from the wilds.

By comparing the signals of closely related species, Lorenz was able to make inspired guesses as to how some displays might have evolved. Some of his interpretations were obviously anthropomorphic. For example, during sexual encounters, the drakes often broke off their courtship routine and vigorously preened their wing feathers. It reminded Lorenz of someone scratching his head in frustration. It occurred to Lorenz that perhaps the display of these mandarin drakes was a highly "ritualized" form of "frustrated" wing preening. Such reactions then became known among European ethologists as "displacement reactions" (inappropriate behavior induced by frustration of normal behavior).

N.W. Moore (1952) evoked this displacement theory to explain the behavior of male dragonflies that perform egg-laying motions following "frustration" resulting from the departure of a courted female.

Actually, such behavior of dragonflies is capable of another directly adaptive interpretation. The male is testing the egg-laying site as a suitable place for "starting a family." In many cases such as this, what was at first considered useless was later found to be useful. Comparative anatomists often called organs "vestigial" if their functions were unknown. For example, the small legs of some snakes were at first regarded as useless. However, the legs were later found by naturalists to be used in the mating process. Some evolutionists argue that rabbits are endowed with notoriously poor digestive systems, since their pellets still contain so much food that the rabbits find them a source of nourishment later. But this may simply represent another method used by animals to store food in a preserved, dried form for later use.

In 1937 Lorenz was joined by Nikolaas Tinbergen (1907–), a Dutch zoologist. While Lorenz sat with his newly hatched geese, Tinbergen hauled across the sky models of various kinds of birds. The goslings reacted strongly to hawk models traveling forward. When the model traveled backward, it resembled a goose, and the goslings did not react. It turned out that this was because the hawk model was a stranger to the goslings, but the goose was not.

Following Nikolaas, another Tinbergen, Niko, joined the growing group of students of animal behavior. He is noted for his studies of the stickleback fish. He found that males fight with other males in territorial defense. It turned out to be the red color of the male that provoked the fighting response.

Following this observation, and others, ethologists concluded that red colors arose in response to stress situations, such as result from territorial threats. Conflict situations were interpreted as being responsible for the origin of sign language, using, for example, bright colors. Other signs were interpreted as being evolved from various useful movements. Courtship-feeding of birds was seen to have been derived from juvenile behavior. Hen finches and gulls beg like babies, and their mates obligingly give them food.

By the 1970s investigators realized that to understand the evolution of mentality, research in comparative behavior of animals in nature must be undertaken. When such studies were finally begun, under the banner of "ethology," it was soon realized that animal behavior is much more flexible than envisioned by the strict mechanists.

Ethology opened the door to the next phase in the study of animal behavior: the "cognition" phase. Students of cognition are interested in the possible manifestation of consciousness in non-humans. Donald Griffin is a leading advocate of the school of animal cognition. This school abandons the taboos against anthropomorphism laid down by the strict mechanists, maintaining that internal processes within the brains or minds are of utmost importance in determining the behavior of humans and animals.

Griffin (1984) decries the tendency of strict mechanists who advocate a total disregard for subjective feelings and conscious thoughts of animals. He insists that such a narrow view restricts students of animal behavior, foreclosing research into the subject. He admits, however, that much research has been conducted by those who aren't motivated by a theory of consciousness.

He cites some examples of possible consciousness among birds: In the genus, *Parus* (the chickadees known in Europe as "tits"), the great tit, *Parus major*, has earned a reputation for having learned how to open the caps of milk bottles at the front doors of houses, then get at the food inside the bottles. Krebs et al. (1972, 1978) and Krebs (1979), using caged great tits, experimented with how the birds acquire the habit of opening containers to obtain food. The birds quickly learn how to pick away the tape over the enclosures and obtain the food. The birds then associate the tape with other tapes elsewhere. Furthermore, their companions learn the habit from them. The birds show individual variations in their methods of opening the containers. Griffin gives this as an example of unusual problem-solving ability of birds, implying that the birds know what they are doing. This might indicate rudiments of consciousness, a concept advanced by Darwin for animals in general.

Actually, this hole-pecking behavior of birds of the genus, *Parus*, may be much more innate than it appears. The black-capped chickadee, *Parus atricapillus*, for example, earns a good portion of its living pecking into soft, natural wood in search for food. Also, both parents peck their way through a rotting snag to create a nest site deep in the snag. The female is especially careful in pecking the entrance hole just large

Left: A female chickadee "sizes up" the diameter of the hole she is constructing.
Right: A female cowbird finds the chickadee hole too small to enter.

enough to fit the parents. In so doing, she steps back and waves her head while examining the hole before resuming her precision pecking. A female cowbird, finding the hole too small for admission, subsequently spends considerable time pecking around the snag as if to find another place to enter (personal observations).

As a further example of apparently conscious mentality of birds, Griffin notes the example of the carrion crows. These birds routinely find and eat mussels, stranded as tides recede, on sandy beaches. Croze (1970) performed experiments to learn how the crows determine which mussel shells contain food. He did this by hiding beef under the bottom sides of empty mussel shells on the beach. The crows quickly answered the question — "Where's the beef?" — by locating the meat. Croze then buried the beef in the sand under the empty shells. The crows soon learned to dig it up. When Croze stopped placing beef under the shells, the crows continued to turn over the shells, attempting to find food underneath. But failing to find food, they gradually lost interest. Suggests Griffin: "When they have just recognized a new searching image, crows and other animals may consciously think about their fruitful discovery."

Griffin next turned his attention to the red-winged and the yellow-headed blackbirds studied by Orians (1980). Both species maintain territories in which more than one female mates and nests. Within extensive areas of marsh, the males choose one small region from which they exclude other males of their species by threats and sometimes actual fighting. When the females arrive, they visit several territories before choosing one. Orians discovered that both males and females choose territories that would only *later* become rich in food. How can the birds predict future productivity? Griffin believes they do some thinking at this point.

Orians, however, does not attribute this blackbird behavior to conscious decision-making. Rather, he surmises that the birds determine the future food supplies and other territorial conditions on the basis of the state of the permanent vegetation in the ordinary "birdly" fashion.

In discussing the relationships between predatory bats and the moths they prey on, Griffin notes the complicated behavior the moths exhibit in escaping predation. He says, "If moths can feel anything, this is time for terror and conscious striving to escape." Also, regarding the complex actions the bats exhibit in capturing moths, Griffin credits the bats with mental conceptualizing prior to their acts.

Use of tools by birds and mammals has long captured the attention of students of animal mentality. Griffin cites such cases with the following observation:

> When chimpanzees fashion sticks to probe for termites, their behavior is considered one of the most convincing cases of intentional behavior yet described for nonhuman animals. When McMahan discovers assassin bugs carry-

ing out an almost equally elaborate feeding behavior, must we assume that the insect is only a genetically pro-grammed robot incapable of understanding what it does? Perhaps we should be ready to infer conscious thinking whenever any animal shows such ingenious behavior, regardless of its taxonomic group and our preconceived notions about limitations of animal consciousness.

In this quotation Griffin is referring to an observation by Elizabeth McMahan (1983). In watching an assassin bug feeding on termites, she notes that the bug pushes the empty exoskeleton of its victim into the nest opening of the termites and jiggles it gently after the manner of a fisherman. Another termite seizes the corpse as part of the normal behavior pattern of devouring the body of a dead sibling or carrying the corpse away for disposal. The assassin bug pulls the exoskeleton of the first victim out with the second worker attached. This one is eaten, and its empty exoskeleton is used in another "fishing" expedition. In one case an assassin bug was observed to thus devour 31 termites before moving away with a bloated abdomen.

But this "fishing" behavior of the assassin bug is wide open for alter-nate interpretations. In this regard, lessons may be learned from the ladybird beetle. The larva of the convergent ladybird beetle, *Hipodamia convergens*, approaching a colony of aphids, feeds on one aphid while capturing others that creep over the victim. One could easily get the impression that the larva is using an aphid corpse as a lure to catch another aphid (personal observation).

Tool use by birds has been observed, not only for woodpecker finch-es (Lack 1947), but also green jays (Gayou 1982). These birds use plant spines and sticks to dislodge insects from holes and crevices under the bark of trees.

Gavin Hunt (1996) reports that the crow, *Corvus moneduloides*, native to the New Caledonian Islands 900 mile east of Australia, prepares sticks for probing insects from crevices. Sometimes hooks are left on the tips of the twigs being prepared for this purpose. Other tools are made from long, tapering leaves with backwardly pointed barbs on their margins. With their beaks, the crows devise sword-shaped instruments with the barbs on one side. Hunt maintains that the differently shaped tools are used for specific purposes. The crows are reported to carry with them some of their specially prepared "tools."

Lest one get the impression that tool-making by birds reflects human-like, consciously directed behavior, it should be emphasized that such use of plant materials may be a mere extension of nest-building behavior. A nest itself may be considered a "tool" for rearing young. An appreciable amount of the complicated behavior that goes into building a nest may be performed unconsciously (innately).

Cooper's hawks show apparent ingenuity in their manipulation of sticks. In 1997 I had the unusual opportunity of observing the behavior of young Cooper's hawks that emerged from a nest on the Goshen College campus in Goshen, Indiana. After leaving the nest, the young hawks fed on the campus for about a month. Characteristically, after feeding, the young hawks played games with sticks that had fallen from trees onto the lawn. The birds often appeared to watch as the ends of the sticks elevated when a hawk landed on the opposite end. On one occasion, two of the hawks played a game of seesaw with a crooked branch lying on the ground. The pair of birds perched on opposite ends of the branch then jumped up and down on the branch, as the opposite partner did likewise. In effect, the birds were using the sticks for gymnastic activity. They were even seen hanging upside down under elevated sticks, much as children use swinging bars.

Many creatures use sea anemones with stinging devices on their tentacles for their own protection against predators. The marine crab, *Melee tessellate*, detaches small anemones from the substratum, holds one in each of its two front appendages and, when threatened, directs the anemone toward the intruder (Thorpe 1963).

Among examples of apparent cleverness is actual "fishing," often observed among herons. David McCullough and Ronald Beasley (1996)

*Two young Cooper's hawks find that a bowed branch serves as a seesaw
on which they can play games after finishing their meal.*

give an account of this behavior. The green heron, *Butorides virescens*, and
the striated heron, *B. striatus*, have been observed worldwide engaging
in such bait-fishing. The bird will drop a small feather, twig, or leaf onto
the surface of the water, wait for a small fish to investigate, then strike.
Green herons will carry a particularly successful lure from place to place,
and keep repositioning it directly beneath their bill should it drift away.
They will use bits of bread, or even fish-food pellets, as highly attractive
bait. Beasley noted similar behavior among black-crowned night herons
in California.

At first, it looks as though the birds have learned the technique from
local anglers. However, fish that share the heron's normal diet are routinely attracted to bread thrown into the water by local residents to
attract fish. The herons are often tempted to investigate floating crumbs
and crusts. In the case of the green heron, the habit of dabbling with
morsels of bread may have been rewarded by the appearance of fish
attracted by the crumbs. The heron may therefore have simply learned
to fish by associating the bread with fish.

Food-dunking has been widely reported for many species of birds. The significance may be to clean the food or to moisten it so it may be more easily swallowed. Dennis (1981), in his review of this behavior, says:

> Food dunking is sometimes carried to extremes by grackles. They commonly dunk not only bakery products in water but also seeds, fruits, and almost anything they eat. Stale bread and yes, pieces of doughnuts are dunked and sometimes left in water until the proper consistency for eating has been attained. ... Other birds that dunk food include the starling, house sparrow, red-winged blackbird, and Brewer's blackbird. Nearly always the food is bread or some other bakery product. But yellow-bellied sapsuckers, using natural food and their own sap wells, which they have drilled in the limbs and trunks of trees, carry on a unique kind of dunking operation during the nesting season. Before offering wads of sticky insects to their young, they are known to moisten the bundle at one of their sap wells. Nearly always a habit that seems wholly artificial, such as dunking food at the birdbath, has its counterpart in the wild.

Chimpanzees are also credited with conscious rationality as they fish for termites by probing the termite mound with a stick. In this case the male chimpanzee may have accidentally discovered the utility of a tool by placing a twig in a hole, only to learn when he pulled it out that it was covered with tasty termites. It is also easily conceivable that the first chimpanzee to crack nuts with an object used as a hammer had learned the trick by watching humans. In warm regions, monkeys are frequently treated as free-ranging pets that associate with wild monkeys. In fact, any inferences drawn about emotions of wild animals as based on observations of pets are subject to question. Any human-like behavior of the pets may simply reflect human imprinting on the pets. In this connection, it is to be remembered that Charles Darwin's evaluation of the minds and manners of wild animals is based largely on observation of pets.

Griffin's reopening of the door to anthropomorphism was what Theodore Barber was awaiting. He soon released his Griffin-inspired book, *The Human Nature of Birds: A Scientific Discovery with Startling Implications* (1993). He supplies numerous examples of the "amazing" abstract mental ability of birds. For example: "A male jay guided a human over a considerable distance to an abandoned new-born of a different avian species that had fallen from its nest. The jay then helped the human raise the young bird to maturity by protecting it, and sharing its own precious food with it."

Of what species was the young bird? How did the jay attract the human to the young bird? What did the jay then do to help raise the young bird? More details would be helpful.

The picture section of Barber's book shows what is purported to be an adult wood thrush teaching a juvenile to sing. In fact, the photo appears to be of two juveniles perched together. One of them has its beak wide open, as if begging for food. The other one is crouched down with its beak closed. At this point a thousand words would indeed be helpful.

Another book along similar lines is one by Jeffrey Masson and Susan McCarthy, *When Elephants Weep* (1995). The title is extracted from Darwin (1872) who reported: "The Indian elephant is said sometimes to weep." The authors claim that Donald Griffin's writings were pivotal in inspiring their book. The authors then go on to present their views:

> Animals cry. At least they vocalize pain or distress, and in many cases seem to call for help. ... But can we feel sure that an old dog with an excellent memory and some power of imagination, as shown by his dreams, never reflects on his past pleasures in the chase? And this would

be a form of self-consciousness. ... Animals love and suffer, cry and laugh; their hearts rise up in anticipation and fall in despair. They are lonely, in love, disappointed, or curious, they look back with nostalgia and anticipate future happiness. They feel.

The authors cite a case in which two calf elephants pressed themselves against the sides of a wounded adult, supporting her as if feeling compassion. The anecdote, however, could be equally interpreted as two calves pressing against their mother, as elephant calves are prone to do under dire circumstances.

The new anthropomorphism espoused during what has been termed the "cognitive revolution" includes up-to-date knowledge of population genetics. Because anthropomorphism involves interpretation of animal behavior in terms of the observer, an understanding of genetic principles on the part of the observer is now transferred to the observed subject. Consequently, the mating behavior of wild animals is now described as though the female of the species has a sophisticated knowledge of population genetics. Females are now interpreted as selecting males on the basis of the fitness of their genes, and they are doing an uncanny job of this. Sexual selection has taken on an ever-more-subtle form. In the "new biology," examples of sophisticated interpretations of female choice are proliferating at an enormous rate. For example, in *A Natural History of Sex* (1986), Adrian Forsyth writes:

> In some butterflies with spermatophores, it appears males discriminate against older females whose worn and dull wings reveal them as a poor, high-risk venture in which to sink a large amount of capital. Fruit fly males, following a similar logic, prefer to court virgins because these females will have more eggs to yield. In *Drosophila melanogaster* the females are wary of depleted sperm

and actively seek out virgin males. Females in species such as fruit flies are called promiscuous. They court many males.

Actually, the reason male fruit flies prefer virgin females is not because such virgins will have more eggs to yield, but because the other available females, the previously mated ones, are repulsive. After mating, the females emit a repulsive vaginal sac when they are courted. The female may then perform her egg-laying activities without interference by extraneous males. Beyond this, young females are more attractive to males than are older females. This selection is probably related to chemical attraction. The phenomenon can be demonstrated with mere heads of females placed in a petri dish (Jacobs 1960).

The other proposition suggested above — that fruit fly females, being wary of the possibility of depleted sperm supply in males that have previously mated, actively seek out virgin males for mating — is also wide open for alternate interpretations. If virgin males mate more readily than previously mated males, this could be because males become less active in courting after their sperm supply has become depleted by prior mating. Dragonfly studies reveal this principle (Jacobs 1955).

Furthermore, in the 30 years I have spent observing the behavior of fruit flies I have never observed anything I would interpret as females seeking out males for mating. The impression that females seek out males may stem from the fact that females encounter males as the females move about. This motion attracts the males. A female passing through a group of quiet males may immediately be pursued by the males, leading to a mass chase. Such attraction by movement may appear intentional on the part of the female, but it is simply the consequence of the female fleeing from a male. In these cases the female is simply not yet ready for mating. When she is ready, she yields to the male's advances.

Wing-flicking by the male during courtship is done in a manner appropriate for forcing air-borne chemicals toward the female. A female may reject a male by wing-flicking, kicking, and lowering her abdomen even after coitus has started, as when a male is deficient in structure and behavior. In the years of observing *Drosophila melanogaster*, the nearest thing I have seen that might be construed as a female performing "courtship" toward a male involved a female spreading her wings and charging a male that had intruded upon her feeding space. This charge appeared to be aggressive. It is not always easy to distinguish between aggressive behavior and courtship.

M.J. Hollingsworth and J.M. Smith (1955) report female refusal of defective males among *Drosophila subobscura*. In that case the males are defective, apparently because of inbreeding. Such cases of female rejection of males are also reported in mate-choice experiments between males and females of different species (Spieth and Hsu 1950).

In the literature there are numerous accounts of females "inciting" males to compete so they can make a choice of the fittest male, in line with Darwinian sexual selection. With mallard ducks, the females are described as flying up near the males to attract them to follow her. But at a local woodland pond where I have been studying wild mallards for 17 years, mass chases of females appear to result from the females fleeing from competing males, rather than from their attempts to incite males to pursue. After the extra males drop out of the competition, a female may accept the remaining male as a mate. Males also perform such flights in territorial defense before the females arrive.

Female birds are frequently described as "seeking extramarital affairs" for various reasons. In a *National Wildlife* article (June-July 1993, p. 43) is a picture of a black-capped chickadee with the following caption: "Among black-capped chickadees a female often will pick a more dominant male than her own mate to sire offspring. Reason: She presumably is getting more fit genes for her young."

However, in this, along with myriad other interpretations, it could well be that the female is seeking food in a nearby territory and has inadvertently encountered a male other than her mate, with the usual consequences.

It is commonly asserted that some arena birds, such as the long-tailed manakin, display altruistic motives in group dancing. Certain subordinate males, it is said, compete in the arena with the express aim of helping the dominant males attract females by enhancing the common display in the arena.

It's unnecessary, though, to invoke this altruistic interpretation. The subordinate males may simply be competing for territorial rights, along with the other males. Any resulting attraction of females to the territory, facilitated by the competing vociferous group, appears to be a mere by-product of such competition. Their gathering is a result of microterritorial grouping, not cooperation to enhance mate attraction.

Subjective interpretations of animal behavior may be as unreliable as the human mind. Such unreliability is conspicuously exhibited by hypnotists who show dramatically how the power of suggestion may warp judgment. There are those who contend that it's impossible for humans to be objective, especially on the subject of sex. But this is no excuse for not trying. After all, is it not an attempt at objectivity that sets the natural sciences apart from mysticism? It is this that has given the public special confidence in science. If humans were natural animals, they might be qualified to interpret the behavior of wild animals subjectively, even anthropomorphically. As it is, humans have plenty of trouble understanding the behavior of their fellow humans, let alone interpreting the motives of non-humans. At least for practical purposes, though, it's important for us to know whether animals are conscious. Griffin (1992) strongly advocates that this problem, while excruciatingly difficult to solve, needs at least to be explored:

> The customary view of animals always being in a state comparable to that of a human sleepwalker is a sort of negative dogmatism. The question of animal consciousness is an open one, awaiting adequate scientific illumination. Many behavioral scientists dismiss this effort as idle speculation; but speculation is where scientific investigation begins. ... Regardless of the degree to which it may come to seem more or less probable that various animals experience particular conscious thoughts and subjective feelings, this approach should open up significant

but largely neglected opportunities to attain a fuller and more accurate understanding of the other creatures with which we share this planet.

Are all animals conscious? If not, animals might not experience pain as we know it, for we experience no pain in the unconscious state — as when sleeping, hypnotized, or anesthetized.

Actually, when it comes to pain perception, nature appears to have done a creditable job in preventing the misery of the antelope captured by the lion. At times like this, when an animal is shocked by capture, the body releases chemical painkillers with effects similar to morphine, which produce a feeling of euphoria. Under these conditions, the prey automatically becomes limp and motionless. This may account for the so-called hypnotic states exhibited by birds when captured and held. Since a lion after capturing prey customarily pauses and surveys the surroundings for some time before beginning to feed, the delay affords an opportunity for the prey to make a quick getaway. Were it not for the painkiller, the prey might have had a hard time remaining motionless under these conditions. Lewis Thomas (1979) says:

> Pain is useful for avoidance in getting away when there's time to get away, but when it's an end game, and no way back, pain is likely to be turned off, and the mechanisms for this are wonderfully precise and quick. If I had to design an ecosystem in which creatures had to live off each other and in which dying was an indispensable part of living, I could not think of a better way to manage.

A baby duck, upon being taken in hand, will struggle violently, but it will finally settle in the hand, close its eyes, and become quiet. In fact, it is conceivable that what is called "freezing" or "tonic immobility" among dragonflies, birds, or rabbits falls into the category of a hypnotic, anesthetic state.

Humans who have had near-death experiences consistently report feelings of euphoria. Timothy Ferris (1992), reviewing such cases, says many involve feelings of light and ecstasy. In a national survey of 8 million persons who reported having similar experiences, two-thirds recalled being in an ecstatic or visionary state. Many reported a profound peace and well-being, which was so blissful they felt grumpy about being returned to life.

Perhaps animals feel pain, but not pain as we know it. But our concern over the well-being of animals goes beyond the problem of acute pain. We are also concerned about whether animals are conscious of such emotions as joy and sorrow. In fact, we wonder whether they are "aware" at all and, if so, what we can do to promote their enjoyment of life and prevent their sorrows. The ultimate question, then, is whether non-humans are conscious. At what point in the evolutionary family tree does conscious experience first manifest itself, or is there no such point — only gradual origin as conceived by Darwin?

Whether or not non-humans are conscious of pain as we know it has long concerned veterinarians, physiological experimenters, naturalists, and those responsible for animal welfare. Bernard Rollin has reviewed the history of this problem in his book, *The Unheeded Cry* (1990).

In a discussion of the origin of consciousness, researchers concentrate on the mating process because it's here that mental activity expresses itself to the fullest. Such ingenuity might be brought out particularly in the exploratory phase of the life cycle, the sexual phase. Indeed, the essential ingredient in sexual procreation is explorative creativity. If conscious-type behavior is exhibited at any point, it would be revealed conspicuously in mate selection. In this selection, choice of mates would be involved in genetically directed evolution of consciousness. Are all animals, from Protozoa to people, conscious of beauty, ugliness, pleasure, pain? In fact, are they conscious at all? And, if so, to what extent?

CHAPTER 7

NATURAL INGENUITY AND THE ORIGIN OF CONSCIOUSNESS

*T*HE PRIME QUESTION ASKED BY SAGES through the ages is: What is consciousness? Is consciousness adaptive for the human species? Will humans ultimately eliminate nature as we know it, creating a completely artificial environment from which there is no turning back? Is the human uniquely conscious, or is wildlife also conscious? What is the adaptive function of consciousness?

In constructing a behavioral continuum, we could start with the behavior of ultimate particles. If we view all of life as a continuum, why not also include the precursors of life? Did consciousness already start back there? Some quantum physicists consider the electron conscious, since it appears to make behavioral choices. (See Herbert 1993.) Are ultimate particles, or atoms, conscious of what the are doing when they seek pairing partners to form stable alliances, to satisfy the natural law of energy conservation? At what point in brain development in the animal lineage does consciousness arise, or is there no point of origin, just a continuum of development?

In his book, *Comparative Physiology of the Brain and Comparative Psychology* (1900), Jacques Loeb defines consciousness simply as associative memory. This definition presumes some sort of putting things together in an internal reflective fashion. This implies that consciousness involves nervous organization and activity.

In small animals, such as insects, the size of the brain is tiny, yet adequate for adaptation. In fact, these clusters of nerve cells (ganglia) do such a remarkable job that what they accomplish in the way of adaptive behavior is ingenious. In fact it's so ingenious that from time immemorial the behavior of wildlife has been viewed with awe, even reverence. This yielded the doctrine of animism (giving to nature spiritual anthropomorphic interpretations)

To see such natural ingenuity in action we need go no farther than our own backyards. We see there a complex ecosystem in which each species survives indefinitely with an average population growth of zero. This is mathematically and ecologically determinative. A greater figure would lead to that species taking over the entire earth, while a lesser figure would result in the extinction of that species. The behavior of each species is attuned to this natural law. The fact that this adaptive ingenuity appears innate does not detract from its fascination. In fact, it is even more fascinating since the behavior, which the organisms might have originated ages ago, is now programmed onto the DNA tapes. Superimposed onto these programs may be observed new additions in the making. Will some of these additions be found in the future as part of the heredity of the species?

On the continuum of complexity, where did consciousness set in? We could start to answer this question by considering the behavior of a simple virus particle. Without any semblance of a brain, it seeks out a specific type of cell and bores into it in search of food. Does this represent conscious behavior? It certainly looks intentional. Does the virus particle reason as it discriminates among cells? After all, it does make choices. Does the organism show evidence of foresight before it responds, or can this behavior be explained simply on the basis of simple direct response to stimuli? The same could be said of a sperm as it seeks out an egg to bore into it and reach the DNA territory within the nucleus. In so doing, it must compete with other sperm. There is a *distant objective* here: for the DNA of the sperm to mate with the DNA of the egg.

Psychologist-philosopher William James (1842–1910) noted that those who most fully base their present activities on *distant objectives* are said to be the most intelligent. In the human the cerebral cortex plays an important role in foreseeing distant objectives. This Chief Executive Officer, the cerebrum, makes a decision to react to stimuli on the basis of suspended judgment. Does consciousness reside here? How much brain matter is necessary for foresight? What behavior indicates foresight? It would be helpful to compare the neural anatomies and behaviors of animals representing a continuum of complexity.

To get some idea of the point at which consciousness may have arisen in the animal kingdom, it may be helpful to examine the line of progression of the human progenitors with a view to evaluating how complicated and flexible is the behavior of the earlier forms of life. We could start with single celled organisms, the Protozoa, and progress to those with more complicated nervous systems.

PROTOZOA

Examining the single-celled protozoan, *Amoeba proteus*, which looks like a mere dot of protoplasm, a tiny speck of Play-Doh, we see already some complicated behavior. To move, the animal simply flows into a long, filamentous extension proceeding from its body. It looks like all brain, a nerve cell with a long antenna extending outward. Does *Amoeba* exhibit any signs of "intelligence"? When the extension comes in contact with an obstruction to its path, it appropriately retracts. The cell, after a little delay, sends out another extension into which the animal flows in a different direction. Does the extension, upon contact with the object, send a neurological-type message into the cell for processing? Does the animal then, by an internal reflection process, make a conscious decision to go in another direction? Nerve cells in our own brains behave similarly. They send out extensions called axons and dendrites in certain directions, appropriate to their functions, in coordinating the incoming and outgoing messages.

Amoeba appears to make decisions. It shows choice in selection of food. It is attracted by the movements of its prey. Does *Amoeba* experience pleasure (joy) when it finds edible food? Indigestible, or undersized, particles may be ejected quickly and selectively. Does *Amoeba* experience displeasure or even disappointment when it discovers its prey is inedible?

All cells, including the cells of our bodies, are highly discriminating in the choices of foods they will ingest or reject. In making their choices, are these cells conscious?

A creeping *Amoeba*, touched lightly with a needle, responds negatively by withdrawing its extension and moving away. When a bright light is switched on, the protoplasm streams away from the stimulus. When *Amoeba* flees from light, is it afraid? If the animal comes repeatedly into a field of intense light, the number of attempts to continue in the original direction decreases as the number of trials increases. This conditioned behavior resembles the learning process of higher animals.

Is *Amoeba* conscious? Is it conscious of pain? When the extension of *Amoeba* is pricked with the needle, does this hurt? If not, why does the extension retract and the animal move away? When it changes direction, is it reasoning? In such a free-living single cell it is unknown how the tactile message, stimulated by touching the cell membrane, is transmitted through the body to the other side. The response makes sense to us; it is purposeful (directed toward appropriate ends). Does *Amoeba* know what it is doing? Is it conscious of its environment?

When we perform such purposeful activities, *we* know what we're doing. We can modify our response to such stimuli at will, in accordance with our reasoning ability. Are we scientifically (as contrasted with poetically) justified in using our own mentalities as a standard to evaluate the behavior of *Amoeba*? On the other hand, is objective physiology (just plain physics and chemistry applied to vital processes) adequate for interpretation of the animal mind? Neurologists are probing this problem. Perhaps they will finally determine, given the necessary techniques, that they can probe the psyche scientifically and thereby remove it from its private domain. So far the progress has been slow. Frequently, it appears they are spinning their wheels and getting nowhere.

The basic question being asked here is whether *Amoeba* is conscious in the same sense as the human is conscious. Are differences in mentality of *Amoeba*, as compared with the human, merely differences in degree of complexity? Is *Amoeba* on the same continuum of development as the human and, if so, what changes are necessary to go up the ladder to achieve a terrestrial existence?

We see here in one free cell all the basic elements of life represented: getting hungry and searching for food, reproducing, smelling (chemoreception), seeing (light detection) and feeling (touch detection). It is amusing to watch this little cell following our same desires. An anthropomorphic novelist could write a book on "The Human Nature of *Amoeba*": how it gets up in the morning, goes out as a hunter-gatherer, runs into trouble with competitors it fears, flees from what causes pain, and is attracted to what causes pleasure. It "hates" certain odors and "loves" others.

Amoeba is a sluggish creature, crawling about on the bottom of ponds, feeding on the products of photosynthetic cells that have descended from above. It lives a quite placid life there. Perhaps, at least for now, we should leave it in peace.

We turn now to *other* Protozoa, the ciliates. They have numerous short cilia, which are involved in movement. The ciliates dart about in search of food. Some ciliates living in the upper zones contain chlorophyll. These have red-pigmented, light-sensitive "eye spots" that aid in the attraction of ciliates to the light.

The behavior of the ciliate *Paramecium* has been studied extensively. The front end is more sensitive than the back end. If the front end is touched lightly with a fine point, a strong avoidance reaction occurs. In a temperature gradient it seeks a temperature of 24 to 28 degrees centigrade. In a culture tube the animals cluster together near the surface with their fronts pointed upward. In gentle water currents they align with their fronts upstream. In an electric current they head toward the cathode from which the electrons stream. They are also attracted to acidic conditions. Nutritionally, this makes sense, for places rich in organic food are frequently acidic. Micro-organisms living there give off carbon dioxide, which forms carbonic acid in water. In mazes *Paramecium* learns from trial and error.

Other Protozoa are the flagellates. Instead of having short cilia over their bodies, they have long, whiplike flagellae. Some of these flagellates form permanent colonies. In so doing they depend on each other. They specialize for different tasks. *Volvox* is a good example of early colonial aggregation and cellular specialization.

In asexual reproduction, certain cells lose their flagellae and enlarge. By repeated division these cells form a hollow mass of very small cells that recede within the colony. Later, when the parent dies and disintegrates, the cluster of reproductive cells escapes to form a new colony.

In sexual reproduction a cell in the colony enlarges to become a female sex-cell "ovum." Other cells divide repeatedly into flat bundles that contain up to 128 minute, slender "sperm." Inside the hollow ball of colonial cells, the sperm seek out the ovum. Of the 128 sperm, only one is selected for the next generation. Do the male sperm compete for the prize, the ovum? Perhaps the ovum does some selection of sperm. Studies of sexual selection are in order here.

The hollow ball of cells is something like a floating brain, with eyes. The pigmented cells resemble the retinal cells in our eyes — and the long, extending, protoplasmic connectors resemble nerve tracts reaching to the other cells of the hollow ball, just as our optic nerve extends from the retinal cells to the brain. In fact, when we go through the blastula stage of embryological development, the outside layer of the ball of cells does indeed become the brain, and some of these cells protrude as eye cups to form the retinas of our eyes. With its structure, *Volvox* is capable of considerable neurological organization and coordination of the cells toward common goals — such as orientation toward light and migration to favorable food supplies.

COELENTERATES

Proceeding from *Volvox*, the colonial ball of cells, we come to the coelenterates. These "jellyfish" represent a hollow ball of cells caved in. The inside cells differentiate into the digestive cavity. The outside layer specializes as nerve cells, forming a nerve network in the epidermis. These outside cells have long, slender processes that join with other cells. Some of the other cells are capable of muscular contraction.

These animals respond to food stimuli. They extend their tentacles and clasp food particles, then quickly retract them toward the mouth. The animal can sense edible objects. When a tiny piece of filter paper is placed around the mouth, it is readily grasped by the tentacles, then rejected. After a number of such experiences, the tentacles "learn" not to grasp the paper, but previously unused tentacles will grasp the paper. Finally, the paper is entirely refused.

When conditions are unfavorable, the metabolic rate is lowered. The symptoms resemble what humans call "depression." Some coelenterates such as *Hydra* have the ability to attach themselves to the substratum and "walk" by looping. As *Hydra* "decides" to walk, it shows some evidence of intentionally driven patterns of behavior, resembling those of highly developed organisms. Evidence of habitation is shown. *Hydra* reacts at first strongly to dripping water, but the response declines as the water continues to drip. Regular periods of light and darkness can induce a diurnal rhythm in *Hydra*.

The coelenterate, *Cassiopoeia*, observed in the waters around the Florida Keys, has brush-like appendages around its mouth. These are impregnated with algae. When the sun is bright, this jellyfish lies on its back, allowing the sun to hit its green algae to produce sugar. When the sun is not out, *Cassiopoeia* turns over and feeds on organic matter at the bottom of the pool.

FLATWORMS

The nervous system of planarian flatworms is more highly organized than the diffuse nerve net of coelenterates. In the head region beneath the eyes are two clusters of nerve cells joined to form the "brain," from which short nerve fibers extend to the eyes. Two longitudinal nerve cords pass backward, with many cross-connections.

Compared with a coelenterate, the planarian shows a much higher degree of coordination in the action of its parts. Planarians are easily taught to turn toward the light by placing food there. When they have been so taught, the information may be transmitted to other planarians by feeding them ground-up tissues of the taught specimens. The digestive tract of planarians is rather open, and food may be absorbed in vacuoles. But how the learned information is absorbed from the food is quite mysterious.

INSECTS

The insect nervous tract contains, in various segments, clusters of neurons equivalent to brains. There is a prominent cluster near the eyes and another between the wings. Insects are capable of associative learning. Only a small cluster of nerve cells is needed for organizing complicated behavior. By comparison, it is little wonder that the greatly enlarged human brain is capable of so much.

TIGER SWALLOWTAIL BUTTERFLY

The male tiger swallowtail butterfly, *Papilio glaucus* (at least the one studied near our home in Goshen, Indiana), establishes his territory to include tulip trees, *Liriodendron tulipifera*. Mating occurs in the vicinity of the tree. The female lays a single egg on a leaf of the tree.

The adult tiger swallowtail butterfly has newly emerged from its pupa case.

The larva is a change artist. It dresses for the occasion. Upon emerging from the egg, the tiny larva wears a brown coat with a ruffled collar and an ivory-colored belt. Before the larva has finished eating its egg case, the coat has changed to black. As a small, black speck, it will go unnoticed among the numerous black specks on the leaves. It spends much of its larval life resting in a little silken nest it spins on the middle of the leaf on which it feeds. As the larva grows, the ivory belt gets bigger and now looks like the insignia of a white eagle on top of the black coat. To a predatory bird, the larva may look like a bird dropping, with its dark background color and white marking. Birds almost certainly would pass up the larva as an inedible dropping. The larva makes short forays to the margin of the leaf to feed, spinning a path of silk from the nest as it goes. It follows the path of silk as it returns to the nest after feeding. Most of its life at this stage is therefore spent immobile on the leaf. Naturally, the bird-dropping disguise works best if the larva is motionless.

But as it matures, the larva feeds more voraciously — and thus becomes more mobile. The bird-dropping disguise is no longer useful. What it needs now is a green coat to match the green leaves on which it feeds for more and more extended periods. What it needs, Mother Nature provides. At the last larval molt of its black coat, it gets a green coat. It also has on its prothorax two large circles around a yellow disk on which is printed, however implausibly, an Arabic #10. It would be nice if every species carried a number. *Papilio glaucus* would then simply be #10 on the playing field of nature.

These yellow disks on which the #10 is imprinted persist through the pupal stage. They are thought to be light receptors. Emergence of the adult occurs at the first light of dawn before the butterfly predators are active — and while the atmosphere is still moist. The damp atmosphere will prevent too-rapid drying of the wings as they pass from the soft, flexible state to the hardened state.

As the mature green larva approaches its pupal stage, the green coat will no longer be appropriate for the occasion. It will attach itself to the bark of a tree and therefore needs a brown coat. After the larva has finished its last meal, it waits to leave the leaf and look for a place to transform itself. Meanwhile, the coat turns brown, without a molt. Upon excreting a drop of reddish-brown fluid, the mature larva heads for the next step of its metamorphosis.

Following emergence, the monarch butterfly also excretes a drop of reddish-brown fluid just before flight. In the age of superstition, such drops — with their origin unknown — were thought to be symbolic drops of blood, warning of ominous things to come.

If the costume changes of the swallowtail larva are considered ingenious, what is to come may be considered super-ingenious. In line with the ingenuity it shows in blending into its background, the larva chooses a place on the tree where, as a pupa, it will resemble a broken-off branch. To achieve an upward-directed position, the larva and subsequent pupa will need a security belt — to hold itself in that position.

How can a larva, with its limited brain, supply itself with a security belt? Mother Nature has the answer.

In producing the belt, the larva spins a pillow of silk and securely fastens it to the bark. After the pillow has been completely formed, the larva faces upward and fastens its abdominal claspers to the pillow. Next it attaches a strong silk thread to the bark on one side of its body, then elevates its foreparts and measuredly fastens the thread to the bark on the other side. After repeating this 20 or more times, the larva ends up with a strong security belt of the proper length. It need now simply crawl through the belt and throw it up over its back. It does this as though it had done it many times before. The belt is rested deep in a groove in the back. The larva now waits for the molt and ensuing pupal condition.

In molting, the body covering is pulled off head first and through the belt. The larva now lifts its abdomen free from the silk pillow, and the entire outer skin, including the claspers, is discarded. Thanks to the strong security belt, the larva does not fall from the bark. The larva then immediately refastens its new abdominal claspers to the pillow and completes its transformation. The larva, now a pupa, assumes a brown, wooden appearance and looks like a little broken twig sticking out of the trunk of the tree. It will overwinter in this condition, unnoticed by predators. How is that for ingenuity?! Even the white-breasted nuthatch will pass it by, despite the bird's search for a protein package to add to its food cache for winter, when protein is in short supply.

How did this ingenious behavior arise? Are we to believe that it arose by trial-and-error selection of mutations over the ages? If you would ask the swallowtail butterfly about this, and it could speak, you would get a very clear answer: "I am here to chew up these leaves and to leave a replacement for myself when I go. Everything I do is directed toward these two ends. Are there any more questions?" If you would ask the wisest man the same question, you doubtless would get an answer as fuzzy as a caterpillar, nonetheless filling many a philosophical treatise.

MONARCH BUTTERFLY

Another butterfly, one which does not overwinter in the north, but flies south for that purpose, is the monarch, *Danaus plexippus*. (One of its kin, *Danaus gilippus*, the queen butterfly, doesn't fly north, but stays put in its tropical home.) A discussion of the life cycle of the monarch butterfly was started in Chapter 4. Resuming that story, within a day or two of mating, the female lays an egg on the underside of the leaf of a young milkweed plant, which she finds after much searching. Usually just one egg is laid per leaf. But nature has its deviations from the normal. In one case a female laid four eggs within a radius of a half-inch on the underside of a single leaf. The entire history of these four was recorded on videotape through all the molts. Emergence of the four adults all occurred on the same morning at nearly the same time.

Again, this study dramatically demonstrates nature's ingenuity. What construction worker would not admire the precision-measuring ability and deft execution of a complicated plan (illustrated by the monarch as it grows up), each step being directed toward adaptive efficiency? I now zoomed in on one of the larvae and followed it through to full maturity.

After eating its egg case, which contains proteins essential for proper growth, the tiny green larva began to chew into the delicate leaf tissues. As the white sap oozed from the chewed areas, the larva chewed a sticky circle around itself, leaving a platform of leaf tissue on which it continued to feed. No ant is likely to cross this sticky barrier and pick up the tiny larva. The milk is not only useful as a barrier, it is repulsive to creatures other than monarch butterflies. There is evidence that birds learn not to eat the larvae. As the larva matures, it develops black and yellow warning stripes, announcing to an experienced bird what lies ahead if this larva is eaten.

As the larva grew, its skin became too tight. It was time to molt, so it crawled out of its skin. As it had eaten its egg case to conserve precious proteins, it now ate its skin. The surrounding milky barrier became a moat, as the larva had chewed through the leaf to leave an empty circle around itself. The larva avoided the mistake of chewing itself out of house and home at this point. It left enough of the leaf veins unchewed to hold the feeding platform. Furthermore, it provided an unchewed pathway for its exit when it had finished eating the platform.

When mature, the larva was ready to become a butterfly. It moved down to the ground and searched for a place to begin its pupal stage. In making its choice, there was plenty of opportunity for individual expression of ingenuity. (Some would call this real genius.) One of the four larvae — the one we're focusing on — found a common ragweed to meet its specifications as a good place for a two-week siesta. This would certainly not be a good location for an overwintering pupa, but the monarch comes from a family of tropical butterflies: the Daneidae. These do not overwinter in the North; rather, they seek their traditional homelands in the South. They require only about two weeks to reach the adult-butterfly stage.

Our larva found that the chosen leaf needed some work before it would remain in a horizontal position when crawled upon. This situation had to be remedied, for the developing pupal stage needed a horizontal perch so it could hang freely. Also, the emerging adult butterfly needed complete freedom while hanging and drying its delicate wings after crawling out of the pupal case. Otherwise, the wings might become permanently bent by obstructions. The larva, with its tiny brain, appeared to recognize all these problems.

The larva spun silk around the leaf stem, well out from the base of the leaf. While still spinning a strong strand of silk from a gland on its lower lip, it crawled up the stem of the ragweed and fastened this strand of silk to the stem above, thus forming a guy wire for supporting the leaf with its larval burden in a horizontal position.

The larva then went down to the underside of the leaf and spun its little pillow of silk, securely fastening it to the leaf stem. It is this pillow that would be needed to hold the delicate pupa through the contortions of its development. Having finished this attachment pillow, the larva waited 12 minutes, then fastened its abdominal claspers into the pillow. These claspers held only the larva, not the pupa. (The pupa is held by a bristle-tipped rod, the cremaster, which the pupa develops and inserts into the pillow. The claspers are discarded with the larval skin covering during the molt to the pupal stage. At this point the cremaster is the pupa's sole means of support.)

After hanging from the tip of its abdomen in a "J" shape for about 11 hours, the larva shed its skin, revealing a green bag with a golden chain and spots. It underwent considerable contortions in casting off its larval skin. It was here that the ingenuity of the larva was put to the test. The pillow supporting the larva hanging onto it by its cremaster had to stick fast to the stem of the leaf. If the green, soft pupa were to drop, it would have splattered like a bag of mush. ... It held!

A couple of weeks later, the adult monarch made its exit from the thin, cellophane-like pupa case. The wings of the newly emerged adult were soft and flexible, not suitable for flying. The adult had emerged just after dawn, before its predators were "on duty." The monarch quivered its wings, thereby eliminating wrinkles and allowing the flexible surfaces to hang out to dry and stiffen. It soon flew away. Fall was approaching, and it had to head south, perhaps as far as Mexico. Ahead lay many more opportunities for the expression of natural ingenuity. The monarch's amazing migration is another long story, already admirably told by others.

CICADA-KILLER WASP

Territorial behavior of the cicada-killer wasp, *Sphecius speciosus*, was also studied. Here are the results obtained by the author and his young assistant, Eric Kirk, at the Merry Lea Environmental Learning Center of Goshen College.

Early in July in four successive summers, 1990–93, male cicada-killer wasps were observed defending individual areas around particular holes in the ground. A male intruding into the territory of another was attacked vigorously with stinging attempts made as the two tussled on the ground near the holes. Occasionally, a male grasped the intruder with his feet and carried him away. The resident male then returned to his territory.

The male stood at attention, his antennae vibrating rapidly over the hole in his territory. When a female emerged from the hole, he dashed after her and captured her quickly. The two fell to the ground, and mating ensued directly. Extraneous males sometimes joined in, jumping on the backs of the mating pair. Such males made stinging thrusts toward the mating male and mating thrusts toward the female. At this time the wasps were marked with a tiny drop of paint on the tip of a long stick.

About two days after mating, the female returned and began looking for a place to dig a burrow. She dug with her front legs, throwing up the sandy soil with her back legs. This produced a trough leading into the burrow. The burrow went to a depth of about 1 foot (and 2 feet long). At the end was a chamber in which cicadas were placed. The chamber was elevated above the deepest part of the burrow. This would prevent flooding of the chamber, and its "booty," during rainstorms.

Having completed the burrow, the female made numerous trial flights and landings at the burrow. She then flew around the burrow in larger and larger circles, finally leaving for the tree area. Finding a cicada, she paralyzed it with stings. Next, she positioned the cicada head first while holding it with her feet. She swayed back and forth as if to sight the home airport. She then flew to the burrow and dragged the cicada in. She placed it in the chamber and laid an egg on the bottom of the thorax near the insertion of the front legs. When the larva hatched, it chewed a hole into the thorax of the cicada and fed on the internal tissues and fluids. Does this complicated behavior require any insight, or is it all "merely programmed" on long ribbons of DNA tapes to be read off by RNA ribosomes? It all looks highly intentional and anticipating.

Having matured, the larva moved away from the cicada and rolled around in the soil, creating the shape of the inside of its cocoon. It subsequently sucked fluid from a large sack at the tip of the abdomen and from the swellings on the sides of the body segments. These swellings arise just before the larva is ready to construct its cocoon. Next, the larva orally emitted fluid into the walls of the inside of the cocoon, creating a pliable, easily molded material. Silk was now spun into the internal layer. The outside wall took on a smooth form, the entire structure resembling a ceramic vase. The wall became hard, but it was still permeable to water and, therefore, air. The wasp, which developed inside this cocoon, emerged the following summer.

The male wasp's responsibilities do not end with mating. While the female dug her burrow, he guarded her, not against intruding males, but against another species of wasp — a large sphecid wasp, a cricket killer. When this cricket-killer wasp approached the burrow of the cicada-killer wasp, it was immediately attacked by the male cicada-killer wasp.

It was found that the modus operandi for the female cricket-killer wasp was to catch a cricket, paralyze it with a sting, and carry it down to the chamber that the female cicada-killer wasp had prepared for her own use. There the cricket-killer wasp laid an egg on the cricket. (A female cricket-killer wasp may attempt to scare off a cicada-killer wasp working on her burrow.)

The female cricket-killer wasp was frequently followed by tachina flies as she entered the burrow with a cricket. In this study a tachina fly laid four of its own eggs into the egg of a cricket-killer wasp. Four tachina fly larvae emerged from the wasp egg on the cricket. The larval tachina flies chewed up the cricket, changed into their pupal form in the soil, and emerged as adult tachina flies. This is one of many examples of parasitism that helps keep the rate of population growth of most species at an average rate of zero.

The behavior of the cicada-killer wasp leaves our minds swimming with intriguing questions. How does the male wasp recognize the cricket-killer wasp as a potential enemy? The cricket-killer wasp is really not much of a threat. All it does is use part of the burrow of the hard-working cicada-killer wasp for its own purposes. This merely spares the cricket-killer wasp some work. Observation shows that the cricket-killer wasp is, in fact, capable of digging its own burrow.

When the female cicada-killer wasp so laboriously digs her burrow far into the ground, does she have any idea why she is doing this? When she so meticulously makes trial touchdowns on the landing pad near the hole to the burrow, does she anticipate landing there with her huge cicada? The landing must be done deftly and quickly. Any other female spotting her landing, bearing a cicada with its bright-white underside, will immediately attempt to seize the prize from her. The flight to the landing pad must be straight and true. The female runs a tight ship. At the departure site, high in a tree, she holds the cicada in the aerodynamically correct position, head first, with the wings spread out like the flight feathers of an arrow. Then, without aid from a control tower, she prepares for the moment of departure. First, she makes sure all systems are go! With her front legs, she carefully wipes any dust from her eyes and antennae. Her wings quiver as she adjusts them for flight. Her checklist complete, she takes off, as if directed by electromagnetic waves, straight to the burrow. Is she on autopilot, or is she operating the controls manually? Indeed, how much, if any, of the total operation is under conscious control?

But much ingenuity is still called for underground. First, the hole must curve upward, so rainwater rushing into the burrow will not flood the chamber in which the cicada is to be placed. This engineering feat accomplished previously, the cicada is brought in, and the egg is carefully placed on the underside of the cicada so that the tiny emerging larva will find a soft spot to drill in.

The larva also has problems to solve. After maturing, it must remain in a dangerous place underground for about a year. Lurking around are chipmunk-like rodents (spermatophiles), that would as soon eat a larva as look at it. If unsuccessful in extracting a larva, the rodents will go after a newly emerged adult wasp. But the larva rests securely in its ceramic-like cocoon, safe from most predators and parasites. The larva has provided its own protection.

The female cricket-killer wasp also demonstrates some ingenious behavior. The cricket she has paralyzed with a sting may recover from the general anesthetic and walk away from the burrow. Apparently anticipating this, the wasp cuts off the back legs of the cricket, which could be used for escaping, before depositing her egg on the cricket's body.

LEAF-CUTTER ANTS

On our visits to Costa Rica, we observed the common leaf-cutter ants cutting out of the leaves small pieces, which they were carrying down to their underground fungus garden. One of the ants cut off an entire leaf. How could the ant manage a whole leaf? Simply! It stood above, holding the leaf firmly, and waited for help. Help soon came. Three other ants sawed pieces out of the leaf and carried them away. The original ant waited until there was only a small piece left. It then carried this small piece down to the underground burrow. The green leaves contain the sugars and other materials the ants need to nourish the fungi they grow underground in their dark garden.

As the ants cut pieces out of the leaves, it was noted that the leaves they cut were more free of visibly dark fungus colonies than were the general leaves of the tree on which they worked. After the cutter ants had finished their work and were carrying the pieces to the underground fungus garden, smaller ants traveled back to the den on the leaf pieces carried by the larger ants (as has been observed by others).

It is reported in the literature that these small hitchhikers actually protect the carrying ant from small flies of the family Phoridae, which become parasites by laying their eggs on the ants. These reports are based on the observation that the hitchhiking ants elevate their mandibles toward approaching flying insects.

But perhaps there is more to this story than that. Perhaps the small ants, being experts at fungus identification, proceed to the tree first and select leaves that are free from foreign fungi. Then, as the larger ants arrive and the cutters cut out their leaf pieces, the small ants simply crawl aboard and ride home on their pieces of leaf. Perhaps they continue to remain associated with that piece of leaf as it is deposited in the garden. These small ants, being experts at chemical identification of fungi, may be highly qualified for their gardening tasks. On exposing one of the underground gardens, I saw individual small ants confining their attention to small areas of the garden. It is reported in the literature that these small insects are gardener ants that weed out foreign fungi from the garden, leaving only the species — or even specific race — of the fungus of their choice, *Leucocoprinus gongylophorus*. This fungus is then consumed by the ants.

In the acts of apparent ingenuity enumerated here, are the insects conscious of what they're doing, or are they simply sleepwalking automatons? As compared with vertebrates, the behavior of insects does appear highly mechanical and stereotyped. Let us now proceed to examine the nervous systems and behaviors of various vertebrates.

FISH

Among the fish, the brain is a simple smooth swelling on the front end of the spinal cord. Large olfactory lobes project forward to near the olfactory and gustatory organs involved in smelling and taste. Much of the behavior of fish appears to be directed by chemoreception. Legendary is the ability of the salmon to remember the smells of home as it migrates from the oceanic feeding ground to the stream of its birth for reproduction. In an aquarium male guppy fish recognize certain females, even in the dark. They home in on them and pick at the dark speck on the brood pouch.

Behind the olfactory lobes are two optic hemispheres involved in processing visual stimuli. Fish have excellent eyesight, especially underwater.

Behind the optic lobes is the huge cerebellum. The fish is thereby equipped for highly organized muscular coordination. The cerebellum, anticipating movements, organizes muscular coordination.

The cerebrum is appropriately positioned between the olfactory and optic lobes. Here is where the incoming stimuli picked up by the sensors are processed. The message goes out to the muscles with instructions to move.

With fish, mental ability can easily be demonstrated with jars of food placed in their environment. The fish quickly learn the location of the jars and how to get into and out of them. They remember the pathway for many months. If perch are placed in an aquarium with minnows, they readily dash at and catch the minnows. If the minnows are separated from the perch by a glass partition, the perch crash into the glass in pursuit. The perch then learn by trial and error to cease and desist from pursuing the minnows, even after the glass partition is removed.

AMPHIBIANS AND REPTILES

Except for the greatly reduced size of the olfactory lobes, the brain of the amphibian or reptile is similar to that of the fish. The behavior of an adult frog is directly influenced by visual perception. It appears to recognize sex by the swollen sack on the throat of its fellow frog. The male is stimulated by a string of eggs to extrude sperm. This behavior appears automatic, as do sense of direction, location in space, and a positional sense of the visual field.

The amphibians learn not to snap at inedible objects. If they are shocked electrically as they begin to eat edible food, they will learn not to eat that food. The memory of the experience may last up to five days. Toads eat bumblebees with the stings removed. They learn to reject bumblebees with stings and afterward will avoid them on sight. (See Thorpe 1963.)

BIRDS

Compared with the brains of amphibians and reptiles, the brain of the bird shows a greatly expanded cerebrum and cerebellum at the front of the spinal cord. In the mammal, this smooth brain is represented as part of the limbic system, which becomes overgrown by a large convoluted cerebrum. In this respect, even we mammals have bird brains "down under." This limbic system may play an important role in the subconscious activities of our minds. The Austrian neurologist, Sigmund Freud (1856–1939), emphasized the importance of this system in our psyches. It appeared to him that many psychological problems arise from conflicts between our subconscious and conscious mentalities. In fact, many of us hide a secret admiration for the simple lives of birds, which lack the large, expanded cerebrum typical of mammals. Perhaps those of us who are critical of a book on "The Human Nature of Birds" would be less critical of any book that may be written on "The Bird Nature of Humans."

The smooth cerebrum, along with the cerebellum of the bird, plays an important role in controlling neuromuscular coordination. Being an aviator, the bird needs quick and accurate autopilot control. In the quicksilver life of a bird, the large, convoluted cerebrum characteristic of a mammal would actually be an encumbrance. The bird must make instantaneous decisions as it flits hither and yon among the branches of the trees. Any time spent "philosophizing" by means of a convoluted cerebrum might well spell doom for a bird. Reasoning its way out of trouble is not important for the bird. It can simply fly from its unanticipated problems. Simple "knee-jerk reactions" appear to play a predominant role in the life of a bird. Who is more adapted to natural living: the bird, or the creature with the most convoluted brain, the human?

The bird has a daily dilemma that is uniquely faced by winged ones. For flight it must keep its weight down. This may be why birds characteristically excrete ballast before taking flight. At the same time it needs a continuous supply of food to support its rapid metabolic rate. The normal temperature of the blood of a bird would spell "fever" for us. This high metabolic rate is needed for the quicksilver life of a bird. Even the mentality of a bird has been described as "flighty," and so it is.

Going along with the bird's snap judgment is a snapshot memory. Click, and it has the picture. Such imprinting in birds is legendary. Along with this memory goes the ability to imitate and recite. These mysterious properties of bird mentality are frequently interpreted as examples of human-like intelligence.

One of the greatest points of confusion in the interpretation of animal behavior concerns the difference between memory and intelligence. The confusion is almost excusable, for memory and intelligence are intertwined. Intelligence involves taking stored memories and synthesizing from them a new creation.

Human educators have a persistent problem here. They are supposed to be able to evaluate the "academic" potential of students. The mistakes made in this area are of historic proportions. Students considered to be of low-grade academic merit included Gauss, the developer of the Gaussian curve (normal curve), which converted hopeless levels of uncertainty about nature into confident levels of certainty; Mendel, who used the binomial theorem to bring order out of chaos in heredity; and Einstein, who developed the equation that clarified relationships between energy and matter. These students refused merely to mirror the thoughts of their evaluators who were trying to make them over into their own images. Gauss, for example, became so obsessed with his curves — which he realized would enable students to deal with the probabilities that pervade all of nature — that he neglected the conventional "exact" mathematical abstractions. Meanwhile, the good grades were going to the students who could best regurgitate the ruminations of their teachers. These were considered the most intelligent — and they were awarded the rights, the rites, and the privileges.

In the world of nature, however, imitation may be a great aid in the quest simply to survive. How many lives of ducklings may have been spared as the ducklings closely imitated the behavior patterns of their mothers? I once made a study of wood ducks in a woodland pond. I observed that the adults imitated each other. When one found some unusual food, such as red buds springing from a fallen maple tree, it was not long before the entire flock joined in the feast. When a male picked up some wood chips on top of a snag, a potential nest site, the female imitated him. The pair then flew together, swam together, fed together, preened together, and, yes, slept together.

The newly hatched ducklings followed each other and closely imitated the behavior of the mother. When she swam, they swam, when she fed, they fed — in the same area and in the same manner. When she perched, they perched, when she preened, they preened, when she slept, they slept. At one point the mother picked duckweed from around the bill of a duckling. Immediately thereafter, the duckling picked the duckweed from around the bill of the mother.

Many birds are quick to imitate vocalizations. The tooth-billed bowerbird of Australia not only learns quickly to imitate the surrounding birds on a daily basis, but also the ringing of a telephone. An Australian naturalist told us that mimicry of the ringing of a telephone may be transmitted from one tooth-billed bowerbird to another throughout the entire series of territories. Some birds, such as the chaffinch, apparently learn the full territorial song from other chaffinches. But they have not been reported to incorporate the song of other species into their full territorial song. They do, however, add such songs to their subsong, a low-volume song of birds not related to territorial communication.

Antiphonal singing is common in birds. Henschel (1903), a famous musician of the day, relates how a caged bullfinch learned portions of "God Save the King." A canary, in turn, learned this song from the bullfinch. The two birds then sang it antiphonally. The bullfinch would pause after the third line, a little longer than the melody warranted, whereupon the canary would take up the tune from where the bullfinch had stopped, and finish it properly. The episode was repeated dozens of times.

The imitative and stereotypical behavior of a bird does not preclude its capacity for associative learning. Birds are highly sensitive to space and shape. This ability can be used to advantage in studying their powers of association. Given the appropriate food as a reward, the birds will perform associated tasks. Such studies reveal that birds can discriminate between circles and triangles — and between small and large shapes. Like humans, they can be fooled by optical illusions that make a shape appear larger or smaller. Thorpe (1963) considers this to be evidence that birds are capable of insight or internalized judgment.

In nature the power of association in birds is most remarkably illustrated by the honey guides. First they associate the buzzing of bees with honey. Then they frequent the habitats of ratels, baboons, or even humans, leading them on by agitated chatterings and flutterings. Reaching the goal, they sit silent and still in nearby cover until the "ally" has opened the beehive and made the contents available. The birds have specialized enzymes for digestion of beeswax.

In Costa Rica, as we were observing a pair of violaceous trogons, the male suddenly flew to a huge wasp nest nearby and entered through a hole in the side. The female perched outside and emitted low clucking notes. (Among birds nesting in holes, one parent closely guards the nest site when its mate is inside.) A predator or egg thief may be reluctant to enter a wasp nest even though the wasps had abandoned the nest. Other birds are known to nest in bee or termite nests, some with termites living in the same nest, though in separate compartments.

The South American spinetail not only builds its nest close to colonies of wasps' nests, but invariably attaches to its nest a portion of a snake's shed skin. The North American crested flycatcher places a snakeskin in the lining of its nest. In Costa Rica, near La Selva Biological Reserve, we found the nest of the yellow-crowned euphonia in a fence post with a snakeskin draped near the hole. Many species of birds, wood thrushes, catbirds, blue jays, and cardinals put conspicuous pieces of plastic on the perimeter of their nest. Such strips of plastic resemble snakeskins. In Arizona the cactus wren may place huge pieces of white or red plastic on its bulky nest.

In building their nests, birds employ both innate and learned behavior. Some birds, such as male African weaver finches, build faulty nests if they are deprived in their youth of nesting materials with which they can learn the finer points of nest-building (Collias and Collias 1984). Young ruby-throated hummingbirds, particularly the females, spend much time picking and probing nesting materials before finally leaving the nest (personal observations).

Most, if not all, insect and bird behavior, such as described above, appears innate (not original). How the behavior originated, and then became innate, is an ethological question. It is the question treated by Thorpe in his *Learning and Instinct in Animals* (1963). He describes his experiments with *Drosophila melanogaster* in which it was found that larvae raised on peppermint-flavored food seek that type of food for mating and egg-laying. This is an example of the transmission of learned behavior. It's a start toward understanding the basis for innate behavior.

Skutch (1996), summarizing his long bird-observation career in which he gave attention to evidence of special intelligence, says, "In many years of watching free birds, I have rarely seen behavior that I was fairly certain was not innate."

The rare exceptions include the gray catbird that nested near his boyhood home in Maryland. When young Skutch placed his hand, palm up, over the nest containing young birds, the parent catbird pecked the top of his hand. But when he turned the palm down toward the bird, the catbird shrunk from the hand. Skutch concluded that the catbird had some idea of how a human hand works.

Recognizing how a hand works, however, would be not especially remarkable for a bird. The bird may have simply recognized the similarities between a human hand and its own foot. After citing a few more examples of "special intelligence," Skutch concludes, "Birds appear to have as much mental capacity, call it instinct or call it intelligence, as would be useful for them. To have more might be upsetting." This is a profound sizing up of the issue of animal intelligence. One species in particular should pay attention to this observation. Is human intelligence upsetting the entire ecosystem?

On a trip to Australia we observed an example of bird behavior that looked novel. In the passion flower, the brush-like stamens are elevated far above the nectary. In Costa Rica, the rufus-tailed hummingbirds were observed getting their heads visibly dusted with pollen from the stamens overhead as they probed the nectary below. Since there are no hummingbirds in Australia, but passion flowers are common, I wondered what would pollinate the passion flower there. It soon became evident that honeyeaters of various species were serving this function in Australia.

Pollen is rather sticky — and hard for the bird to remove from its own head. This situation calls for some ingenuity. Among 12 Lewin's honeyeaters being observed, one apparently had originated a scheme to

A honeyeater gets its head dusted with pollen from the stamen brush of the passion flower.

avoid head-dusting by the pollen. Wherever it flew over the stand of passion flowers, it used its beak to pinch off the stamen brush, allowing the pollen-bearing anthers to fall free from the flower. The bird then proceeded to probe the nectary below, while keeping its head free from the sticky pollen grains.

Such a habit (perhaps discovered by trial and error) might, by an imitation process, be transmitted throughout the entire honeyeater population. Though we saw only one example of stamen-clipping at Lake Eacham, birds are prone to imitate behavior, especially behavior involved in feeding. There may even be some such feeding imitation *between* species. What would be the fate of the passion flower if stamen-clipping were practiced extensively by birds?

In Florida we did observe imitative bird behavior in connection with feeding. Approaching a quiet pool along the road, we spotted a snowy egret, *Egretta thula*, flying back and forth, dangling its yellow feet just above the surface of the water. Occasionally, the bird bent its long neck down near the surface and caught a fish with its beak.

Meanwhile, a common egret, *Casmerodius albus*, perching on a snag nearby, appeared to be observing the fishing methods of the snowy egret. The snowy egret has a black bill and *yellow* feet, whereas the common egret has a yellow bill and *black* feet.

Presently, the common egret made a pass over the water in the same area where the snowy egret had been successfully fishing. It lowered its black feet close to the surface of the water after the fashion of the yellow-footed snowy egret. The common egret repeated this fishing technique two additional times, without success. Finally, it perched again.

We had earlier observed a snowy egret using its yellow feet in search of prey in the tide pools of the Pacific Ocean. If the yellow feet are indeed used as lures, perhaps the yellow bill of the common egret is also used as a lure. Many fishing birds have attractive red bills. The black skimmer, in fishing, dips the bill into the water in flight. The part of the bill just above the water is bright red. The part that enters the water is black. Perhaps the red just above the water attracts fish, while the inconspicuous black part actually does the catching. Numerous other fishing birds have brilliantly colored red or yellow legs and colored beaks. Some waders, such as the reddish egret and little blue heron, have beaks with distinctive dark tips. The African yellow-billed stork appears to use its bill as a fish lure. The bird inserts its wide-open beak into the water and holds it there until fish swim into it. The roseate spoonbill moves its red bill back and forth through the water where fish gather. The bright-yellow or red legs of wading birds may serve as lures for fish. Flamingos are similarly equipped with colored bills having dark tips.

There are some cases in which birds might be expected to imitate feeding behavior of other species, but do not. Among these are the house finches. In winter, the slate-colored juncos at our bird feeder actively scratch snow off the sunflower seeds. House finches, watching them, chase the juncos away and eat the exposed seeds. In no case, however, have I observed a house finch scratching away the snow. These finches originally inhabited the southwestern US, where snow is seldom encountered. It would be interesting if house finches living in the Snow Belt ever do acquire the snow-scratching habit. Of course, it must be noted that the general feeding habits of the junco involve more scratching on the ground than do those of the house finch. But even in ground-scratching situations, the house finches appear to learn little, if anything, about scratching from the juncos. House finches feed regularly on the same piles of sunflower seeds at our tray feeders. The house finches benefit directly from the juncos' habit of exposing the fresh seeds by scratching, but they do not appear to imitate this junco behavior.

In our front yard in Goshen, Indiana, are some anthills on which numerous ants swarm in late summer. Above them a rather listless robin, with beak partly open on a hot day of July 22, 1994, was perched in a spruce tree. Suddenly, the robin flew down and landed squarely on the hill over which the ants were running around. Soon the ants began creeping over its feathers. The robin spent 22 minutes picking up ants as they walked upon its feathers, crushing the ants with its bill, then depositing them into the downy feathers on its body. It was clear that the robin was squeezing the ants, not merely picking them up. In some cases the squeezed ant dropped to the ground, immobilized by the squeeze.

This behavior has been observed by scientists among 40 families of passerine birds, comprising some 200 to 250 species. Ants secrete formic acid, which is an effective repellent of insect parasites. Wood ants can spray formic acid as far as a foot.

Are there benefits to be derived from this behavior and, if so, how would a bird evaluate these benefits? It has been theorized that birds perform this ritual of "anting" to repel parasites. It is thought that the formic acid squeezed from ants serves to discourage lice, fleas, etc. In support of this theory, grackles have been reported to pick up mothballs placed by gardeners around plants as insect repellents, then rub the mothballs into their feathers. Some birds use flowers, such as the marigold (which contains the insecticide pyrethrum), to rub over their bodies. Other birds use the peelings of citrus fruits, particularly limes, to press into their feathers. The peels contain D-limonene, another powerful insecticide.

In addition to the anti-parasite theory, Dennis (1981) offers a further interpretation of anting behavior. In his view, the behavior is primarily related to stimulation of skin metabolism during the molting period. Not only are irritating substances applied for this stimulation, but also for heat itself. A remarkable, almost incredible, report is given of the use of fire in the preening operation:

> Maurice Burton, an English writer with the British Museum of Natural History, topped any accounts of birds anting with fire with his stories of tame rooks. One, on its own initiative, learned to hold a match in its toes and peck at the head until it burst into flames. The lighted match was then applied to the undersides of the wings. Another bird not only anted with lighted matches but "wallowed" in burning straw. It performed its fire act many times and was said never to have been burned.

If this story is true, it certainly gives the impression that the bird is conscious of what it is doing. Is the rook conscious, or is its behavior programmed onto its DNA tapes in the process of natural selection? We simply do not know enough to make a judgment on this. Is it possible that all the complicated behavior we observe among animals is programmed into their nervous system to be performed unconsciously, automatically?

Birds are most famous for their incredible powers of space perception. Without maps or instruments, birds fly from their breeding sites thousands of miles to winter homelands, only to return to the exact spot the following spring. For these activities the smooth brain of the bird appears adequate. The logic produced by this brain is simple and direct, as contrasted with the logic of the mammal brain. It may be partly this simple logic that makes us love the bird: It is such a relief from the complicated, and often "convoluted," logic of our own brains.

MAMMALS

The cerebral cortex of the mammal's brain is a neocortex. It overarches all other brain structures and further expands the layer of its integrating surface cells by convoluting the surface. The mammal, in contrast to the bird, must stand its ground and solve problems with foresight and strategy, outwitting prey and predator. The expansive cerebral cortex performs this function as a gigantic computer might.

This development of the cerebral cortex has proceeded so far as to set one mammal, the human, apart from nature itself. It may be at this point that consciousness has arisen. Cerebration has instigated an awakening, an enlightenment. This expansion of the cerebral cortex, however, comes with a price. Even brief deprivation of food or oxygen from this rapidly metabolizing tissue mass leads to permanent brain damage. The brain is the chief focus of disability among humans. Considerable time and effort are devoted to producing drugs intended to eliminate mental anguish.

It is the cerebrum that is responsible for far-reaching decisions. It is this part of the brain that is of special interest to students of cognition and consciousness. It is this part of the brain that has led to human civilization. Most important is its capacity for memory and integration.

Short-term memory involves chemical facilitation of the switches between one neuron and another, the synapses. The chemicals involved in this facilitation, or inhibition, are called neurohumors. The chemical effects of these neurohumors are temporary, as the chemicals are soon removed enzymatically. Long-term memory involves structural changes in the neurons. Just as *Amoeba* extends its pseudopodia in moving, the neural cells extend their processes when stimulated. This brings the dendrites closer to the axons that receive the nervous stimulation. Finally, the connection may become fixed as in long-term memory. If this fixation is genetically controlled, the memory may become part of the fixed behavioral patterns known as instincts.

The extension of neuronal processes, of course, requires protein synthesis. A characteristic of aging is a slowdown in protein synthesis. This helps explain why aging is associated with decreased ability to form new memory pathways. Meanwhile, the older fixed pathways still persist. It is therefore important for younger individuals to have pleasant experiences and memories, then through repetition ensure their fixation. This will be their senior-citizen cache of life's experiences.

Why a decrease in rate of protein synthesis is characteristic of aging is being investigated. A prominent theory is that the flow of nutrients to the cells slows during the aging process. This is in turn due to the accumulation of waste products of metabolism collecting in the connective tissues of the body, causing these tissues to become hardened and more impenetrable to nutrients from the body fluids. In youth the connective tissues are more soluble and elastic than they are in old age.

If an old-age mammal suffers a fracture of its neuronal fibers involved in reflexes between sense organs and muscles, restoration of the neuronal connection is difficult. At this point a younger animal (or human) can form alternate reflexes quickly — to restore nerve/muscle coordination. The older creature remains shaky and uncoordinated. Many neurological diseases can lead to similar behavioral abnormalities.

Actually, the aging process begins already shortly after birth, possibly even before. A young embryonic cell, not yet determined for its fate of colonial living in the body, is well-nourished and highly flexible. As the cells specialize for their adult tasks, they lose their youthful flexibility. Free-living cells, such as *Amoeba*, do not experience the aging process. Any difficulties in absorbing nutrients through their thin outer coverings, due to accumulation of metabolic wastes, are minimized by cell division.

Beneath the cerebral cortex are subliminal brains, the thalamus and hypothalamus. These give the emotional "go" signals and control flight-or-fight behavior. The cerebral cortex ultimately controls activity of these lower neuronal centers. Decerebrate cats, lacking the inhibition that the cerebrum normally exercises in control of the hypothalamus, fly into immediate rage in response to meager stimuli. The hypothalamus has appropriately been called the seat of the emotions.

The sensory and motor nerves that control vital bodily functions — such as breathing and heartbeat — operate almost automatically. This autonomic nervous system is located diffusely throughout the entire body. In this respect it resembles the primitive condition seen in colonial Protozoa or a flatworm. It runs the body on autopilot, with minimal (backup) "conscious" control by the pilot, the cerebrum.

In this comparative review of the increasing complexity of the nervous systems of animals, it is obvious that the human nervous system is the most complex. This might indicate that the human is the most conscious of all animals. It is obvious that consciousness is related to elevated activity of the nervous system, this is why elimination of stimuli such as noise and light contributes to sleep. Various drugs which inhibit activity of the nervous system also contribute to unconsciousness.

Griffin (1992) argues that any animal may be conscious to some extent. They do not slavishly follow genetic instructions but modify their actions on a basis of experience, and succeed in obtaining an apparently desired result. Some modern scholars maintain there may be a conscious component in the behavior of any animal, but we err in our interpretations only in going too far when we use higher human consciousness to interpret lower animal consciousness. John S. Kennedy, in *The New Anthropomorphism* (1992), claims such interpretations are often extremely misleading. He supports "neobehaviorist" interpretations. Though maintaining a mechanistic approach, he accepts internal processing in the causation of behavior. Many behavioral scientists support this sort of interpretation of animal psychology. Perhaps the differences between the conscious states of the various animals represent only differences in degree of complication. Regarding consciousness of pain and suffering on one hand and pleasure and joy on the other, the degree of these feelings may differ only in degree among the various animals. Regarding this, *Homo sapiens* may indeed be the chief primate.

The debate over human primacy has raged since the time of Darwin and has abated little since. Even today, few give the spotted owl and the human creature equal primacy. Addition of human consciousness appears to be the straw that breaks the back of nature. Is this good? The debate is reflected today as the biosphere-centered environmentalists take on the human-centered environmentalists. What is the place, if any, for the human being in nature? If the human species does not properly perceive this place and put itself into it, nature will do the job — with nature's traditionally inhumane methods. The future will determine who is right: the biosphere-centered or the human-centered environmentalists.

Focusing attention on the earth's ecosystems, Stephen Gould (1940–), in his book, *Full House* (1996), likes to view evolutionary success not in terms of individual species, but in terms of entire ecosystems. He complains that many evolutionists place the human animal as the chief representative of evolutionary progress. Gould would rather see the gamut of all species representing this progress. Maintaining that *Homo sapiens* is a mere twig on the big bush of evolution, Gould decries the fact that this species has made such a big deal of itself. But while extolling the virtues of Mozart and Beethoven, he inconsistently minimizes the role of individual initiative in promoting such excellence. Such initiative has been involved also in the advancement of science.

Gould, obviously promoting a socialist agenda, deplores the tendency for certain classes to dominate other classes. He claims that Charles Darwin at heart did not like this either, but as a beneficiary of British imperialism, he moderated his opinion on this matter. (What, incidentally, would the British royalty think about reducing the far-flung British empire to the status of a little twig on the evolutionary bush?)

It should be pointed out here that Wallace — though a commoner and not a member of the royal class — supported a view of the primacy of *Homo sapiens* far in excess of anything Darwin might have suggested. Though Wallace had collaborated closely with Darwin in developing the theory of natural selection, he refused to believe that humans and apes had a common ancestry. To him, the human is so unique that a special-creation theory must be invoked to explain the origin of *Homo sapiens*.

The question of the primacy of humanity is intimately involved in the debate over sexual selection. Was it sexual selection, natural selection, or a combination of both that pushed humans to a position of dominance over nature? In his *Origin* book Darwin emphasizes natural selection for general evolution, though he had mentioned sexual selection as a way of explaining a few select cases. He later added the *Descent* book in order to elaborate on these select cases. Some authors evidently believe that Darwin combined his discussions on sexual selection and the descent of man into a single book simply to put both discussions behind him in a single housecleaning. Whether Darwin realized it or not, however, the two discussions are directly related. Was it natural or sexual selection that led to the origin of human consciousness, or was it a combination of both, with sexual selection providing the impetus? Could the human intellect, once developed, consciously speed up continued expansion of itself by a process of artificial selection?

H.J. Muller warned that a free society, not bound by traditional taboos about playing God with the germ plasm, might practice artificial selection for superior intellect, thereby enabling that society to rule the world. Would this be good? The basic question is: What is the brain for? Is it for adaptation to nature, or are their more ethereal aims for development of human-type intellect?

With respect to adaptation to nature, single-celled animals get along quite nicely, thank you, without brains. But there may be additional adaptive advantages to be gained by the grouping of cells into adaptive cooperatives. Such colonial living would require some means of integration of these cells as a unit, some type of administrative headquarters. This calls for specialization of some of the colony's cells into a nervous system. Is consciousness the inevitable outcome of this process carried to its logical, or illogical, conclusion — as in the human brain?

What is the destiny, or fate, of the human intellect? This is a hard question to answer, but we aren't precluded from trying. Historically, those who have tried to probe these questions were called prophets. Prophets, generally, can be grouped two ways: the pessimists and the optimists. The former are called "naturalists," hopeless predictors of doom. The latter are called "mystics," hopeful saints of salvation.

Intuitively, we know there is a creature that has taken animal ingenuity beyond the programmed stage of behavior to the stage of hindsight, insight, and foresight — the stage of consciousness. *We* as humans are capable of reflective imagination, of putting mental images together to draw conclusions. In our daily activities, we are aware of the increased efficiency to be derived from planning ahead, in light of past experience, instead of relying solely on trial and error in the performance of tasks. This is commonly known as "wisdom." In this, an element of "consciousness" (*knowing* what we are doing) appears to be involved.

Consciousness is a strange state. It is perceived as being public, but it is experienced only privately. Universalizing one's private experience to the outside world is intellectually dangerous. Therein lies the pitfall of anthropomorphism. This subjective evaluation of other creatures is responsible for many misunderstandings. How can we objectively judge whether a living organism outside ourselves shares our conscious experience? With humans, speech is helpful. With other species, behavior tends to be the key.

Consciousness is like electricity. It is not observed directly, but is related to turning on a light bulb. Our consciences tell us what to do and what not to do. Is it conceivable that all the mystery connected with consciousness is simply due to the apparently immense complexity of the nervous system, and that once consciousness has been deciphered, it will turn out to be as simple as DNA? In *Scientific Search for the Soul* (1994), Francis Crick appears to have aspirations along these lines.

It is staggering to realize that there is only one individual on earth I can be sure is conscious. That individual is myself. Any other conclusion is merely an inferential deduction. I can be reasonably sure, however, that most fellow humans are conscious. The evidence is based on the fact that they can speak. By means of words (mental images) they can communicate their perceptions of consciousness. By comparing their perceptions with my own, I infer that they are conscious. Certain behavioral patterns that parallel these perceptions are also helpful in drawing these conclusions. Yet, a dentist, who has the mouth of a patient loaded with clamps, is not quite sure whether the patient is conscious of pain, since the patient cannot speak. Likewise, because wild animals don't effectively speak to us, we can't be sure they're conscious. We have only behavioral analogies to go on, and these analogies can be deceiving.

In a way, it would be comforting to know that wild animals are not conscious. If they are conscious, it may be presumed that they are capable of experiencing misery. This is a sobering thought. The entire method of operation of nature appears to be competition for survival of the fittest. This process extends up to and includes *Homo sapiens*. How much misery, frustration, and downright pain are involved in this process of survival of the fittest? All individuals are continuously frustrated in their attempts to realize their maximum potential. As a result, the struggle for existence includes the possibility of limitless suffering.

From a humanitarian point of view, this scene appears awful. From an ecological point of view, though, it is awesome. How the marvelous adaptive behavior of animals can be derived from a simple process of competition is a perpetual source of wonder. A totally favorable view of nature as wondrous and awesome (not awful) would result if it were determined that nature is not conscious of misery — perhaps not conscious at all.

Viewing the complexity of nature's nervous systems, along with the equally marvelous behavior patterns under nervous control, leaves us in awe. Still more awesome is the question of how all this originated, along with its purpose. A poem by William Cullen Bryant beautifully bespeaks the longing many of us have to understand not only our own destinies, but those of *all* Mother Nature's children:

TO A WATERFOWL

Whither, midst falling dew,
While glow the heavens with the last steps of day,
Far, through their rosy depths, dost thou pursue
Thy solitary way?

He who from zone to zone,
Guides through the boundless sky thy certain flight,
In the long way that I must tread alone,
Will lead my steps aright.

Poets have a way of asking profound questions, then giving less profound answers. Will the same natural laws that lead a waterfowl aright also lead the human aright, or is the human too "unnatural" for this?

In the world of nature, the law of energy conservation controls behavior. But in the world of the human, the mind controls behavior. The destiny of the waterfowl is determined. It remains only to work out the details. What, if any, destiny is outlined for the human? Definitive answers to this question have escaped the probing human mind from the dawn of civilization. What is the utopia (niche) for the human? The utopia of the larval monarch butterfly is simply delineated — a healthy milkweed leaf. But the question of a human utopia is as complicated as the human mind itself. We may initially ask how this special problem of human destiny arose in the first place.

A reader following the arguments presented in this book may be struck with a nagging question: If, in the process of sexual competition, exhibitory embellishment and ostentatious display confer selective mating success, what is to keep the display traits from developing indefinitely? A partial answer may be "natural selection," which counteracts the excesses of sexual selection in the natural world. Mother Nature has rules on this point. Her children can go just so far in selection for a trait, then the natural law of energy constraints will stop further development of that trait. It is not necessarily the most ostentatious, but it is the most energy-efficient which will inherit the earth.

If the trait involved is the brain itself, however, that brain may be used to eliminate natural controls to population growth. The result may be freedom from Mother Nature's inhumane methods of birth control: parasites, predators, and a plethora of pernicious forces that can't wait to bump you off in the night (or day). But, according to the law of compensation, there must be a downside.

The free (liberal) consuming stage of the life cycle, the sexual generation, stands in marked contrast to the conservative, producing, vegetative generation. Whereas the vegetative phase actually stores energy in the form of food, the sexual phase exploits this store of energy. Expenditure of energy in the sexual phase is, of course, for a good cause. Gained from the sexual phase are new genetic combinations for use in exploring alternate lifestyles. All species balance the vegetative and sexual phases of the life cycle at optimal levels for survival of the fittest. Biologically, this is known as the alternation of generations.

Since the sexual phase is so energy-consuming, it is of little wonder that successful species reduce sexual activity to the bare minimum deemed necessary for adaptation. An extreme example of this is the 17-year cicada. Out of the 17 years of the life cycle, only about a month is dedicated to the sexual phase.

Nature uses various strategies for minimizing sexual activity. One of the most ingenious methods is to have the sexual phase triggered by environmental change itself. Common plant lice are good examples of this. Under the uniformly warm, sunny conditions of summer (optimal for plant growth), aphids reproduce rapidly by birth not involving sex. But when the environment changes drastically, as when fall approaches, the sexual phase is initiated. Even crowding may trigger this response as the aphids develop into winged males and females. They leave the plant, mate, and explore new environments. The adult female may over-winter in this stage. The following spring the mated female's offspring, now genetically variable, try out for the new environmental conditions. Only the genetically fittest offspring will succeed in the competition, as the new vegetative phase is reinstituted.

As an extreme case of this alternation of generations, naturalists exploring the wildlife of Lake Baikal, a deep body of water in Russia (a uniform environment), found a rotifer species consisting just of females. This was described as an all-female species. However, when the rotifers were grown in the laboratory (under changed conditions), males and females developed. They mated, and the sexual generation was inaugurated.

Any species not assuming an optimal balance between the producing (vegetative) and consuming (sexual) phases of the life cycle will naturally suffer extinction in the face of natural competition for the limited energy supplies in its niche. This is in accordance with the law of natural selection.

In this scheme the human appears to be an exception — at least temporarily. Having a greatly expanded cognition potential, the human can become an unnatural outlaw and proceed indefinitely with the sexual phase of the life cycle. Only the sky seems to be the limit. The entire earth is becoming studded with artificial displays of glitter and glamour, which confer temporary political prowess and competitive advantage. Outside of the limitations of nature what could stop this "progress"? One can hope that the human intellect itself may recognize the economic imbalance resulting from competition within the human species. We see this re-enacted in human history as empires rise and fall; there is constant political strife between the liberals and conservatives (spenders versus savers). Prophets of doom arise under these conditions. Their views are based on observing historical examples of the rise and fall of civilizations, as well as on observations of nature. It is often those who have lived close to nature who make attempts to keep artificiality under control. These prophets begin to ask whether it is the meek — or the self-aggrandizing — who will inherit the earth. At this point such prophets may head back to nature in search of a more simple lifestyle. Such movements are often backed with religious zeal, as in monasteries.

The Protestant Reformation in Europe included movements protesting the dominance of state churches. This state-church system was not slow to use force (physical, psychological, and economic) to promote its own politico-religious-economic interests. Individual liberties were trodden underfoot. After this state-church system had become sufficiently ripe, it was time for revolt. Among those who revolted were the Anabaptists, so-called because they nullified state-church baptism and rebaptized members of their own communities. This, of course, could not be tolerated by the state-church system, jealous as it was of political power. The Anabaptists paid dearly for their disregard for the prevailing "powers-that-were." The deaths of some 6,000 Anabaptists are recorded in their thick book, *The Martyrs Mirror*. Some of those who escaped the massacre fled to other lands, such as America, land of the free. In fact, their presence in the colonies of United States was influential in framing the separation-of-church-and-state concepts in the US Constitution. (See Sweet 1930.) They attempted to operate with the premise that it is not the self aggrandizing but the meek who will finally inherit the earth.

There are also attempts to solve crowding problems by advocating more moderate solutions than total escape. In competition for the dwindling natural resources of the earth, the human intellect, which is responsible for the uniquely human predicament, may in turn be the guide out of the metabolic morass — or so we might hope. Whether the human intellect will be used for constructive conservation, as well as for controlling population growth, only time will tell. If the human species succeeds in adapting to its eventual destiny, the name *Homo sapiens* (the wise man) may be justified.

As humans overrun the ecological niches, an essentially human monoculture is developing. This progression may eventually lead to only one species on earth. Lacking plants, of course, an alternate food source would need to be found. Such an artificial life does not represent nature as we know it, but it appears to represent the overall aspirations of what we call the utopias (ideal places) of modern civilizations. Will these utopias become dystopias? The jury is still out. Who among us would be so arrogant as to declare the destiny of the human race? Humanity, meanwhile, awaits at the crossroads.

Fortunately, we now have lessons taught by former civilizations. Very early peoples left pictures on rocks showing a predominant interest in nature, particularly in sources of the foods on which these ancient societies depended — large game animals, for example. The populace spent the day primarily in food procurement and storage. We need go no farther than western South America to see this historic scenario re-enacted. Early American tribes subsisted there for centuries, close to nature. Although they made efforts to keep their population growth at the natural zero rate, using birth-controlling plant extracts, the populations did show slow growth. Consequently, competition within the various factions arose. The end result was development of a huge, pretentious empire under the auspices of the Inca tribe. The Incas' history shows how the elaboration of ostentation may spell doom for a civilization.

Like the amber-winged dragonflies described in this book, the Incas were lovers of the sun. They worshipped Father Sun as the golden orb beneficently bestowing both light and heat energy for driving all vital forces on earth. The Incas correctly recognized their direct dependence on solar energy for light and heat and — indirectly — for metabolic energy contained in food. Members of the tribe loved the warm sunshine as it entered through the windows of stone houses perched atop the cold Andean peaks. Since firewood was scarce at such high elevations, the sun was the central heating system. Sunshine was instrumental in warming and tanning their bodies. (The role of pigments in heat regulation is discussed in the chapter on fruit flies.)

But the windows were for much more than central heating. They were openings through which Father Sun could enter and illuminate his golden image as the nobility worshipped in the stone temples. This was a type of *living* image, in contrast to the stained-glass images to be substituted later by Christendom.

Through some windows the nobles could view the terraced agricultural fields from whence their chosen foods were derived. Father Sun was responsible for these crops. He had donated the golden corn, and he continued to supply the vital forces for growth of the corn, the staff of life. They could also view their chosen llamas, which the agricultural members of the tribe had sexually selected from the small, wild American camel, some bred for carrying packs, others for providing wool. Inside the castle walls sat the chosen nobility of both sexes. The chosen men were waiting to be of noble service, as directed by Father Sun. The chosen women were waiting to be of service to the sons of Father Sun. Yes, the nobility knew all about sexual selection.

Father Sun also knew about sexual selection. He had chosen the male nobility who in turn had chosen the female nobility of worthy lineage. The "chosen women" were kept secluded. Before the age of modern biology, after all, the conception of life was given a spiritual interpretation. It was thought that the intimate approach of a male to a reproductive female might allow his spirit to influence the heredity of the offspring. It was feared that even a natural catastrophe could leave an adverse impression on the unborn.

Such superstitions may have been based on the observation that a comb rubbed through the hair would later attract the hair toward the comb — and the closer the comb, the greater the attractive force. This "animal magnetism" theory persisted for many generations. There were some who claimed that the natural environment could directly influence the development of an embryo. In our modern day of X-rays, this view has proved prophetic, as developing embryos are shielded against irradiation.

If one of these "secluded" chosen women bore a son which she could prove was of Solar parentage, that son was another son of The Sun and was worshipped as such. So much for positive selection. But the Incas also knew about negative selection. If one of these chosen women bore a son that the tribe could prove was *not* of noble lineage, she was buried alive, and her bastard son was promptly executed along with the perpetrator of the crime and all his relatives. But the Incas did not stop there. They destroyed the whole town from which the criminal had sprung and scattered stones over the remains. To the Incas, anything worth doing was worth doing well. This primitive form of eugenics, in connection with ethnic cleansing, illustrates that there is little new under Father Son.

The nobles were chosen to be an aggressive, domineering type. According to tradition, Father Sun had instructed the Incas to be plunderers of humankind. They did a thorough job of this: despoiling, dominating, and ruling all the pre-Inca tribes they could lay hands on in a 2,500-mile stretch on the western coast of South America. Along with the inspiration from Father Sun went a lot of perspiration; the gold so laboriously collected was the sweat of their celestial father. Their architectural masterworks were dedicated to The Sun. The Incas exerted such effort in finely measuring and hewing the huge rocks of the castle walls that those finished walls were able to withstand the tests Father Sun put to them with his earthquakes.

Sacrifices of gold, and expensive clothing adorned with gold, were all burned on altars in homage to Father Sun. Gold dust was dedicated by throwing it into Lake Titicaca, near the place the Incas had originated. Their ancestors, before being chosen by Father Sun, had been cave-dwelling savages. So much "holy gold" was stored out of reverence for Father Sun that the Spanish ships almost sank carrying it back to the Old World to fill the coffers of the Holy Roman Empire. (See McIntyre 1975.)

Not all of the gold was hauled to Europe. Much of it was used by the Spanish conquerors to bedeck their new version of the Inca temples, the Roman Catholic cathedrals, which were elaborate expansions of the Inca temples. In view of these displays, vast numbers of the Inca tribe joined the Catholic vision of utopia.

The Incas had put much time and effort into ceremoniously exhibiting their favorite foods on the altars in their temples. These displays also were replicated and embellished in the Catholic cathedrals. They may be viewed in Cusco, the ancient Inca capital. One must be there personally to absorb the scene, which is so magnificent as to be obscene. All around are guards who make sure the spectacle is not photographed. The entire history of sexual selection may be viewed there at a glance as one huge wedding festival. The simple family altar, where a virgin had met her mate over a bowl of tribal delicacies in company with the tribal dignitaries, had gone through stages to include Father Sun as a guest. As he entered through the window of the Inca temple, the delicacies were ceremonially and sacrificially heaped up for him. Occasionally, even a "chosen woman" was offered to Father Sun, thus perpetuating the line of sons of The Sun for the Inca nobility. In modern parlance, this amounted to introduction of some more Godly genes into the family gene pool.

The simple altars became more and more elaborately decorated with riches and ornate (even gaudy) representations of tribal delicacies. All this energy-consuming display was awaiting bankruptcy. Soon it would be plundered by outsiders.

The plundering and rebuilding of ancient temples has been repeated many times in the history of humankind, the "other mammal." The same scenario may be viewed among bowerbirds, "the other birds." The males build magnificent structures within which they display special foods and ornamental facsimiles thereof. These displays are often plundered by invading, rival males. (See Chapter 3.)

With regard to the premise of this book, the Incas have two important lessons to teach us. First is the role of sexual selection in the fates of human civilizations. Second is the role of skin pigmentation in temperature control. The amber-winged dragonflies provide simple illustrations for both of these lessons. Let us hope that these dragonflies, with their glittering, golden wings, do not suffer the same fate as the Incas, but continue to flit about under Father Sun at their chosen spots, above their chosen waters, with their chosen mates, all in their chosen niches. Let us also hope that sexual selection is adaptive for them — and does not do them in.

A case may be made that the fall of ancient empires has been preceded by an emphasis on the sexual phase of the life cycles. This is to be expected if the sexual phase is both a cause and a result of economic stress. Paleontologists observe that the immediate extinction of many fossil species was presaged by elaborate development of structures such as antlers, or even large bodies, which may have developed by a process of competition. Specialization, which may result from a process of sexual selection, could confer "maladaptation" upon a species if carried too far. Evolutionary ecologists note that highly specialized species are in special danger of extinction as a result of sudden environmental changes.

In the Western Hemisphere, Americans, bent on not repeating the mistakes of their ancestors, fostered environmental movements. Many pioneering groups, having fled the tyrannies of European systems, made attempts to develop simple-life communities close to nature. These refugees had learned much in the Old World about the disaster of environmental degradation. This they did not wish onto America the beautiful. National parks, such as Yellowstone, were established to preserve nature, as well as to satisfy human longings for the natural life. Despite the fact that these parks are often at considerable distances from cities, environmentalists are continually on guard to ensure that the growing populace does not obliterate these cherished treasures. The same is true for the more accessible local parks. Recently, there has been an emphasis on promoting greenways, sometimes on abandoned railroad corridors. Such linear parks assist in migration of wildlife from one localized community to another. This mixing of populations helps prevent the stifling effects of inbreeding. The preservation of greenways is a giant step toward integrating human civilizations with nature.

Civilized humans are eternally nostalgic for their roots. In every human there may be vestiges of an ecological conscience. This is plainly evident in children, who appear to have an especially strong love of nature. Some of this love of nature may disappear as the individual approaches adulthood. But generally, there is something within us that loves, even envies, a bird. What is this? Why do we equip our angels with feathered wings? Is this an attempt to escape our mortal bondage to a tyrannical, artificial creation of our own making? Perhaps we aspire to fly from our problems as the birds appear to do. Future-minded peoples, such as those of ancient Egypt, painted birds on their walls. In the Viennese palace of Prince Eugene, we see pictured the highest form of human enlightenment in the form of humans equipped with the wings of birds.

Near the town of Epps in Louisiana, we viewed the knolls of the mound-building Native Americans. Buried in the mounds were numerous small pendants of birds, each with a little hole for hanging it from the body as an ornament. Also found were clay pipes molded into the form of birds. Tribe members had painstakingly, with baskets of their own making, piled neat, semicircular, concentric rings of earth to construct what looked like a large amphitheater. On these ridges, elevating their huts above the wetland, they spent their natural lives. They did not clutter their countryside with tombstones. Instead, they recycled their bodies in burial mounds. The centerpiece of the amphitheater was a huge mound representing the chief bird, with a 640-foot wingspan. This provided an appropriate spot for the ceremonial celebrations of the tribe. Other Native Americans, as near Portal in southern Arizona, painted their huge eagles on the walls of their caves. Of course, it is common knowledge that even historic Native Americans bedecked their bodies with feathers in preparation for their ceremonies.

This heritage lingers on. On the visits my wife and I make to various birding areas, we are continually inspired by the dedication and enthusiasm of the bird watchers. They do not complain. Rather, they celebrate the opportunity of waking early to spend the day pondering the lives of birds. Part of what modern bird watchers are recording is data on birds invading and vanishing from ecological niches. Much of this effort is motivated by sheer love of nature. A good deal of support for environmental protection has come from the bird watchers. In fact, present-day humans may have a more "pure" love of nature than their prior savage counterparts. The love is not contaminated by a desire for food. It is an ethereal form of appreciation of nature's beauty, design, and rhythms.

Today, bird watchers are not just a paltry few; their numbers have increased greatly in modern times. Not much escapes their notice. It is an inspiration to read popular accounts of the pure exhilaration expressed by these bird watchers. Their accounts often end up in the scientific literature. All this gives hope that modern humans will never become completely artificial creatures.

Birds seem to have it all: relative freedom, functional art and music, and natural ingenuity, as defined by ability to adapt to nature. Best of all, they don't need to depend to any large degree on education for this ingenuity. The information is on their DNA tapes. Birds express their remarkable ingenuity without the aid of a convoluted cerebral cortex, such as the mammals' brain structure. The fact that much of bird behavior is merely programmed does not detract from its remarkable fascination. In fact, this actually adds to the appeal. What carpenter wouldn't admire the precision with which the acorn woodpecker makes its hole just the proper size to fit the acorn that is to go into it? Furthermore, the woodpecker need not be troubled with a long period of education and apprenticeship. Who is more adaptable to the natural world — the

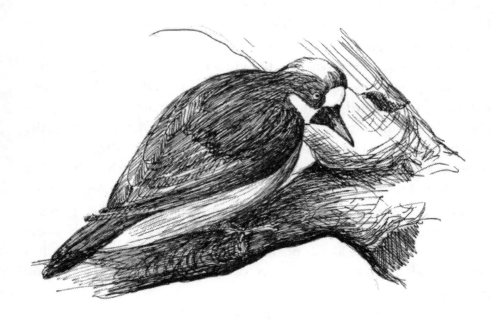

Acorn woodpeckers store huge caches of acorns of various sizes.

human, which we know exhibits a high level of conscious mentality, or the protozoan, not so highly endowed?

A final assessment of the value of human-type consciousness must await an evaluation of the very destiny of humankind itself. If the aim of life is adaptation to the natural environment, we may look for no more than bird mentality for an ideal. But if adaptation to an artificial setting, or perhaps an extraterrestrial environment, is the goal of life, human-like mentality may indeed be in order. Consideration of the ultimate destiny of the human species, however, goes beyond the scope of this book.

Having spent several months videotaping a family of goldfinches, I, though not in possession of a poet's license, felt inspired to summarize the observations with, yes, an anthropomorphic poem:

TO A GOLDFINCH

On vaulted sky he writes his song,
Sailing cheerfully along.
With sunshine on his golden back,
Trimmed with jetty plumes of black.

His demure mate of gentle green,
With tempered voice, almost unseen,
Her thistled domicile she binds
Among the needles of the pines.

In this cozy, fluffy bed,
Red mouths gaping to be fed,
Anxious parents watch them feather,
Talking quietly together.

As in undulating flight,
Leaving trails of pure delight,
Over field and over wood,
They even do the cynic good.

REFERENCES

Alatalo, R.V., J. Höglund, and A. Lundberg, 1991. Lekking in the black grouse: a test of male viability. *Nature*, 352 (6331):155–156.

Andersson, M., 1982. Female choice selects for extreme tail length in a widowbird. *Nature*, 299:818–820.

Andersson, M., 1994. *Sexual Selection*. Princeton University Press, Princeton, New Jersey.

Averhoff, W.W., and R.H. Richardson, 1976. Multiple phermone system controlling mating in *Drosophila melanogaster*. *Proceedings of the National Academy of Sciences* (USA), 73:591–593.

Barber, T.X., 1993. *The Human Nature of Birds: A Scientific Study with Startling Implications*. St. Martin's Press, New York.

Barbosa, P., and T.M. Peters, 1972. *Readings in Entomology*. W.B. Saunders Co.: Philadelphia, London, Toronto.

Basolo, A., 1990. Female preference predates the evolution of swords in swordtail fish. *Science*, 250:808–810.

Basolo, A., 1990. Female preference for male sword length in the green swordtail, *Xiphophorus helleri* (Pisces: Poeciliidae). *Animal Behaviour*, 40:332–338.

Bischoff, R.J., J.L. Gould, and D.I. Rubenstein, 1985. Tail size and female choice in the guppy. *Behavior, Ecology, and Sociobiology*, 17:253–255.

Borgia, G., 1986. Satin bowerbird parasites: A test of the bright male hypothesis. *Behavior, Ecology, and Sociobiology*, 19:355–358.

Brodsky, L., 1988. Ornament size influences mating success in male rock ptarmigan. *Animal Behaviour*, 36:335–342.

Burley, N., 1986. Comparison of the band-colour preferences of two species of estrildid finches. *Animal Behaviour*, 34:1732–1741.

Burley, N., 1988. Wild zebra finches have band-colour preferences. *Animal Behaviour*, 36:1235–1237.

Burley, N., and C.B. Coopersmith, 1987. Bill colour preference of zebra finches. *Ethology*, 76:133–151.

Campbell, G.D., 1867. *Reign of Law.* In Autograph Manuscripts of Sir R. Owen, British Museum, London, Owen Collection, 59.7.

Clutton-Brock, T.H., 1989. Mammalian mating systems. *Proceedings of the Royal Society of London* (B), 236:339–372.

Conner, W.E., T. Eisner, R.K. Vander Mee, A. Guerrero, and J. Meinwald, 1981. Precopulatory sexual interaction in an arctiid moth, *Utetheisa ornatrix*: Role of a phermone derived from dietary alkaloids. *Behavior, Ecology, and Sociobiology*, 9:227–235.

Conner, W.E., B. Roach, E. Benedict, J. Meinwald, and T. Eisner, 1990. Courtship phermone production and body size as correlates of larval diet in males of the arctiid moth, *Utetheisa ornatrix. Journal of Chemical Ecology*, 16:543–552.

Crews, D., 1975. Effects of different components of male courtship behaviour on experimentally induced ovarian recrudescence and mating preference in the lizard, *Anolis carolinensis. Animal Behaviour*, 23:349–356.

Crick, F., 1994. *The Astonishing Hypothesis: The Scientific Search for the Soul.* Charles Scribner's Sons, New York.

Cronin, H., 1991. *The Ant and the Peacock: Altruism and Sexual Selection from Darwin to Today.* Cambridge University Press, New York.

Croze, H., 1970. Searching image in carrion crows. *Zeitschrift Für Tierpsychologie* (suppl.), 5:1–86.

Darwin, C.A., 1859. *On the Origin of Species by Means of Natural Selection.* John Murray, London.

Darwin, C.A., 1868. *The Variation in Animals and Plants Under Domestication.* John Murray, London.

Darwin, C.A., 1871. *The Descent of Man and Selection in Relation to Sex.* John Murray, London; A.L. Burt Publ., 2nd Ed., 1874, New York.

Darwin, C.A., 1872. *The Expression of Emotions in Man and Animals.*

Longmans, London.

David, J.R., P. Capy, V. Payant, and S. Tsakas, 1985. Thoracic trident pigmentation in *Drosophila melanogaster*: Differentiation of geographic populations. *Génét. Sél. Evol.*, 17:211–224.

Davison, G.W.H., 1981. Sexual selection and the mating system of *Argusianus argus* (Aves: Phasianidae). *Biological Journal of the Linnean Society*, 15:901–904.

Davison, G.W.H., 1982. Sexual displays of the great argus pheasant *Argusianus argus*. *Zeitschrift Für Tierpsychologie*, 58:185–202.

Davison, G.W.H., 1983. Behavior of the Malay peacock pheasant *Polyplectron malacense*. *Journal of Zoology*, 201:57–66.

Dawkins, M.S., 1993. *Through Our Eyes Only, The Search for Animal Consciousness*. W.H. Freeman — Spektrum: Oxford, New York, and Heidelberg.

Dennis, J.V., 1981. *Beyond the Bird Feeder*. Knopf, New York.

Diamond, J.M., 1986. Animal art: Variation in bower decorating style among male bowerbirds, *Amblyornis inornatus*. *Proceedings of the National Academy of Sciences* (USA), 83:3042–3046.

Diamond, J.M., 1991. Borrowed sexual ornaments. *Nature*, 349:105.

Dobzhansky, T., 1937. *Genetics and the Origin of Species*. Columbia University Press, New York.

Dugatkin, L.A., and J.-G. J. Godin, 1998. How females choose their mates. *Scientific American*, 278:56–61.

Easterbrook, G., 1995. *A Moment on the Earth*. Penguin Books, New York.

Einstein, A., 1905. On the motion required by the molecular kinetic theory of heat of particles suspended in fluids at rest. *Annalen der Physik*, Vol. 17.

Elton, C.S., 1927. *Animal Ecology*. Sidgwick & Jackson, London.

Endler, J.A., 1980. Natural selection on color patterns in *Poecilia reticulata*. *Evolution*, 34:76–91.

Feder, J.L., C.A. Chilcote, and G.L. Bush, 1990. Regional local and microgeographic allele frequency variation between apple and hawthorn populations of *Rhegoletis pomonella* in western

Michigan. *Evolution*, 44:595–608.

Ferris, T., 1992. *The Mind's Sky*. Bantam Books, New York.

Fisher, R.A., 1930. *The Genetical Theory of Natural Selection*. Clarendon Press, Oxford.

Forsyth, A., 1986. *A Natural History of Sex*. Charles Scribner's Sons, New York.

Fricken, M.S., and R.W. Fricken, 1987. Bill sweeping behavior of a Mexican chickadee. *Condor*, 89:901–902.

Frisch, K. von, 1974. *Animal Architecture*. Harcourt Brace, New York.

Frith, C.B., and D.W. Frith, 1990. *Emu*, 90:136–137.

Gayou, D.C., 1982. Tool use by green jays. *Wilson Bulletin*, 94:593–594.

Gilliard, E.T., 1958. *Living Birds of the World*. Doubleday & Co., Garden City, New York.

Good, P.P., and L. Stoltzfus, 1991. *The Best of Mennonite Fellowship Meals*. Good Books, Intercourse, Pennsylvania.

Gould, J.L., 1982. *Ethology*. W.W. Norton: New York and London.

Gould, J.L., and C.G. Gould, 1989, 1997. *Sexual Selection*. Scientific American Library, New York.

Gould, S.J., 1993. *Eight Little Piggies: Reflections in Natural History*. W.W. Norton: New York and London.

Gould, S.J., 1996. *Full House*. Harmony Books, Crown Publishers, New York.

Grahn, M., G. Goransson, and T. von Schantz, 1993. Territory acquisition and mating success in pheasants *Phasianus colchicus*: An experiment. *Animal Behaviour*, 46:721–730.

Griffin, D.R., 1984. *Animal Thinking*. Harvard University Press: Cambridge, Massachusetts, and London, England.

Griffin, D.R., 1992. *Animal Minds*. University of Chicago Press: Chicago and London.

Haines, S.E., and J.L. Gould, 1994. Female platys prefer long tails. *Nature*, 370:512.

Herbert, N., 1993. *Elemental Mind*. Penguin Books, New York.

Hill, G.E., 1990. Female house finches prefer colourful males: Sexual selection for a condition-dependent trait. *Animal Behaviour*, 40:563–572.

Hill, G.E., 1991. Plumage coloration is a sexually selected indicator of male quality. *Nature*, 350:337–339.

Hilty, S., 1994. *Birds of Tropical America*. Chapters Publ. Ltd., Shelburne, Vermont.

Hingston, R.W.G., 1933. *The Meaning of Animal Colour and Adornment*. Edward Arnold, London.

Hollingsworth, M.J., and J.M. Smith, 1955. The effects of inbreeding on rate of development and on fertility in *Drosophila subobscura*. *Journal of Genetics*, 53:295.

Hopkins, T.L., T.D. Morgan, Y. Aso, and K.J. Kramer, 1982. N-beta-alanyldopamine: major role in insect cuticle tanning. *Science*, 217:364–366.

Houde, A.E., 1988. Genetic difference in female choice between two guppy populations. *Animal Behaviour*, 36:510–516.

Houde, A.E., 1997. *Sex, Color, and Mate Choice in Guppies*. Princeton University Press, Princeton, New Jersey.

Hunt, G.R., 1996. Manufacture and use of hook-tools by New Caledonian crows. *Nature*, 379:249–251.

Huxley, J.S., 1938. Darwin's theory of sexual selection and the data subsumed by it in the light of recent research. *American Naturalist*, 72:416–433.

Huxley, J.S., 1942. *Evolution, the Modern Synthesis*. Allen & Unwin, London.

Jacobs, M.E., 1955. Studies on territorialism and sexual selection in dragonflies. *Ecology*, 36:566–586.

Jacobs, M.E., 1960. Influence of light on mating of *Drosophila melanogaster*. *Ecology*, 41:182–188.

Jacobs, M.E., 1968. Beta-alanine use by ebony and normal *Drosophila melanogaster* with notes on glucose, uracil, dopa, and dopamine. *Biochemical Genetics*, 1:267–275.

Jacobs, M.E., 1974. Beta-alanine and adaptation in *Drosophila*. *Journal of*

Insect Physiology, 20:859–866.

Jacobs, M.E., 1978. Influence of beta-alanine on mating and territorialism in *Drosophila melanogaster*. *Behavior Genetics*, 8:487–502.

Jacobs, M.E., 1980. Influence of beta-alanine on ultrastructure, tanning, and melanization of *Drosophila melanogaster* cuticles. *Biochemical Genetics*, 18:65–76.

Jacobs, M.E., 1982. Beta-alanine and tanning polymorphisms. *Comparative Biochemistry and Physiology*, 72:173–177.

Jacobs, M.E., 1985. Role of beta-alanine in cuticular tanning sclerotization and temperature regulation in *Drosophila melanogaster*. *Journal of Insect Physiology*, 6:509–515.

Jacobs, M.E., and K.K. Brubaker, 1963. Beta-alanine utilization of ebony and non-ebony *Drosophila melanogaster*. *Science*, 139:1282–1283.

Johnsgard, P.A., 1986. *The Pheasants of the World*. Oxford University Press, Oxford.

Johnsgard, P.A., 1994. *Arena Birds*. Smithsonian Institution Press: Washington, D.C., and London, England.

Karlson, P., and C.E. Sekeris, 1962. N-acetyl-dopamine as sclerotizing agent of the insect cuticle. *Nature*, 195:183.

Kilham, L., 1968. Reproductive behavior of white-breasted nuthatches (1). Distraction display: bill-sweeping and nest hole defense. *Auk*, 85:477–492.

Krebs, J.R., M.H. MacRoberts, and J.M. Cullen, 1972. Flocking and feeding in the great tit (*Parus major*) — an experimental study. *Ibis*, 114:507–530.

Krebs, J.R., and N.B. Davies, 1978. *Behavioral Ecology: an Evolutionary Approach*. Blackwell, Oxford.

Krebs, J.R., 1979. Foraging strategies and their social significance. In *Handbook of Behavioral Neurobiology*, Vol. 3, Social Behavior and Communication, P. Marler and J.G. Vandenbergh (Eds.), Plenum, New York.

Lack, D., 1947. *Darwin's Finches*. Cambridge University Press, New York.

Lack, D., 1968. *Ecological Adaptations for Breeding in Birds*. Chapman and

Hall, London.

L'Heritier, P., Y. Neefs, and G. Teissier, 1937. Apterisme des insects et selection naturelle. *Compt. Rend*. (Paris), 204:907–909.

Löfstedt, C., N.J. Vickers, W.L. Roelofs, and T.C. Baker, 1989. Diet related courtship success in the Oriental fruit moth, *Grapholita molesta* (Tortricidae). *Oikos*, 55:402–408.

Masson, J.M., and S. McCarthy, 1995. *When Elephants Weep*. Delacorte Press, Bantam Doubleday, New York.

McCullough, D., and R. Beasley, 1996. Bait-fishing herons. *Bird Watchers Digest*, 18:48–51.

McIntyre, L., 1975. *The Incredible Incas and Their Timeless Land*. National Geographic Society, Washington, D.C.

McMahan, E.A., 1983. Bugs angle for termites. *Natural History*, 92(5):40–47.

Mitchell, R.W., N.S. Thompson, and H. Lyn Miles (Eds.), 1977. *Anthropomorphism, Anecdotes, and Animals*. State University of New York Press, Albany.

Moore, N.W., 1952. On the so-called territories of dragonflies (Odonata-Anisoptera). *Behaviour*, 4:85–99.

Morgan, C.L., 1896. *Habit and Instinct*. Edward Arnold, London.

Morgan, T.H., 1903. *Evolution and Adaptation*. Macmillan, New York.

Orians, G.H., 1980. *Some Adaptations of Marsh-nesting Blackbirds*. Princeton University Press, Princeton, New Jersey.

Peck, M.S., 1978. *The Road Less Traveled*. Simon & Schuster, New York.

Petrie, M., T. Halliday, and C. Sanders, 1991. Peahens prefer peacocks with elaborate trains. *Animal Behaviour*, 41:323–331.

Pruett-Jones, S.G., and M.A. Pruett-Jones, 1988. The use of court objects by Lawes' Parotia. *Condor*, 90:539–545.

Reznik, D.N., and J.A. Endler, 1982. The impact of predation on life history evolution in Trinidadian guppies, *Poecilia reticulata*. *Evolution*, 36:160–177.

Rimlinger, D.S., 1984. Display behavior of Temminck's tragopan. *World Pheasant Association*, 9:19–32.

Ripley, D., 1942. *Trail of the Money Bird*. Harper & Brothers, New York.

Robertson, D.R., and S.G. Hoffman, 1977. The roles of female mate choice and predation in the mating systems of some tropical labroid fishes. *Zeitschrift Für Tierpsychologie*, 45:298–320.

Rollin, B.E., 1990. *The Unheeded Cry*. Oxford University Press, Oxford.

Romaines, G., 1882. *Animal Intelligence*. Kegan Paul, London.

Rowland, W.J., 1989. Mate choice and the supernormality effect in female sticklebacks (*Gasterosteus aculeatus*). *Behavior, Ecology, and Sociobiology*, 24:433–438.

Ryan, M.J., 1990. Sexual selection, sensory systems and sensory exploitation. *Oxford Surv. Evol. Biol.* 7:157–195.

Ryutova-Kemoklidze, M., 1995. *The Quantum Generation*. Springer Verlag: Berlin and Heidelberg.

Sayre, A., 1975. *Rosalind Franklin & DNA*. W.W. Norton, New York.

Selous, E., 1907. Observations tending to throw light on the question of sexual selection in birds, including a day-to-day diary on the breeding habits of the ruff. *The Zoologist*, Vol. 11.

Sherald, A.F., 1981. Intergenic suppression of the black mutation of *Drosophila melanogaster*. *Molecular and General Genetics*, 183:102–106.

Skutch, A.F., 1992. *Origin of Nature's Beauty*. University of Texas Press, Austin.

Small, M.F., 1993. *Female Choices*. Cornell University Press: Ithaca, New York, and London, England.

Snow, D.W., 1976. *The Web of Adaptation: Bird Studies in the American Tropics*. The New York Times Book Co., New York.

Spalding, D., 1872. Instinct with original observations on young animals. Reprinted from *British Journal of Animal Behaviour*, 1954, 2:2–11.

Spieth, H.T., 1968. Evolutionary implications of sexual behavior in *Drosophila*. *Evolutionary Biology*, 2:157–193.

Spieth, H.T., and T.C. Hsu, 1950. The influence of light on the mating behavior of seven species of the *Drosophila melanogaster* species group. *Evolution*, 4:316–325.

Sweet, W.W., 1930. *The Story of Religion in America*. Harper & Row: New

York, New York; Evanston, Illinois; and London, England.

Thomas, L., 1979. *The Medusa and the Snail*. Viking, New York.

Thornhill, R., 1976. Sexual selection and nuptial feeding behavior in *Bittacus apicalis* (Insecta: Mecoptera). *American Naturalist*. 110:529–548.

Thorpe, W.H., 1963. *Learning and Instinct in Animals*. Harvard University Press, Cambridge, Massachusetts, 2nd Ed. (1st Ed., 1956).

Tinbergen, N., 1963. On the aims and methods of ethology. *Zeitschrift Für Tierpsychologie*, 20:410–433.

Wallace, A.R., 1856. On the habits of the orang-utan of Borneo. *Annals and Magazine of Natural History* (2nd Series), 18:26–32.

Wallace, A.R., 1871. Review of Darwin's Descent of Man. *The Academy*, 2:177–183.

Wallace, A.R., 1889. *Darwinism*. Macmillan, London (3rd Ed.).

Weiner, J., 1994. *The Beak of the Finch*. Knopf, New York.

Williams, G.C., 1997. *The Pony Fish's Glow*. HarperCollins, New York.

Witmer, M., 1996. The telltail tale. *Living Bird*,15(No. 1):16–20.

Wright, T.R.F., 1987. The genetics of biogenic amine metabolism, sclerotization, and melanization in *Drosophila melanogaster*. In *Advances in Genetics: Molecular Genetics of Development*, John G. Scandalios (Ed.), 24:127–209. Harcourt Brace Jovanovich, New York.

Zahavi, A., and A. Zahavi, 1997. *The Handicap Principle*. Oxford University Press: New York and Oxford.

AUTHOR INDEX

SUBJECT INDEX